Phenomenology and Future Generations

SUNY series in Contemporary Continental Philosophy

Dennis J. Schmidt, editor

Phenomenology and Future Generations

Generativity, Justice, and *Amor Mundi*

Edited by

MATTHIAS FRITSCH,
FERDINANDO G. MENGA,
and REBECCA VAN DER POST

Published by State University of New York Press, Albany

© 2024 State University of New York

All rights reserved

Printed in the United States of America

No part of this book may be used or reproduced in any manner whatsoever without written permission. No part of this book may be stored in a retrieval system or transmitted in any form or by any means including electronic, electrostatic, magnetic tape, mechanical, photocopying, recording, or otherwise without the prior permission in writing of the publisher.

Links to third-party websites are provided as a convenience and for informational purposes only. They do not constitute an endorsement or an approval of any of the products, services, or opinions of the organization, companies, or individuals. SUNY Press bears no responsibility for the accuracy, legality, or content of a URL, the external website, or for that of subsequent websites.

For information, contact State University of New York Press, Albany, NY
www.sunypress.edu

Library of Congress Cataloging-in-Publication Data

Names: Fritsch, Matthias, editor. | Menga, Ferdinando G., editor. | van der Post, Rebecca, editor.
Title: Phenomenology and future generations : generativity, justice, and *amor mundi* / edited by Matthias Fritsch, Ferdinando G. Menga, and Rebecca van der Post.
Description: Albany : State University of New York Press, [2024] | Series: SUNY series in Contemporary Continental Philosophy | Includes bibliographical references and index.
Identifiers: ISBN 9781438499499 (hardcover : alk. paper) | ISBN 9781438499512 (ebook) | ISBN 9781438499505 (pbk. : alk. paper)
Further information is available at the Library of Congress.

Contents

Acknowledgments — vii

Introduction: Why Phenomenology and Future Generations? — 1
Matthias Fritsch, Ferdinando G. Menga, and Rebecca van der Post

Section 1.
Generativity: The Future Is of Us and in Us

1. Generativity and Ethics: A Phenomenological Approach — 27
   Mario Vergani

2. Responding to the Claims of Those Who Shall Come After Us — 47
   Bernhard Waldenfels

3. Generativity, Generations, and Generative Intergenerational Solidarity: Untimely Reflections on the Way We Live After One Another, With One Another, and For One Another, in Its Unforeseeable Historicity — 73
   Burkhard Liebsch

Section 2.
The Politics of Human Generations

4. Absences that Matter: Phenomenological Insights into (the Predicaments of) Intergenerational Justice — 109
   Ferdinando G. Menga

5. How Can We Take Claims of Future Generations Seriously? Combining Different Perspectives in Our Action 133
   Eva Buddeberg

6. Jonasian Grounding of Future-Oriented Responsibility and the Idea of the Human 151
   Hiroshi Abe

7. "The Race of the Poor": Intergenerational Lessons from Anarchist Eugenics 163
   Anne O'Byrne

Section 3.
Amor Mundi in Presentist Modernity

8. Critical Theory, Natal Alienation, Future People 181
   Matthias Fritsch

9. In Our Element 207
   Rebecca van der Post

10. From Love of World to Love of Earth: Taking Responsibility for the Future of the Planet 239
    Kelly Oliver

Contributors 259

Index 263

Acknowledgments

This book has been on an extended journey from its first conception to its arrival at the printer's desk, and we are indebted to all those who have helped it on its way. We would especially like to thank our contributing authors, as well as our principal editors at the press, series editor Dennis J. Schmidt and SUNY Press's senior acquisitions editor, Michael Rinella. Without their enthusiastic and enduring support, this project could surely not have reached its final destination. We would also like to express our immense gratitude to our two anonymous reviewers for the remarkable generosity of their time, their comments, and their insight. Finally, we would like to extend our heartfelt thanks to Nicholas Walker, translator extraordinaire, for the English versions that appear in this volume of papers by Burkhard Liebsch and Bernhard Waldenfels, and to extend our gratitude to the Social Science and Humanities Research Council of Canada (SSHRC), whose generous financial support made these translations possible. Earlier versions of these two works and the chapter by Anne O'Byrne were first published in *Metodo. International Studies in Phenomenology and Philosophy* 5 (2) (2017), and appear here in revised form.

Introduction

MATTHIAS FRITSCH, FERDINANDO G. MENGA,
AND REBECCA VAN DER POST

Most especially in the context of climate change, future-oriented duties are now high on the agenda of the global public, as can be seen, for instance, in sustainability targets and cuts to greenhouse gas emissions that increasingly find justification not only in terms of our obligations to our contemporaries but also on the basis of what we owe to future generations.

This collection of essays seeks to emphasize the fertility of the phenomenological tradition for intergenerational ethics and environmental justice. To the extent that the current destabilization of the environment and the climate threatens overlapping and more distant future generations with significant and direct harms, as well as the attendant problems of economic debt, political instability, weakened public institutions, and the like; and to the extent that sustainability can and should be understood to center in and around justice between generations (Holland 1999, Habib 2013), intergenerational ethics and environmental justice are key issues of our time. Our current situation urgently demands that we, the presently living and accountable, understand ourselves as only one generation in a chain of others, with obligations stretching forward and backward in time. But in ethics and politics, time tends to be understood in ways that challenge standard accounts of harms, duties, and responsibilities. Time seems to separate parties that would otherwise stand in a moral, social, legal, or political relation.

But time also links generations to one another. The tradition of philosophical phenomenology, especially when taken in its full breadth, is ripe with possibilities internal to its own methods, frameworks, and developments that are strikingly well suited to the exploration of temporal relations among different generations. In this, two avenues in particular stand out. The first is phenomenology's focus on embodiment, and hence upon birth and death that connect and separate generations. The second is its rich reflections on the role of time in the constitution of individuals and of the social world, which extend from Dilthey's history of worldviews (1990), Husserl's time-consciousness (1964), and Schütz's historical lifeworlds (1980) to Heidegger's being-towards-death (1962/2008), Gadamer's hermeneutics of tradition (1992), Arendt's natality (2005), de Beauvoir's reflections on sexuality and on aging (2011), Merleau-Ponty's flesh of the world (1968), Levinas's fecundity (1979), Derrida's living-on or *sur-vivance* (1979), and Carr's phenomenology of history (2014). Building on and from within this tradition, the volume as a whole strives to advances phenomenological accounts of historical time and sociality in long-term lifeworlds while emphasizing the self-understanding and experience of humans as generational and generative beings, and takes as its purview not the critical interrogation of current politics, laws, and institutions *per se*, but rather, and within a more fundamental register, an investigation into their conceptual and phenomenological underpinnings.

At the conceptual level, intergenerational ethics and environmental justice over time have moved from a peripheral or "applied" field in the 1970s, mostly concerned with nuclear waste, to more widespread and central concerns in ethics and related disciplines today. It would be hard to deny that, at least in part, these academic developments track worldwide political and environmental changes. We have only to think of teenagers and climate activists—not only Greta Thunberg from Sweden, who tends to hold center stage so far as the press is concerned, but also Vanessa Nakate (Uganda), Disha Ravi (India), Autumn Peltier (Wikwemkoong/Manitoulin Island), and many others—lecturing politicians and business leaders on the enormous problems that the decision-makers of today are leaving to their own generation to address. Despite what are often dishonest or self-interested denials, an awareness of the urgency of achieving a sustainable environment—including the social, economic, and political conditions needed to ensure a life worth living for our immediate successors and for inhabitants of the earth in the distant future—seems to have entered the collective imaginary as well as the international political agenda. At the level of sociopolitical practice, it is increasingly recognized that there is a widespread and growing demand for responsibility in these areas, even if voters and politicians alike often seem unwilling to walk the talk. Thus, the overarching purpose of this volume is to tap the tremendously rich resources of phenomenological approaches for rethinking intergenerational responsibilities at this crucial historical juncture, with a view to furnishing and elaborating conceptual and philosophical material for a revised understanding of intergenerational justice and ethics that is capable of informing social praxis and of finding political, legal, and institutional expression into the future. The hope is that, in so doing, it can help to bring the extraordinary wealth of the phenomenological tradition directly to bear upon the environmental and social crises that, in recent years, have pulled questions of intergenerational justice (or IGJ) out from their relative obscurity at the margins of thought and action and have shown them to be absolutely central to, and deeply problematic for, both theory and society.

In both areas, in academia and in society, many questions remain open and unresolved from ethical, political, and legal points of view. Since nonoverlapping future others are absent from the present, are obligations towards them really justifiable? And if so, what are the most appropriate political-institutional instruments with which to articulate such obligations and through which to establish a framework for their implementation? Is it enough merely to extend and amend present theoretical and politico-legal accounts, methods, and devices, or is a radical reconfiguration necessary? These and similar questions are gaining an increasing urgency and a broadening foothold within theoretical and public debate, and together, given all that is at stake with the issues they raise, they reflect a need to illuminate the fundamental aspects and structural properties of genuine understanding of our responsibility to future generations—and, hence, the need for intensive and sustained philosophical discourse (Gardiner 2011, 45ff.; Jamieson 2014).

However, resistance to recognizing intergenerational obligations is fed by several sources, including economic and sociopolitical short-termism and self-interested views that, in turn, are fostered by the increasing instrumentalization of action orientations (Horkheimer 1974; Habermas 1984, 1985). But in addition, any such recognition, like the motivation to act, is certainly not helped by the challenges that a radically future-oriented ethics poses to traditional moral theories. At the risk of oversimplification, we are dealing with a demand for a responsibility towards future individuals that, no matter how strongly perceived, is more or less homeless within the presentist matrix—the mesh of extant normative theories of moral obligation and political legitimacy that largely presuppose interacting parties who are living contemporaries—that underlies most approaches to modern moral theory in the West. As a result, moral relations between the living, the

4 | Matthias Fritsch, Ferdinando G. Menga, and Rebecca van der Post

dead, and the unborn (meaning the not-yet-conceived) face many obstacles and a number of so-called ontological problems. We outline these here, in brief, by way of providing context and background to the central issues as represented within the existing literature, and which are explored in detail within the chapters to follow (Gardiner 2011; Jamieson 2014, chapters 5 and 6; Fritsch 2018, chapter 1; see also Vergani and Menga, in this volume).

The scholarly literature on obligations to those who do not yet exist is largely in agreement that existing concepts of moral duties, political legitimacy, and human rights face special and fundamental challenges when expanded to cover obligations to future generations. The challenges that distinguish inter- from intragenerational justice include:

a. The *absence of temporal overlap* between the parties: an absence that gives rise to the nonreciprocity argument, which holds that because there can be no mutually advantageous interaction between present and future generations, the present has no or few obligations to the future (Beckman and Page 2008, Page 2007). In addition, it raises the argument from temporal complexity, according to which duties to the future are hampered by the fact that both the causal responsibility for harm and the effects of present actions stretch across generations in such a way that the agents bearing the duties are difficult to identify (Garvey 2008: 59ff.) and are caught in a particularly vicious collective action problem (Gardiner 2006, 2011).

b. The *remoteness in time* that has led to (i) the uncertainty argument, according to which we do not know enough about either the effects of our actions on future generations—in particular distant ones—or their needs, which might be radically altered by as yet unknown technologies (Garvey 2008: 90ff.; Routley and Routley 1979); and (ii) the incommensurability argument, which suggests that the notion of justice itself may undergo possibly radical change (Ball 1985).

c. The *nonexistence challenge* that leads to the argument from the unidentifiability of interests, according to which there can be no individual (but at most, only collective or generational) rights where they are not backed by identifiable interests (Weiss 1989)—interests that rights-holders must, in principle, be able *themselves* to defend (Pogge 1995; Feinberg 1970), at least on a choice-conception of subjective rights (Steiner and Vallentyne in Gosseries and Meyer 2009).

d. The *indefinite number of future people*, an indefiniteness or infinity that poses great challenges for all aggregative theories of distributive justice seeking to divide the intergenerational cake equally.

e. The *nonidentity problem* (Kavka 1981; Parfit 1984: 351ff.; Woodward 1986; Page 2006: 132ff.), which, it is generally agreed, acts as the persistent shadow from which all work on future duties seeks to emerge (Humphrey 2009; Roberts and Wasserman 2010). Highlighting the further problem of power asymmetry between the present and the future (Barry 1989b: 189, 246), the nonidentity argument suggests that because the existence and identity of future individuals is contingent on the actions and decisions of the currently living, even actions that arguably harm them, such as increases in CO_2 emissions, contribute (if only indirectly) to their very existence; as a result, future people are not in a position to complain of these actions as they themselves would, otherwise, never have existed at all (Roberts and Wasserman 2010; Tremmel 2009, 2010).

To respond to this formidable web of challenges, moral and political theorists have largely sought to amend extant accounts of justice. Arguably, however, the presentist matrix is thereby merely adjusted, rather than fundamentally reconsidered. For example, various impersonal consequentialist theories have been put forward that escape the nonidentity problem by promoting an increase in overall (i.e., nonperson specific) happiness, though that has generated the so-called "repugnant conclusion," according to which it would be better to engender more future people even if individual happiness or utility decreases significantly (Parfit 1984: 381ff.). Contractarian views (based on mutual advantage) and contractualist views (based on fair cooperation) have been refined to avoid both the nonidentity problem and the nonreciprocity problem (Heyward 2008; Fuji-Johnson 2007). However, contract theory still assumes the existence of subjects oriented to the pursuit of self-interest in a relationship of reciprocity and co-presence so as to secure the ability to enter into, and fulfill, agreements with one another. The counterargument has been made that future generations are characterized precisely by the fact that they do not yet exist and cannot cooperate (Gardiner 2009, 81ff.; Hiskes 2009, 50ff.; Barry 1978; Pontara 1995, ch. 3; Beckermann 2006). This issue also raises a problem for discourse ethics and deliberative democracy, both of which typically assume the presence of discursive partners in settings where the fundamental norms and policies that affect them are discussed (Fritsch 2021).

Hence, the underlying impression persists that generation-oriented adjustments to existing theories of justice tend to be afterthoughts that do not fully take account of the fact that human beings come to be what they are only in historical lifeworlds that continue to be inherited and bequeathed. The worry is that the presentist matrix prevents scholars from addressing the ontological problems head-on and from rethinking the role of generational time. A number of strategies of avoidance might be discernible. First, as mentioned, a theorist may begin with an existing account of justice developed by assuming only contemporaries, and then extend the resulting account to past and future generations (e.g., Rawls 1996, 20ff.; Gosseries and Meyer 2009). On this view, future people do not belong to the core problem of justice; and relations between generations—such as birth and death—concern more or less contingent features of human agents. Similarly, generational relations can be misconstrued by defining generations in such a way as to model away their overlap. Many theorists suggest that, to understand the problem of why and what we owe future people in its pure form, we should model generations as temporally unified such that they enter the historical arena *en bloc* (Gosseries 2009b; Gardiner 2011). As Vergani and others argue (in this volume), this approach does not take the "inter" of "intergenerational relations" seriously enough, and downplays generativity and natality, or the fact that future generations emerge in (discontinuous) continuity with ongoing historical practices that take place among overlapping generations.

The "inter" may also be seen to be denied or sidelined when issues of *intra-* and *inter*generational justice are separated from one another (e.g., Meyer and Roser 2009). If justice could be either nongenerational or intergenerational, then generational relations again are not seen as a defining feature of human beings as the subjects of justice. Similarly, generational historicity is marginalized by approaches to intergenerational justice that suggest we imagine a legislative meeting of generations outside of history (Rawls 1971; Birnbacher 1977; Partridge 1978; Barry 1991; Beckermann 1999; Tremmel 2013). The parties who devise principles for intergenerational justice would then, as the drafters, not be generational beings; they themselves would be removed from time, birth, death, and history. Last, a theory of justice may seek to cover future people by way of generic categories, such as "humanity." If we owe moral respect to all members of humanity without regard to time, actual existence, and so on, then future people are owed duties as well (e.g., Weiss 1989; Caney 2010). Again, however, the generational features of human beings and the specificity of historical situations in which generations are addressed are sidelined.

Extensionism, abstraction from overlap, the split-theory approach, dehistoricization, and generic universalism thus contribute to the impression that intergenerational relations are treated in a secondary way—a way that avoids grasping humans as what our contributor Anne O'Byrne has called "generational beings" (2010, 6, 41). In its sum, this anthology can be seen to argue that the theoretical task consists in taking fully into account the role of social and historical time, including the time of birth and death that both separates and links generations. If globalization—however it is conceived and however problematic it might be—calls into doubt the spatial assumption that moral and political parties are domestic co-citizens, then the so-called Anthropocene (again, however conceived and however problematic the notion may be) questions the temporal assumption according to which the parties involved are living contemporaries. Phenomenology can help with this questioning, for it generally shows, as this volume illustrates, that the meaningfulness of the present lifeworld depends on nonpresent times that are co-implicated in the present (see van der Post, in this volume). Accordingly, rather than having to be covered by extensions, ahistorical notions, or piecemeal adjustments to moral or political concepts, future people are to be seen as of us and with us in our present time, in fact, co-implicating the nonpresent in the present (see Fritsch, in this volume).

All in all, then, the importance of future justice in our time means that phenomenology ought not to be absent from recent attempts to reorient moral and political philosophy, and so the volume presented here hopes to remedy a lacuna in the literature. In addressing the ontological problems and their potentially demotivating implications, there is the suggestion that we should not begin by focusing exclusively on the calculative question as to how much we owe future people, but by approaching them—and then, perhaps, with a difference—in line with a better understanding of how our lives are connected in morally significant ways to future people. The special challenges of intergenerational justice should lead us to explore the social-ontological basis of ethics and justice; and, having already undertaken its own explorations of ethics from the social-ontological angle of what it is to be a human being, and of ways in which human beings are connected across time—principally by exploring the themes of both death and birth as instituting relations to previous generations as well as to future people—this is an area in which phenomenology promises to make important contributions. However, although the phenomena of birth and death have received much-needed attention in phenomenology, as the chapters demonstrate (see esp. O'Byrne, Fritsch, Waldenfels, and Liebsch, in this volume)—especially in connection with accounts of human subjectivity, agency, and community—it has generally been the case that the attention paid has overlooked one of the great questions of our time, that is, the question of our duties to future people, to which we turn directly in this collection.

We believe the time is ripe for such a volume, not only for reasons that are external to phenomenology but also for reasons arising internally within the discipline itself. From within phenomenology, intergenerational justice can be seen as the next logical focus, given four key developments: (i) some thirty years of ecophenomenology concerned with the human relation to the earth (Howarth 1995; Foltz 1995; Brown and Toadvine, eds. 2003; McWhorter and Stansted, eds., 2009); (ii) a recent flurry of new work on the phenomenology of intersubjectivity (Steinbock 1995; McMullin 2013; Zahavi 2014), though largely without mention of specifically intergenerational intersubjectivity; (iii) work on phenomenology, time, and the feminine, especially with respect to birth, natality, and motherhood (see Chanter 2001; Guenther 2006; Fielding et al., eds. 2011; LaChance, Adams, and Lundquist, eds. 2013; Cavarero 2014; Oksala 2016), although this, too, is rarely bent on addressing relations with future people; (iv) the recent development of a critical phenomenology that makes issues of justice central (see the recent founding of the journal *Puncta: Journal of Critical Phenomenology*, and its first issue, especially Salamon 2018; see also Guenther, 2013, 2020, 2021; DeRoo 2022). Sitting at the intersection of these four key developments, the question of IGJ is thus a crucial fulcrum of one of the most pressing issues we confront today: relations with future generations in the context of the environmental crisis. The present volume, then, may have the effect of nudging phenomenologists towards further contributions on the vital topic of intergenerational justice.

Above all, however, the hope here is that nonphenomenologists, whether or not they are philosophers, will be encouraged and motivated to consider phenomenology's contributions to the subject. In this vein, we now move onwards to an overview of the chapters, which fall loosely into three sections.

Section 1: Generativity: The Future is Of Us and In Us

The three chapters that make up the first section of the book speak directly to the relevance of phenomenology to the theme of relations between generations and the vectors of intergenerational sensibilities and responsibilities. Emphasizing the phenomenological significance of generativity—or the emergence of each generation from the context and conditions of another—in its sociocultural as well as biological aspects, each of the first three chapters explores the continuities and disjunctures, the elisions and interstices, that are among the entailments of our finitude and that shape the confrontation of the subject with its own self and others, past, present, and future. Where the central thread that weaves between the chapters concerns the nonlinear temporality of generativity and ways in which the dynamic exertions of past and future are active within the present as potent and formative structures of human subjectivity, the overarching suggestion is that even generations far removed from our own are neither externalities nor addendums but are in fact *integral* to the self-experience and ethical constitution of the living. Thus, as an ensemble, the first three chapters trace the impact on the present of the dense intergenerational and temporal matrix in which subjectivity takes form and that complicates the scope and temporality of responsibility as it has more generally been conceptualized within the prevailing theoretical paradigms. Taken together, the chapters sound a clarion call for robust theoretical frameworks capable of responding without internal contradiction or compromise to the question of intergenerational justice at a time of a social and environmental crisis.

In the opening chapter, "Generativity and Ethics: A Phenomonelogical Approach," Mario Vergani finds that the inappropriability of the moments of birth and death between which our biological lives extend serves to delineate and perforate the framework of human existence, so that although successive generations overlap with one another their historical sweep is punctuated by diachronic fissures and *inter*generational interruptions. But there is also, he points out, a synchronic or *intra*generational separation that cuts through age-based cohorts and divides each generation within itself, with the result that the living do not conform to any single set of unifying commitments and understandings: there is always, Vergani argues, a "plurality of generations in the contemporary." Far from rendering each generation a discrete and anonymous entity that relates to itself and others as an autonomous totality—which, as he argues, is the fundamental shortcoming of the mainstream theories in the intergenerational justice debate—Vergani finds that the spaces between generations are precisely what make relationships, and therefore the ethical, possible. Intergenerational discontinuity furnishes the dimensions of ethical time; and the irreducible gaps between present and future, and between the different generations that overlap within the present, liberate the future to be the future rather than an endless extension of the present, and, as he writes, "to belong to the other." In our discontinuity, the retrieval of the past by subsequent generations, as the interplay of self and other, is the basis of sense-making and of a profound intergenerational connection that releases the unfinished threads of the past to reach us in the present as the ethical claims of a future that calls upon us to respond. Showing ways in which generativity exposes the plurality of time that is partly recognized—but generally denied the substantial role it warrants—by the mainstream positions he critiques, Vergani underscores one of the important Levinasian lessons that overturns Heidegger's fundamental ontology. History and generations do not draw their substance from temporality, but rather the other way around: temporality derives from historicity, and historicity from generativity.

The second chapter, "Responding to the Claims of Those Who Shall Come after Us," by Bernhard Waldenfels—masterfully translated by Nick Walker—describes the ineliminable alterity of the future that, in touching each of us, imprints itself within the question of how and why we respond to the claims of others and modulates it towards future others in far-distant times. Taking his point of departure from Levinas, who finds that humanity in its entirety addresses each of us through the face of the other, Waldenfels asks whether, in the triangulation of the originary encounter between the self and other through the others of the far-distant future, the ethical claim of the other upon us is diluted—stretched and anonymized beyond its power to elicit the pathos with which we receive it and have already, thereby, responded to it. When, as now, our day-to-day lives unfold as part of a contractual, prearranged social reality that strives to codify the alterity of the other and bring the future to contractual order, we are insulated from the pathic interplay of ethical claim and response, and the expression of the future within the present is stunted. In contrast, Waldenfels argues, if the present time is not cut off from past and future, then birth and death link us, the living, to nonpresent generations. Drawing on his rich and extensive work on responsivity in phenomenological ontology and ethics, and using Levinas's "double accord" of time and the other as his guide, Waldenfels gives special place to biological and nonbiological generativity as he traces the future within the present, in its continuity and its alterity, to show that generativity both links generations and separates them, beginning with the difference in age. Here, as in Levinas's fecundity, present selves live on in future others whose alterity cannot be wholly appropriated. The face of the future can neither be separated from, nor reduced to, today's living faces. With and beyond etymology, Waldenfels argues that generativity is inseparable from generosity.

In the final chapter of this section, "Generativity and Intergenerational Solidarity" (also translated by Nick Walker), Burkhard Liebsch applies a phenomenological approach to generativity to bring the problem of intergenerational conflict to the question of IGJ. Reminding us of Kant's suggestion that each generation receives not only life but also enlightenment from its predecessor, whose influence thereby exceeds its own mortal life span, and observing that this speaks of an underlying diachronic solidarity between generations that is "world-historical" in its reach, Liebsch addresses more recent discussions tracing ways in which disruption to the historical-hermeneutic connections between generations is accelerating in modernity. Finding that today these discussions frequently depict intergenerational relations in terms of oppressive burdens, and often take the form of economic calculations that accuse the elderly of living "too long" at the expense of the younger generation, Liebsch argues that this discourse forgets the connective generativity without which any such talk of generations makes no sense. Both corporeal-biological and historical-hermeneutic, generativity means that each lives from another before one's birth and towards another after one's death; hence, relations between generations cannot just be antagonistic. And yet generative connectivity is not yet intergenerational solidarity: for that, we need to understand better how and why giving birth implies the responsibility to render acceptable the life thus given—that is, how the next generation can come to reaffirm the acts that generated them. Liebsch argues this generative responsibility precedes all ethics: to reconcile others to a life that will always have remained insufficiently justified. Beyond Levinas's fecundity, which Liebsch accuses of dropping the historical profile of generations, and with the help of Hans Jonas, the chapter concludes that the promise of birth extends into a time beyond one's own and so depends for its realization on others and, thus, on social and political conditions that themselves extend across history and generations.

Section 2: The Politics of Human Generations

The dynamics of political responsibility across generations comes to the fore in the four chapters that comprise the second part of this volume. In the previous chapter, Liebsch shows that although the complex chain of dependencies and responsibilities entailed by the promise of birth makes it hard to understand how this promise can *not* be broken, it does, however, impose precautionary principles that express a fundamental solidarity across generations. In turn, the following four chapters apply themselves to the theme of our confrontation in the present with the indefinite extension of dependencies and responsibilities into the future to consider whether or how such challenges might be met in ways that do not, themselves, become forces of oppression. Foregrounding the power that the living hold over the material, conceptual, and institutional conditions that are passed onwards into the future, and the attendant asymmetry of power relations between each generation and the generations that follow, the section as a whole raises questions concerning the object, nature, scope, and mechanisms of responsibility and justice *if* the claim of future generations on the living is to elicit responses that are fit for purpose, durable and adaptable in the face of the uncertainty, alterity, and inappropriability of the future.

The second section opens with Ferdinando G. Menga's chapter, "Absences That Matter: Phenomenological Insights into (the Predicament of) Intergenerational Justice." Menga draws on phenomenology to engage with one of the most pressing questions today concerning intergenerational responsibility: how or whether future generations can be represented politically. What kinds of changes are required for any such representation of future people to be adequate? Noting that in the liberal democratic state today, the right to political inclusion and representation conflates with the right to be considered human, Menga suggests that the absence of future generations from the democratic political sphere exposes the extent to which current theoretical and institutional frameworks fail to regard future people as being fully human. Arguing that although the prevailing theoretical frameworks are beginning, in some areas, to recognize the imperative of including future generations, they generally find themselves unable to do so without internal and potentially self-sabotaging compromise. Thus he finds that the precondition for the fulfillment and continuity of intergenerational responsibility requires nothing short of an ethico-anthropological revolution capable of bringing a new configuration of ethical subjectivity and moral motivation, radically oriented to the future, into the ambit of politics and law—and without, in principle, excluding the reverse possibility that where certain trajectories of politics and legal praxis are already sustained by some such ethico-anthropological reconfiguration, they might facilitate the broader revolution. Drawing from Levinas's ethical exposition of the subject, Waldenfels's account of responsivity, and Arendt's notions of plurality and natality, Menga shows how a "presentist" conceptualization of subjectivity can (and should) be eroded and deconstructed by a future-oriented understanding that, when applied to the question of intergenerational responsibility, yields new politico- and legal-philosophical insights subtended by two main concepts: a future-oriented understanding of participation in the polity, and a notion of political representation as a responsive substitution for future others.

In the next chapter, "How Can We Take Claims of Future Generations Seriously?–Combining Different Perspectives in Our Action," Eva Buddeberg argues that both the increasing scope of human action and its reach into ever further and greater dimensions of the future make it clear that moral considerations must, themselves, transcend our own immediate context to reflect the claims of all those potentially affected by our actions and to include future generations. Questioning the need for a totally new ethical framework, the overarching suggestion of Buddeberg's chapter is that phenomenology has resources that can be applied to discourse ethics in such a way as to expand the present sphere of moral consideration and to address the ethical claims of future generations from within the existing institutional framework of liberal democracy. Buddeberg begins with a call for ethical theory to be underpinned by Levinas's description, taken from the vantage point of the first-person, of an unconditional obligation of the subject to the other human being. Showing how, for Levinas, it is in conjugation with more general third-person reflections that the first-person perspective comes to cognition in ways that allow the subject to universalize their responsibility, she argues that in this way the subject receives the claim of *all* humanity, including future generations, in ethical relations of profound asymmetry. Where Levinas's account stops short of providing a concrete answer to the question of how to *respond* to the claim of all others upon us, Buddeberg proposes that core elements of Apel's and Habermas's discourse ethics are able to incorporate Levinas's account and would, thereby, furnish a theoretical framework capable of expanding the temporal horizons of political and ethical discourse and of embedding intergenerational responsivity and responsibility within legal and democratic practice. In so doing, she affirms Menga's suggestion that the changes required for intergenerational responsibility to be recognized and for future generations to be included within the political and theoretical consciousness of the present need not exclude the contribution, where appropriate, of existing theory; but the approach she advances seeks not to revolutionize but to expand an important theoretical framework and the possibility for IGJ to be an integral part of its institutional expression.

As we have mentioned in previous pages, there is increasing agreement in many quarters that we find ourselves in a position of responsibility towards future generations, and we are beginning to see that calls for this to be reflected in action are growing exponentially. Nonetheless, considerable uncertainty persists as to the basic constitution and most suitable expression of this responsibility, both of which come into focus in the next chapter of this section, "Jonasian Grounding of Future-Oriented Responsibility and the Idea of the Human" by Hiroshi Abe. Turning, in particular, to Jonas's opus magnum, *The Imperative of Responsibility*—which is among the canonic works addressing the issue of responsibility to future generations—Abe draws our attention to a central enigma: on the one hand, Jonas urges that we have a moral imperative to include "the future wholeness of the Human being" (1984, 11) in the exercising of our thoughts and actions; on the other, he states that "we are not at all responsible toward future people but toward the idea of the Human" (1989, 91; translation by Abe). In a quest to make sense of the significance of these two outwardly discordant statements, Abe begins his investigations with an outline of the two paradigms of responsibility that Jonas holds to be exemplary, namely the political and the parental. Despite certain differences, the two paradigms share the traits of totality, continuity, and futurity that constitute the most basic or primordial phenomenon of responsibility. For Jonas, as Abe shows us, the exercise of responsibility towards people who are not directly present to us, as with future people, entails drawing not only from the present but also from the past to remake for ourselves, generation after generation, an image of the whole human being. This, then, is the "idea of the human" *to* which we are therefore responsible in the very exercise of responsibility. Where the danger, here, lies in the concretization of a normative image of the human being that would ossify our image-making and shut down the field of future possibility, Abe argues that, for Jonas, we therefore have a responsibility in the present *for* the horizon of possibility, which, if kept open, enables the responsibility to the idea of the human to be passed onwards from generation to generation. In this way, as Abe concludes, our fundamental futural responsibility is for responsibility itself.

This second section of the book ends with Anne O'Byrne's chapter, "'The Race of the Poor': Intergenerational Lessons from Anarchist Eugenics." Where Abe, as we have seen, draws from Jonas the imperative to hold open the world of possibility that each generation inherits from the previous, O'Byrne asks whether generativity itself cannot *but* reproduce and affirm sociohistorical attitudes and divisions and, thereby, conflict with the project of freedom and an open future. While every social and political vision that strives to sustain itself into the future and across generations is, in itself, a narrowing of the general horizon of possibility, there is a notable tension in those visions that promote themselves as the optimal route to achieving freedom, including freedom for future generations. This is particularly heightened in the radical, nonstatist concept of freedom espoused by nineteenth- and twentieth-century anarchist politics—especially in relation to eugenics—which seems, therefore, to furnish a promising avenue for pursuing this tension. In the context of the biopolitical futurism that is also touched upon by Liebsch, and in ways that speak to the asymmetry of intergenerational power relations, O'Byrne pursues this tension at the forefront of anarchist thought as one between present and future: if we reject authority in the name of present freedom and free love, how can we accept the authority we inevitably have over those who come after us?

Although "anarchist eugenics" sounds like an oxymoron, O'Byrne follows its developments within Spanish anarchist thought of the 1920s and 1930s and the struggle to sustain revolutionary practice, where it was believed that the cause of freedom and equality could be served, and "the race of the poor" eliminated, by sex education, free love, and conscious generation. And yet the commitment to ensure equal freedom—including freedom from the biopolitical promotion of sex for procreation and for long-lasting politics—can hardly, itself, avoid becoming tradition-forming and institution-founding. In this way, anarchist commitments are forced to take a stance on generativity, even if the task is to interrupt the biopolitically naturalized and racialized rhythm of reproduction in poverty. Debating present-day queer anarchist politics "against the Child," and thus against generativity, O'Byrne argues that resistance in the name of freedom still takes place "against the backdrop of generational life" and, thus, in the context of inheritance and bequest and the power of the older generation to shape both the younger generation and the conditions in which they must find their way. For the anarchist, however, the crucial focus is not placed on reproduction and conservation, but, as she concludes, on "protecting the contingency and otherness of the inheritors and conferring on them the responsibility to achieve the capacity for freedom and revolutions of their own."

Section 3: *Amor Mundi* in Presentist Modernity

The final section of the book turns to relations between self and world, humans and the earth on which they live, integrating questions of social, political, and temporal environment and bringing them into the orbit of questions concerning our material environment and the conditions of human and planetary flourishing. As we saw previously, O'Byrne shows that the struggle for freedom and open horizons continues to unfold "against the backdrop of generational life." But, clearly, it also unfolds against the backdrop of the nonhuman. Drawn into three different focal points in the final three chapters of the book, the interplay between generativity and the nonhuman world emerges as a vital, dynamic fabric of human subjectivity and self-understanding that shapes relations between past, present, and future and, in itself, raises further questions about the nature and possibility of human freedom and the role of the nonhuman within it.

The section begins with Matthias Fritsch's chapter, "Natal Alienation, Critical Theory, Future People." The term "natal alienation," which was famously deployed by Orlando Patterson to capture a catastrophic dimension of the many harms of slavery, refers to the forced separation of individuals from their families, their communities, and their historical and cultural context. Where Patterson emphasises the sociocultural aspects of natal alienation, Fritsch points out that divorce from the land and profound rupture between people and place are not only endemic to natal alienation but, as the precondition for dispossession and capitalist accumulation, are all too often among its primary motives. Tracing the threads connecting land dispossession, natal alienation, primitive accumulation (Marx 1992), and the manufacture of the "docile bodies" (Foucault 1995, 294/301) that propel capitalist society, the chapter shows us that in grasping the impact of intergenerational rupture and the insertion of the individual into an arbitrary, alien world from which meaning, history, and symbolic significance have been severed, we can begin to see that our intergenerational context is a primal fulcrum of agency. Drawing upon the phenomenologies of human time in Heidegger, Arendt, and Levinas, Fritsch outlines a concept of agency grounded in the facts of being born of preceding generations (natality) and of leaving the world to succeeding generations upon death (mortality and generativity, or fecundity). In this way, mortality, natality, and generativity relate an agent intrinsically to ancestors and descendants, and are shown by Fritsch to be constitutive of human freedom. He concludes that a critical-phenomenological theory of society that heeds this insight must overcome various forms of presentism or short-termism that hamper our responses to the ongoing environmental crisis.

The next chapter, "In Our Element," by Rebecca van der Post, describes the crisis of modernity in terms of a confrontation with a future from which possibility itself has withdrawn, to argue that the well-being of the future and of future generations requires an urgent restoration of meaning to the present. van der Post begins by outlining Alphonso Lingis's account of the awakening of self-awareness in response to sensorial enjoyment of a "sustaining medium" (Lingis 2018) whose elements—as light, air, sound, terrestiality, and so on—infuse our being from the outset and hold us within an elemental present into which the sentient self is ever emerging. Where Western modernity takes the self-contained, autonomous agent to be axiomatic, van der Post argues that this is a highly specific sociohistorical development in human self-experience, which has more generally taken porous exchange and sensorial interplay with the world to be the foundations of selfhood, meaning, and possibility. Drawing from key works in anarchist anthropology and from Charles Taylor's discussion of the impact of Protestant reform and proto-capitalism on the evolutions of subjectivity (Taylor 2009), van der Post finds that the historical consolidation of human agency—as a telic form and as the purview of the rational, sensorially dissociated individual—has had the effect of displacing meaning from the world and the present and of repositioning it within the human mind and the future where, under the doctrine of progress, it is suspended within the "better world" that ever mobilizes our efforts but is always just beyond our reach.

However, van der Post continues, our knowledge of the damage that the world has sustained at human hands and must carry with it far, far into the future has profoundly altered the way in which the future brings itself to bear upon the present, gesturing to us not from the shorelines of its eventual utopian fulfillment but from the brink of its own elemental dissolution. With reference to recent phenomenological investigations into depression, van der Post proposes that the telic, Western subjectivity is not only vulnerable to the strictures of depression, but also *expresses* them, and draws us ever further from a world in which *possibility* itself remains a possibility, so that our bequest to future generations is becoming a world and a mode of being that are increasingly unliveable. Pointing out that Marcuse and Bachelard have suggested that in reverie we retrieve vital dimensions of both self and possibility that have been submerged beneath our adaptations to modernity, van der Post turns to Toadvine's account of the apocalyptic imagination to conclude that since the imagination is, itself, now succumbing to the depressive operations of modernity, it is to our most basic sensorial interactions with the world that we must turn if the horizon of meaning and possibility is to open anew.

The book draws to its close with Kelly Oliver's chapter, "From Love of World to Love of Earth: Taking Responsibility for the Future of the

Planet." In the previous chapter, van der Post explores the possibility of a renewal of the present and the future to which it points based in a subliminal love of the world that avails itself to our primal, pre-reflective sentience. In the final chapter, Oliver transposes love of the world into the realm of consciousness. Reminding us that in her meditation on education Hannah Arendt asks if we can love the world enough to take responsibility for it, Oliver reflects upon Hannah Arendt's notion of a human world that is "always the product of man's *amor mundi*" (Arendt 2005, 203) to explore the possibility for "love of world" to extend its roots into our ethical and political commitments and to nourish the foundation of our relations with future generations. Drawing from Arendt's distinction between world and earth, the human world and the earth on which it is radically dependent, Oliver raises the question of what happens when we begin to consider ourselves as belonging *first of all* to the earth—as earthlings before and beyond humans—and to imagine responsibility in relation not only to the human world, but also to the earth with all of its creatures. If, as Oliver proposes, to be home is to belong, then, as earthlings, to be at home is to be part of a rich and complex cohabitation, which, she argues, along with its multiplicity of creatures and species, is the subject of ethics, including intergenerational ethics. In conclusion, Oliver proposes an earth ethics based on a love of earth, which commits us to our earthbound existence and fellow earthlings. The project, then, is to avow our *amor mundi* so that it is in profound love of the earth that future worlds continue to be born.

Bibliography

Arendt, Hannah. 2005. *The Human Condition*. Chicago: University of Chicago Press.
Ball, Terence. 1985. "The Incoherence of Intergenerational Justice." *Inquiry* 28: 321–37.
Barry, Brian. 1978. "Circumstances of Justice and Future Generations." In *Obligations to Future Generations*, edited by R. Sikora and B. Barry, 204–48. Philadelphia: Temple University Press.
———. 1989a. "Justice as Reciprocity." In *Liberty and Justice*, 211–41. Oxford: Oxford University Press.
———. 1989b. *Theories of Justice. A Treatise on Social Justice*. Vol. 1. Berkeley: University of California Press.
———. 1991. *Liberty and Justice: Essays in Political Theory II*. Oxford: Clarendon Press.
———. 1999. "Sustainability and Intergenerational Justice." In *Fairness and Futurity*, edited by Andrew Dobson. New York: Oxford.

de Beauvoir, Simone. 2011. *The Second Sex.* Translated by Constance Borde and Sheila Malovany-Chevallier. New York: Vintage Books.

Beckerman, Wilfred. 1999. "Sustainable Development and Our Obligations to Future Generations." In *Fairness and Futurity*, edited by Andrew Dobson. New York: Oxford.

———. 2006. "The Impossibility of a Theory of Intergenerational Justice." In *Handbook of Intergenerational Justice*, edited by Joerg Chet Tremmel. Cheltenham: Edward Elgar.

Beckman, Ludvig, and Edward A. Page. 2008. "Perspectives on Justice, Democracy, and Global Climate Change." *Environmental Politics* 17 (4): 527–35.

Birnbacher, Dieter. 1977. "Rawls' Theorie der Gerechtigkeit und das Problem der Gerechtigkeit zwischen den Generationen." *Zeitschrift für philosophische Forschung* 31: 385–401.

Brown, Charles S., and Ted Toadvine, eds. *Eco-Phenomenology: Back to the Earth Itself.* Albany, NY: State University of New York Press.

Caney, Simon. 2010. "Climate Change, Human Rights and Moral Thresholds." In *Climate Ethics: Essential Readings*, edited by Stephen Gardiner, Simon Caney, Dale Jamieson, and Henry Shue, 163–77. Oxford: Oxford University Press.

Carr, David. 2014. *Experience and History: Phenomenological Perspectives on the Historical World.* Oxford: Oxford University Press.

Cavarero, Adriana. 2014. "'A Child Has Been Born unto Us': Arendt on Birth." *philoSOPHIA* 4 (1) (Winter): 12–30.

Chanter, Tina. 2001. *Time, Death, and the Feminine: Levinas with Heidegger.* Stanford, CA: Stanford University Press.

DeRoo, Neal. 2022. *The Political Logic of Experience.* New York: Fordham University Press.

Derrida, Jacques. 1979. "Living On: Borderlines." In *Deconstruction and Criticism*, edited by Harold Bloom et al. New York: Seabury.

Dilthey, Wilhelm. 1990. *Die geistige Welt: Einleitung in die Philosophie des Lebens; Erste Hälfte; Abhandlungen zur Grundlegung der Geisteswissenschaften.* Edited by Georg Misch. Kornwestheim: Vandenhoeck and Ruprecht.

Feinberg, Joel. 1970. "The Nature and Value of Rights." *Journal of Value Inquiry* 4: 243–57.

Fielding, Helen, Christina Schües, and Dorothea Olkowski, eds. 2011. *Time in Feminist Phenomenology.* Indianapolis: Indiana University Press.

Foltz, Bruce V., ed. 1995. *Inhabiting the Earth: Heidegger, Environmental Ethics, and the Metaphysics of Nature.* Atlantic Highlands, NJ: Humanities Press.

Fritsch, Matthias. 2017. "'La justice doit porter au-delà de la vie présente': Derrida on Ethics Between Generations." *Symposium* 21 (1): 231–53.

———. 2018. *Taking Turns with the Earth: Phenomenology, Deconstruction, and Intergenerational Justice.* Stanford: Stanford University Press.

———. 2020. "Asymmetrical Reciprocity in Intergenerational Justice." In *Future Design: Incorporating Preferences of Future Generations for Sustainability*, edited by Tatsuyoshi Saijo, 17–36. Berlin: Springer.
———. 2020. "Response to Critics of *Taking Turns with the Earth*." *Etica & Politica/ Ethics & Politics* XXII (2): 557–88.
———. 2021. "Discourse Ethics and the Intergenerational Chain of Concern." *Journal of Continental Philosophy* 2 (1): 61–91.
Foucault, Michel. 1977. *Discipline and Punish: The Birth of the Prison*. Translated by Alan Sheridan. New York: Vintage Books. Originally published as *Surveiller et Punir: Naissance de la Prison*. Paris: Gallimard, 1975.
Gadamer, Hans-Georg. 1992. *Truth and Method*. 2nd ed. Translated by Joel Weinsheimer and Donald G. Marshall. New York: Crossroad.
Garvey, James. 2008. *The Ethics of Climate Change*. London: Continuum.
Gardiner, Stephen. 2006. "A Perfect Moral Storm: Climate Change, Intergenerational Ethics and the Problem of Moral Corruption." *Environmental Values* 15 (3): 397–413.
Gardiner, Stephen. 2009. "A Contract on Future Generations?" In *Intergenerational Justice*, edited by Axel Gosseries and Lukas H. Meyer, 77–118. Oxford: Oxford University Press.
Gardiner, Stephen. 2011. *A Perfect Moral Storm: The Ethical Tragedy of Climate Change*. Oxford: Oxford University Press.
Gosseries, Axel, and Lukas H. Meyer, eds. 2009. *Intergenerational Justice*. Oxford: Oxford University Press.
Gosseries, Axel. 2009b. "Three Models of Intergenerational Reciprocity." In *Intergenerational Justice*, edited by Axel Gosseries and Lukas H. Meyer, 119–46. Oxford: Oxford University Press.
Guenther, Lisa. 2006. "'Like a Maternal Body': Emmanuel Levinas and the Motherhood of Moses." *Hypatia* 21 (1): 119–36.
———. 2013. *Solitary Confinement: Social Death and Its Afterlives*. Minneapolis: University of Minnesota Press.
———. 2020. "Critical Phenomenology." In *50 Concepts for a Critical Phenomenology*, edited by Gail Weiss et al. Evanston: Northwestern University Press.
———. 2021. "Six Senses of Critique for Critical Phenomenology." *Puncta: Journal of Critical Phenomenology* 4 (2): 5–23.
Habermas, J. 1984. *The Theory of Communicative Action, Vol. 1. Reason and the Rationalization of Society*. Cambridge: Polity.
———. 1985. *The Theory of Communicative Action, Vol. 2. Lifeworld and System: A Critique of Functionalist Reason*. Cambridge: Polity.
Habib, Allen. 2013. "Sharing the Earth: Sustainability and the Currency of Inter-Generational Environmental Justice." *Environmental Values* 22: 751–64.
Heidegger, Martin. 1962. *Being and Time*. Translated by John Macquarrie and Edward Robinson. New York: Harper and Row.

Heyward, Clare. 2008. "Can the All-Affected Principle Include Future Persons? Green Deliberative Democracy and the Non-Identity Problem." *Environmental Politics* 17 (4): 625–43.

Hiskes, Richard P. 2009. *The Human Right to a Green Future: Environmental Rights and Intergenerational Justice*. New York: Cambridge University Press.

Holland, Alan. 1997. "Substitutability: Or Why Strong Sustainability Is Weak and Absurdly Strong Sustainability Is Not Absurd." In *Valuing Nature?*, edited by John Foster, 119–34. London: Routledge.

———. 1999. "Sustainable Development: Should We Start from Here?" In *Fairness and Futurity*, edited by Andrew Dobson, 46–68. Oxford: Oxford University Press.

Horkheimer, M. 1974. *Eclipse of Reason*. London: Seabury Press.

Howarth, J. M. 1995. "The Crisis of Ecology: A Phenomenological Perspective" *Environmental Values* 4 (1): 17–30.

Howarth, Richard B. 1992. "Intergenerational Justice and the Chain of Obligation." *Environmental Values* 1 (2): 133–40.

Humphrey, Mathew. 2009. "Mapping the Moral Future: Environmental Problems and What We Owe to Future Generations." *Res Publica* 15: 85–95.

Husserl, Edmund. 1964. *The Phenomenology of Internal Time-Consciousness*. Translated by James S. Churchill. Bloomington: Indiana University Press.

Jamieson, Dale. 2014. *Reason in a Dark Time: Why the Struggle against Climate Change Failed—and What It Means for Our Future*. Oxford: Oxford University Press.

Jonas, Hans. 1984. *The Imperative of Responsibility: In Search of an Ethics for the Technological Age*. Translated by Hans Jonas with the collaboration of David Herr. Chicago: University of Chicago Press.

Johnson, Genevieve Fuji. 2007. "Discursive Democracy in the Transgenerational Context." *Contemporary Political Theory* 6: 67–85.

Kavka, Gregory. 1981. "The Paradox of Future Individuals." *Philosophy and Public Affairs* 11 (2): 93–112.

LaChance Adams, Sarah, and Caroline R. Lundquist, eds. 2013. *Coming to Life: Philosophies of Pregnancy, Childbirth, and Mothering*. New York: Fordham University Press.

Levinas, Emmanuel. 1979. *Totality and Infinity: An Essay on Exteriority*. Translated by Alphonso Lingis. Dordrecht: Kluwer Academic Publ.

Lingis, Alphonso. 2018. "The Elements." In *The Alphonso Lingis Reader*, edited by Tom Sparrow, 43–54. Minneapolis: University of Minnesota Press.

Marx, Karl. 1992. *Capital*. Vol. 1. Translated by Ben Fowkes. London: Penguin.

McMullin, Irene. 2013. *Time and the Shared World: Heidegger on Social Relations*. Evanston, IL: Northwestern University Press.

McWhorter, Ladelle, and Gail Stansted, eds. 2009. *Heidegger and the Earth: Essays in Environmental Philosophy*. 2nd ed. Toronto: University of Toronto Press.

Merleau-Ponty, Maurice. 1968. *The Visible and the Invisible*. Translated by Alphonso Lingis. Evanston: Northwestern University Press.
Meyer, Lukas, and H. Dominic Roser. 2009. "Enough for the Future." In *Intergenerational Justice*, edited by Axel Gosseries and Lukas H. Meyer, 219–48. Oxford: Oxford University Press.
O'Byrne, Anne. 2010. *Natality and Finitude*. Bloomington: Indiana University Press.
Oksala, Johanna. 2016. *Feminist Experiences: Foucauldian and Phenomenological Investigations*. Evanston: Northwestern University Press.
Page, Edward A. 2006. *Climate Change, Justice and Future Generations*. Cheltenham, UK: Edward Elgar.
Parfit, Derek. 1984. *Reasons and Persons*. Oxford: Clarendon Press.
Partridge, Ernest. 1978. "Beyond 'Just Savings.'" Unpublished manuscript. www.igc.org/gadfly/papers/swsabf.htm.
Pogge, Thomas. 1995. "How Should Human Rights Be Conceived?" *Jahrbuch für Recht und Ethik* 3: 103–20.
Pontara Giuliano. 1995. *Etica e generazioni future: Una introduzione critica ai problemi filosofici*. Rome-Bari: Laterza.
Rawls, John. 1971. *A Theory of Justice*. Cambridge, MA: Harvard University Press.
———. 1996. *Political Liberalism*. New York: Columbia University Press.
Routley, Richard, and Val Routley. 1979. "Nuclear Energy and Obligations to the Future." *Inquiry* 21: 133–79.
Roberts, Melinda A., and David T. Wasserman, eds. 2009. *Harming Future Persons: Ethics, Genetics and the Nonidentity Problem*. Berlin: Springer.
Salamon, Gayle. 2018. "What's Critical about Critical Phenomenology?" *Puncta: Journal of Critical Phenomenology* 1 (1): 8–17.
Schütz, Alfred. 1980. *The Structures of the Life-World*. Translated by Richard M. Zaner and Tristram Engelhardt Jr. Evanston, IL: Northwestern University Press.
Steinbock, Anthony. 1995. *Home and Beyond: Generative Phenomenology after Husserl*. Evanston: Northwestern University Press.
Steiner, Hillel, and Peter Vallentyne. 2009. "Libertarian Theories of Intergenerational Justice." In *Intergenerational Justice*, edited by Axel Gosseries and Lukas H. Meyer, 50–76. Oxford: Oxford University Press.
Taylor, Charles. 2009. *A Secular Age*. Cambridge: Harvard University Press.
Tremmel, Jörg Chet, ed. 2006. *Handbook of Intergenerational Justice*. Cheltenham: Edward Elgar.
———. 2009. *A Theory of Intergenerational Justice*. London: Earthscan.
———. 2010. "Review of Melinda A. Roberts, David T. Wasserman (eds.) *Harming Future Persons: Ethics, Genetics and the Nonidentity Problem*" *Notre Dame Review of Books*, no. 4. https://ndpr.nd.edu/reviews/harming-future-persons-ethics-genetics-and-the-nonidentity-problem/.
———. 2013. "The Convention of Representatives of All Generations under the 'Veil of Ignorance.'" *Constellations* 20 (3): 483–502.

Weiss, Edith Brown. 1989. *In Fairness to Future Generations: International Law, Common Patrimony, and Intergenerational Equality.* Dobbs Ferry, NY: Transnational Publishers.
Woodward, James. 1986. "The Non-Identity Problem." *Ethics* 96: 804–31.
Zahavi, Dan. 2014. *Self and Other: Exploring Subjectivity, Empathy, and Shame.* Oxford: Oxford University Press.

Section 1

Generativity:
The Future Is of Us and in Us

1

Generativity and Ethics
A Phenomenological Approach

Mario Vergani

Generativity

Generativity is the trace that birth leaves on history. It prevents us from thinking of history as a linear, irreversible, and fated process. Dotted as it is with deaths and births, generativity tells us that history cannot be totalized, that it has no right to the last word. Something will always elude history, something will always exceed it and, bursting into it and fracturing its course, will alter its direction and sense.

As the trace of birth, generativity does not renew time, but rather—each time—the opening up of time, and always in the form of an impossible separation from and relationship with the other: that is to say, as both a definitive and uncomposable *caesura*—death—and a *going beyond* it. Birth interrupts the neutral and irreversible course of time; the impossible possibility of upsetting the temporal flow, of decomposing, arresting, and deviating, it introduces a new beginning. Hence, although we may view the production of time as more than the anonymous flow of homogeneous points along a line, as a figure of time, this misses out precisely on what constitutes its enigma, that is to say, the succession of instants. Yet we should avoid seeing time as dependent on an isolated subject who synchronizes lived experiences and arranges events in a sequence. On the contrary, the time of generativity presents itself as the relationship of self with other, the other-who-is-to-come, one who—albeit another—is also me. It is a time that concerns me, but does not belong to me: a time that anticipates me and is antecedent to me but is not and never can be at my disposal.

At this level of analysis, a temporalization that pertains both to me and to the other, that is mine insofar as it is of the other, is not to be confused with the time that governs the genesis and circular generation of forms. This is because it is not an anonymous time, indifferent to the singularities that produce it but, rather, is given uniqueness by uniqueness, without ever composing a totality that completes it or sums it up. Human time can never be reduced to the reproduction of the living: the other is at stake in it. And my relationship with the other is not extrinsic, insofar as it does not happen over time, but rather generates time.

Thus, generativity cannot be reduced to historical time, whether in terms of history (*Historie*), historical happening (*Geschichte*), or historicity (*Geschichtlichkeit*) as a human existential made up of time that measures time and synthesizes it around itself. Yet we need to distinguish between *generativity* and our specifically human way of measuring social time: that is to say, the periodization of time based on *generations*. This requires us to take two steps in our thinking: first, before addressing the concept of generation itself, we need to focus on the generating of generations; next, we should draw a distinction between this generating of generations and genesis conceived as an ongoing anonymous process that is indifferent to the unknown and the unheard-of in each new birth.

In other words, we can never come to understand birth if we take generativity as our point of departure; on the contrary, birth is key to our conceptualization of generativity and history, because births are the secret, forever secret, of generativity and history. Indeed, birth is an inappropriable antecedence, with respect to which I always arrive late; it is an absence that I carry inside myself and that makes this existence mine. A waiting for good on the part of a past that calls from the future.

Where Classical Approaches Falter: The Synchronic and Diachronic Dimensions

The question of the existence or inexistence of ties of responsibility among generations, and especially towards future generations, is currently debated within the contractualist, utilitarian, and consequentialist paradigms; or, alternatively, on a variety of ontological-metaphysical grounds.

In the former set of approaches, responsibility is conceived as an intergenerational pact, based on the logic of aggregate interest, or else—foundationally—on the assumption that we all belong to one and the same humankind. By way of example, let us take a brief look at two representative perspectives, those of Rawls and Parfit, respectively.

First, how may we theorize a duty towards future generations that conserves the Rawlsian postulates of justice, namely rationality and impartial agreement?

> Now when the parties consider this problem they do not know to which generation they belong (. . .) The veil of ignorance is complete in these respects. But since we take the present time of entry interpretation of the original position (§24), the parties know that they are contemporaries; and so unless we modify our initial assumptions, there is no reason for them to agree to any saving whatever. Earlier generations will have either saved or not; there is nothing the parties can do to affect that. So to achieve a reasonable result, we assume first, that the parties represent family lines, say, who care at least about their more immediate descendants. (Rawls 1971, 254–25)[1]

In arguing for intergenerational responsibility, Rawls himself needs to resolve the issue of the non-contemporaneity of the generations implicated in his theorized pact. Hence, he must necessarily focus on the decisive point of the intergenerational *between*, which we may also term generativity. The consequence is not a question of slightly adjusting his perspective, but of radically shifting it, to acknowledge that the discontinuity between successive generations may nevertheless bind them together in some sense. Thus, in proposing some form of responsibility towards future generations, Rawls appeals to additional motivational assumptions to explain the mysterious "bond of care" between successive generations of humankind that cannot be seen as forming one single, integrated generation.

Parfit—taken here as the most extreme proponent of the nonexistence of intergenerational responsibility—concerned himself with the moral theory surrounding our influence on the generations that come after us. If we accept his "non-identity argument" concerning those who are to come, any framework that appeals to the rights of persons is inappropriate, especially when we find ourselves in a situation in which not only do our choices have an impact on other (future) individuals, but the very number of individuals who come into existence in the future can be expected to vary as a function of these choices. While the former is strictly a question of establishing criteria of preference (concerning the relative quality of life of two possible generational groups of equal number), the latter requires the introduction of additional criteria of discrimination. Parfit raises the issue but does not claim to have found a solution for the second scenario. However, his overall approach to the topic is already significant: a theory that establishes the existence of responsibility for the future would paradoxically apply a "charity principle" (which assumes a situation unhampered by nonidentity problems) and, at the same time, accept the premise of "no-difference," that is to say, the notion that allowing someone to be brought into existence is not in itself to confer a benefit to them, given that—at the time the decision is made—there is no actual beneficiary as yet in existence. But for Parfit it is impossible to overcome this impasse. Indeed, in relation to the future, what would it be rational for us to be concerned about? "I should be egoistically concerned about this person's future if I could justifiably believe that this person will be me, rather than being someone else who is merely physically continuous with me. But, as I have argued, this belief is not justified" (Parfit, 253).[2] Nonetheless, in *Reasons and Persons*, Parfit raises—and leaves aside—questions about hypothetical future experiences that are somehow connected to our present through our death, which severs the bond between us and ourselves, and between us and the other. Death is assumed to represent the interruption of all connection, while also being the turning point in the transition from one generation to the next. This dual perspective softens the harshness of death in its absolute authenticity: "Thinking hard about these arguments removes the glass wall between me and others. And, as I have said, I care less about my death" (Parfit, 252). Again, as we can see, the blind spot in theories of intergenerational responsibility—which deal with the generating of generations and the relationship between one generation and another—is touched upon but assumed to be unfathomable.

Turning now to ontological-metaphysical lines of inquiry, which lead us closer to a phenomenological approach, let us examine the position of Jonas, who clearly abandons the assumptions of symmetrical or reciprocal links between generations that are the very axioms of contractualist or utilitarian theories. Jonas focuses on the most crucial—and correspondingly most problematic—aspect of the intergenerational relationship. He devotes considerable space to discussing the nonreciprocity of our obligations towards the future: if our duty towards descendants is not reciprocal, the logic of the acknowledgment of rights—which are in any case impossible to claim—must give way to that of an anticipated duty. "It is in this one-way relationship to dependent *progeny*, given with the biological facts of procreation, and *not* in the mutual relationship between independent adults (from which, rather, springs the idea of reciprocal rights and duties) that one should look for the origin of the idea of (basically one-sided) responsibility in general" (Jonas, 39).[3] Here, Jonas attempts to base his theory of responsibility for future generations on the archetype of the father-son relationship; however, this solution comes across as problematic and inelegant, because the "principle" that he is seeking to define is simultaneously ontological and metaphysical. That is to say, on the one hand it is based on a fact (i.e., on a self-evident givenness, which is the being-there of a newborn); and, on the other hand, on the metaphysical idea that is expressed in this fact (i.e., the intrinsic incompleteness of being human, which no one man can fully accomplish in himself).

All the leading approaches that we have just outlined present insurmountable obstacles that derive from their starting assumptions. Hence, the theory that a bond of responsibility exists between generations may only be accepted in a reduced or partial sense. The stumbling block for each model that we have examined is typically always the same: even when it is not satisfactorily addressed, the theme of generativity is implicitly recognized as the crucial concept to be investigated and on which the failure or success of the various theories ultimately depends. Last, when we attempt to define the relationship between generations based on assumptions of "presence," "contemporaneity," and "continuity," the case for an intergenerational link is weak. We are forced to rely on fallback solutions that dilate the present and broaden the terms of contemporaneity to encompass both parties to the relationship; or, alternatively, to reformulate the notion of temporal continuity by interpreting it as the overlapping of contiguous dimensions.

Again, this leads us back to the crux of the matter: the intergenerational *between*, or generativity. Arguing that there is such a thing as responsibility for future generations requires us to rethink the mysterious link that binds successive generations together by virtue of their very discontinuity and, thereby, to shift our inquiry to an entirely new level, recognizing that the generations are bound together by virtue of their very unbinding, as they succeed one another, and by virtue of death as the disruption of all connection between them. Because at the most concealed point of generativity, continuity is inevitably broken: it is interrupted by the mortal event that is death, but also by the miracle of birth. This calls into question our conceptualization of time as an irreversible one-way flow. The human time of generativity rebels against and challenges the present, rejecting continuity and making no claim that those to come will be its contemporaries. It does not anticipate the future and does not prejudge it, but allows this future—which nonetheless concerns it—to belong to the other, leaving it unfinished. Generativity measures time without enumerating it, endowing with content each instant that would otherwise be empty. It recognizes that it is waiting to be redeemed by those who are yet to come. Ethics come into play at this level of analysis, as we come to think of the time in which generations are generated as an ethical time that carries within itself a plea for justice.

Breaks within and between Generations

Within the wide-ranging phenomenological debate—which, whether more narrowly or more broadly defined, has engaged with both the philosophies of history "upstream" from it and the field of hermeneutics "downstream," speaking to thinkers as various as Schütz, Mannheim, and Ortega, along with Dilthey and Heidegger before them and Ricoeur after them—it is possible to observe a general shift from conceptualizing a generation as a container to viewing it as a living interweaving of relationships, while recognizing the divisions that can occur within a given generation and, in particular (although this has received less attention), the inevitable discontinuity if not outright rupture that is produced between one generation and another. Or to express this in terms more suited to our purposes here: the discontinuity that generates generations. A generation is conventionally defined in terms of a cohort's period of birth or association with a given time span, such that, for example, a century might see the advent of three generations—parents, children, and grandparents—with a time frame of approximately thirty years per generation. However, phenomenologically informed theorizing suggests that, even at the intragenerational level, contemporaneity alone is an insufficient criterion for defining the members of a given generation.

When Ortega wrote that "the changes in vital sensibility which are decisive in history, appear under the form of the generation" (7),[4] he described this primary historical phenomenon as part of an ongoing rhythmic succession, while arguing that all those who are committed to the key theme of their age (irrespective of whether they are "pro-" or "anti-" it) belong to the same generation, and thereby implying that not all those who live in the same period will meet this criterion. Mannheim (303) distinguished between "location" (in time) [*Lagerung*], the "actuality" of a generation united by a specific bond (in Heidegger's terms, a generation marked out by its participation in a common destiny), and "generation units." And Schütz (142) proposed that *Mitmenschen* (fellow men) and *Nebenmensch* (contemporaries) are not equivalent, insofar as an individual will entertain a typical relationship with the latter but not the former. From each of these three perspectives, the criterion of aggregation on the basis of contemporaneity is shown to have failed. And all three scholars were informed by Dilthey, who had, earlier, theorized two different definitions of generation, the first being "a concept for measuring internal time [*von innen*], subordinate to that of human life," and the second being "a designation for a *relationship of contemporaneity* [*Verhältnis der Gleichzeitigkeit*] among individuals" (36–37).[5] For Dilthey, an "explanatory study" of the generations as coordinated phenomena should take both the diachronic and synchronic dimensions into account, assessing the impact of the legacy handed down by previous generations as well as the multiple new social and cultural conditions onto which it is grafted. Such an approach would allow the exploration of time from a human perspective without leading us into the trap of taking an extrinsic view of history but, instead, and in keeping with Dilthey's philosophy of history, prompting us to see history as embedded in social relations. The difficulty, as Dilthey himself acknowledged, lies in understanding how the various generations may be viewed "as a whole joined together through continuity" (38). The notion of continuity (*Kontinuität*) is subject to limits, and so we need a more nuanced conceptual framework for the imperfect connections (*Zusammenhang*) that are possible across intergenerational time. In this regard, Dilthey does not hesitate to speak of "a real and complete interruption [*Unterbrechnung*] of continuity" (39), given that a generation is a center of incomprehensibility that encapsulates procreation, birth, development, and death.[6]

Heidegger's position was informed by the work of Dilthey (who was also important for Husserl). He too strove to develop a single overarching framework for conceptualizing temporality and historicity, but with a key difference vis-à-vis the others: Heidegger introduced historicity (*Geschichtlichkeit*) as a step towards framing the temporality of *Dasein* as totalizing, that is to say, as extending from beginning to end (from birth to death). He further conceptualized *Dasein* as connected with an even broader totality, within a semantic chain that he saw as linking historical happening (*Geschichte*) with fate (*Schicksal*), and therefore with one's shared destiny (*Geschicht*). Participating in a generational bond represents the recovery

(*Wiederholung*) of that which has gone before, in authenticity, by a singularity: "Dasein's fateful destiny in and with its 'generation' goes to make up the full authentic historizing of Dasein" (Heidegger, 436).[7] The aspects of unicity (recovery) and totalization are related to one another. In the words of Ricoeur: "The Heideggerian analytic of *Dasein* gave us the opportunity to formulate this aporia in terms of an antinomy between mortal and public time. The notion of a succession of generations provides an answer to this antinomy by designating the chain of historical agents as living people who come to take the place of dead people. It is this replacement of the dead by the living that constitutes the third-time characteristic of the notion of a succession of generations" (Ricoeur 1983, 109).[8] Now, Ricoeur's account emphasizes elements of rupture, framing filiation as both a breach and a suture, in both biological and social terms: in other words, it entails both substitution and at the same time something that is irreplaceable, at both the biological and cultural-symbolic levels. Hence, the generation is an intermediate figure that helps us to conceptualize time in the human sense, from the collective rather than the individual point of view. Now, while the aspect of rupture between one generation and the next is key to avoiding an extrinsic perspective on our time consciousness, the social (in the symbolic-cultural sense) dimension of this model is preceded by the "for-the-other" element of generation and as such risks reducing the concept of generation to a form of anomy.

The scholarship reviewed to date allows us to deduce that phenomenological approaches identify a plurality of generations in the contemporary: that is to say, a "non-contemporaneity" with respect to itself in a given time period or multiple generations in the same era. Another key phenomenological insight is that the generations are given precisely by means of a discontinuous succession. The latter assumption, however, leaves us with an anomic definition of generation. It makes it difficult for us to conceptualize the relationship between successive generations other than as the partial overlap of different groups. Ultimately, along with solving the problems raised by the continuity-hypothesis, we also need to shift our focus from "generation" (in the singular) to the pluralization of the concept of generation, that is to say, to the notion of plural generations, and generations of generations. In other words, we need to replace a view of a generation as static to a view of a generation in the sense of generating. Not generation in the natural sense, but rather generation understood as that which passes between one and the other, between a death and a birth, between one name and another name. At this point, the crucial question is no longer how we may define a generation, but how we may define plural generations, or the generativity by which generations are produced. In sum, then, we must ask how we might conceptualize generations in terms of impossible passages from one to the other, or as a plurality of uniquenesses that, although they are other than me, also concern me.

Genetic and Generative Phenomenology

From Husserl's perspective, the basic distinction between *genetic phenomenology* and *generative phenomenology* is clear: the former entails a regressive inquiry or questioning-back (*Rückfrage*) into the active-passive dimensions implicated in the constitution of the transcendental subject; the latter, more specifically, investigates the themes of generative temporality and historicity—understood in the phenological sense—recognizing them as border or threshold problems (*Grenzprobleme* and *Randprobleme*). Hence, generative phenomenology is focused on the historical phenomenological constitution of sense, which concerns both my own self, taken as the transcendental subject and the origin of sense, and also the transcendental generativity of predecessors and successors. By taking this approach, Husserl enables us to conceptualize generativity from a perspective that is neither naturalistic/biological nor historical-cultural/spiritualistic (idealistic or romantic). In so doing, he steers us clear of certain pitfalls, for in their own way each of these alternative perspectives leads us into the domain of procreation and proliferation or even—in the second case—into the domain of human history, and thus induce us to historicize the concept of generation. In either case, we would still be constrained to approaching generativity in terms of succession among members of the same "genus."[9]

Hence, adopting a rigorously phenomenological perspective means acknowledging the uniqueness of the viewpoint from which the generational relationship/nonrelationship is to be described. This in turn raises a preliminary question: is it phenomenologically possible to access the theme of generations? For Husserl, generativity (*Generativität*) or the "generative" (*das Generative*) are broad terms that include the themes of sociality, history, and inheritance.[10] Given their liminary status, such themes may be investigated as figures of interweaving and transgression between ownness and otherness. Thus, the production of sense exceeds the transcendental subject and constitutes it. This is made crystal clear in the intricate depictions of generativity offered to us by Husserl, such as the following: "It is like a sea, in which men and peoples are the fleetingly formed, changing, and then disappearing waves, some with richer, more complicated ripples, others with more primitive" (Husserl, 274).

The figure of ever-returning and ever-breaking waves represents the differences underpinning the differential constitution of sense thanks to the position of each subject as the origin of sense. Husserl strives to combine this insight with a broader overall perspective by using the image of the sea, but also, elsewhere, by drawing upon other equally classical images, such as that of the community of generations, which he describes as forming a chain and being chained together: "The infinite chain of generations and the continuation of one's life in that of one's successors, a concatenation [*Verkettung*] via originary instinctive love bonds. If I know myself to be part of a humanity that endlessly maintains itself, the thought of death loses its sting, death its lack of value" (Husserl 2013, 317). Husserl frequently resorts to the idea of a generative constitution of the world that extends before me and after me, before us and after us, in a community of generations, presenting this, in a sense, as a nonthematized, pre-predicative process that is passively constituted. Yet, at the same time, human generativity involves the reflexive recovery, by the living, of the legacy of the dead, giving rise to an intergenerational connection. In sum, within the extended horizon of the living present (*lebendige Gegenwart*), returning to what is already settled represents a reliving of it, and a "generative connection that constitutes itself iteratively" (Husserl 1973, 199).

Hence, the challenge with which Husserl grapples is that of conceptualizing the unitary process whereby sense is generated, and occasionally expressed in strong terms, such as ancestry or lineage (*Stamm*), mostly in reference to the familial dimension and in relation to both "from-where" and "towards-where." At the same time he is also addressing the need to associate this broader process with the contribution made to it by each newly arrived, singularly occurring individual, who represents a transgression (*Beschreitung*) and an excess—simultaneously a recovery and an irreducible novelty.

However, Husserl's theoretical configuration is made unstable by the paradox of a genesis of sense that relies on an overarching generative dynamic that moves from generation to generation, yet, time and again, is accomplished "in one's own name." Birth is a fact: it is, in the first place, a biological, natural fact and therefore also a historical and social, cultural fact. Phenomenologically speaking, it is an empirical fact and, at the same time, it is transcendental, to the extent that it is the condition of possibility for any phenomenal givenness. Without distinguishing between birth and death, Husserl investigates birth as an "event [*Vorkommnis*] in the world transcendentally constituted by me," along with its "transcendental meaning" (Husserl 2013, 1). He asks: "Are these casual factual events in the world?" [*zufällige faktische Vorkommnisse der Welt*] (Husserl 2006, 427), but does not come up with a satisfactory answer. Birth, he finds, is a "transcendental enigma" [*transzendentale Rätsel*] (Husserl 2013, 81).

With respect to this more open theoretical questioning, Husserl never deviates from his core assumption of a transcendental horizon of experience, which—inevitably—has the effect of radically reducing the scope for the novelty of generation. On the other hand, however, he introduces the figure of generating generations of generations without an ultimate, totalizing perspective that would include them all. He thus introduces us into a regime of plurality. And this finally allows us to pose not only the problem of inheritance, but also that of the *to-be-done*.

Non-contemporaneity in the Present

If birth is the secret of the time of generation, then this will not be an empty time composed of homogeneous and unrelated instants, because between one birth and another, between those who are separated, a relationship is given. The time of the generations is an ethical time. Reflection on the generations has mainly been focused on the relationship between contemporaries. Yet if we are to concern ourselves with the future, a thorough reappraisal of our relationship with those who come after us is undoubtedly required. In other words, we need to discuss the "contemporaneity-continuity assumption" and to explore what occurs both within and between generations. *Within*, or intra, because a generation is not a compact unit but divided in itself; but also *between*, or inter, generations. If there were no relationship between the generations, we would have no reason to argue that one bears duties towards the other; yet, at the same time, if we were to adopt a continuity perspective as the minimum requirement for justice for the future, we would nullify the very concept of future, stripping it of its defining characteristic of unforeseeability. There must be an irreducible gap of discontinuity with the future, for the future to be the future. But this makes it difficult for us to understand why we might have duties towards that which is not there. "A genuine ethic for the future undoubtedly depends on taking into account the appeals and demands by future generations and populations even before their representatives are able to enforce their rights and demands. What is required here, therefore, is a radical form of substitution, which presupposes the fact that each individual allows himself to be called into play beyond his death by an alien future" (Waldenfels 2006, 333).[11] The folds and curves of time become twisted and entangled when time, instead of presenting itself as a flow of homogeneous time-points situated along the line that comes from the past and is directed towards the future, begins to weave the past, present, and future into a more complex pattern. Then, perhaps, the impossible can happen: past and future can combine unpredictably together, challenging the rigid requirement for entropy, the irreversibility of becoming. Of course, time always runs in the same direction and the outcome is certain. This is a constant that the phenomenological tradition has never forgotten. Irreversibility and entropy define the direction of the arrow of time, and this marks all choices, decisions, and responsibilities, imbuing them with due gravity, because—"beware!"—what is done is done!

This remains so unless the time of generativity can be assumed to be a social time, characterized by the relationship between different uniquenesses that is produced by birth, a bond that is composed of both separation and relation with respect to the unattainable. From such a perspective, it might be possible to reconceptualize the temporalization-irreversibility equation, without either denying it or attempting to solve it by dialectical reconciliation of the reversible with the irreversible, but, rather, by appreciating the fact that through—that is to say, both despite and thanks to—the irreversibility of historical time, the time of the generating of human generations achieves the impossible: it reverses the arrow of time.

The past has passed. Normally speaking, we tend to think that our ethical disposition only comes into play in relation to what we ourselves have done or not done, when an action is ascribed to us as done or not done, and when, with respect to this, we are recognized as accountable. But thanks to generativity, in relation to the past, I can have an ethical relationship with things that *did not happen*: with actions that were *not* carried out by others and not just with those that were *not done* by me personally. Even though a relationship with the past of the other belongs to the other, it also concerns me. In other words, without going backward through the relevant sequence of events, we can relate to this past in terms of something there that, by virtue of *not* being been done, remains as an incompleteness, an emergency, an urgency: a hidden call that is addressed to me. In this way, the past is not empty, it is no longer merely the irreversible past that has elapsed but a past that calls to us from the future, appealing to us to respond on its behalf, because it is there waiting, still unfinished, as a past that concerns us, that has been there for generations, and is still awaiting an answer.

Incompleteness and the Call for Justice

Thus, we may begin to think about generating and generations in terms that cannot be reduced to any unitary form of temporalization subsuming the flying splinters of every death and every new birth. This means departing from Heidegger's assumption that the theme of generations relies on the question of temporality. When generation is treated in *Being and Time*, specifically in reference to Dilthey's model, the direction is clear: "In analysing the historicality of Dasein we shall try to show that is not "temporal" because it stands in "history," but that, on the contrary, it exists historically and can so exists only because it is temporal in the very basis of its Being" (Heidegger, 428).[12] Heidegger proposes taking time as our point of departure for conceptualizing history. But if we wish to focus on the process of generation that occurs between generations—the *Zwischenzeit* of generations of generations—then perhaps we need to radically revisit our approach and attempt to view time as starting from history rather than vice versa; and ultimately, not to take generations as a measure of history, but to view history as coming to us courtesy of the generations. Such a reversal of perspectives is proposed by Levinas: "The encroachment of the present on the future is not a feat of the subject alone but of the intersubjective relationship. The condition of time lies in the relationship between humans or in history" (Levinas 1948, 79); or again: "Transitive existence—this is the notion of existence that presides over all my philosophy and that underpins participation. It is history that is the source of time. I take time from others [Je prends le temps chez autrui]. My transcendence in fatherhood is the real relationship—which is time. My assimilation of the second moment to "the other" [autrui]—means nothing more than the priority of the concept of history over the concept of time" (Levinas 2013, 203). Taking time from the other implies thinking about the generations without denying the radical separation that the abyss of death imposes between each given name and each lost name, and thus involves radically transgressing the phenomenological transcendentalist assumption, or a totalizing perspective on generativity. Therefore, this undeniable disruption reminds us to take seriously the irreducible otherness of the *between* whose name is death and whose name is birth. A nothingness between us, an absence that sends us towards the other at each unique death and holds us to the other at each unique birth. Separating us and making us inaccessible to each other is my birth and my death. Perhaps Derrida is getting at something like this in his complex meditations on the theme of genesis, genealogies, and generations: "There, at the heart of the alliance [*alliance*], of the alloy [*alliage*], of the semblance [*semblance*], of the resemblance [*ressemblance*], the wire is cut (. . .) Between them, there is at the same time the cut wire and the identifying substitution" (Derrida 2003, 92).

But no word can be the first or the last. It will always be the penultimate, given the operativity of dead time: "The nothingness of the interval—a dead time [*un temps mort*]—is the production of infinity" (Levinas 1961: 284). The passivity of death is operative, not in terms of a passage from potentiality to actuality, but in terms of the operativity of that which can do nothing, the operating of absolute passivity. The impossible is in operation here, it is the "opus" of dead time. Despite the similarity between one and the other, between a parent and child, in assuming the notion of a cutting off, of a radical interruption, of the abyss of death that separates one from the other, we take the first step towards understanding the relationship without a relation between generations, the generating of generations, and generations of generations. This entails abandoning all totalizing perspectives and adopting a more radical phenomenological viewpoint, via a key theoretical shift from the category of totality to that of plurality joined with uniqueness.

A uniqueness that is mine before the other's, a uniqueness that makes me alone. That which is mine is exposed to the strangeness that constitutes it, to that which I cannot appropriate: my own birth and death. Thus, every living present implies a noncoincidence or a non-contemporaneity with oneself. In the words of Derrida:

> No justice—let us not say no law and once again we are not speaking here of laws—seems possible or thinkable without the principle of some *responsibility*, beyond all living present, within that with disjoins the living present, before the ghosts of those who are not yet born or who are already dead (. . .) Without this *non-contemporaneity with itself of the living present*, without that which secretly unhinges it, without this responsibility and this respect for justice concerning those who are not there, of those who are no longer or who are not yet *present and living*, what sense would there be to ask the question "where?" "where tomorrow?" "whither?" (Derrida 1993, XIX)[13]

Thanks to non-contemporaneity, not only between generations but preliminarily in the living present—because all presents have always been and will always be unfulfilled and inhabited by the inappropriate otherness of birth—every now represents an awaiting for the good and for those who will do justice.

Classical approaches to the problem of responsibility for the future are overturned from this perspective: non-contemporaneity rather than contemporaneity is the prerequisite for justice and responsibility for the future, and this is only possible if non-contemporaneity is inscribed in the living present, which, given that my own birth is inappropriable by myself, cannot be closed upon itself.

> The identity of the present splits up into an inexhaustible multiplicity of possibles that suspend the instant. And this gives meaning to initiative, which nothing definitive paralyses, and to consolation for how could one sole tear, though it be effaced, be forgotten, how could reparation have the least value, if it did not correct the instant itself, if it did not let it escape in its being, if the pain that glints in the tear did not exist "pending," if it did not exist with a still provisional being, if the present were consummated? (Levinas 1961, 238)[14]

Generativity is thus the trace left by birth on history because it illustrates that time is human insofar as it is social, fecund, and thus plural. It prompts us not to "define the other by the future but the future by the other" (Levinas 1948, 82). Conceptualizing responsibility and justice for the future by postulating the existence of an appeal to us from the future that is analogous to the appeal that reaches us from the past maintains the concept of linearity in relations across time. But if we wish to think about it phenomenologically, we must turn back to the generating of generations; and thus identify an infinite responsibility for an unassignable injustice, which is such because of the interruption that is inherent both in the chain of generations and in the living present. The appeal for justice is *already-there* and *to-be-done*, because the past and the rupture with the past, those tears that I have not seen, concern me; and they concern that future that—thanks to the other who is me despite being other than me—will still be me. Generations of generations: such is the tally of human time, an intermittence of births and deaths, and of names of names, the almost nothing of a hyphen. A fleeting stroke of nothingness, of the *between* us and in us, the nonadherence of self to self, a self that receives from the other its very breath, a breath that imparts the future, a future that will be given to us by the otherness of the other—coming from the other and going towards the other—when we shall no longer be.

The experience of time is ordinarily understood as the anonymous flow of homogeneous points along a line. But this is an image of time that misses out on its key enigma: the succession of the instants. The traditional undergirding image of flow, and thus of movement and its measurement, does not resolve the problem. On the contrary, since the idea of movement assumes what it needs to explain, it traps us in a vicious circle or the concept of time. Thus, the question of the amphibolic nature of time, which is structure and process, duration and transformation, the coexistence of change and non-change, continuity and discontinuity remains unresolved. And generativity is located at the exact center of this paradox: by allowing reversibility and irreversibility to stand face to face, without attempting to compose them dialectically, we are able to conceptualize the homogeneous, neutral, anonymous course of time as being broken and interrupted by countless new beginnings—and therefore as being otherwise oriented.

A human being's passage through time is a passing-through, from one side to the other, in and out, from past to future and from future to past. It is one of an infinite number of dots piercing the irreversible fabric of time. These many separate "stitches" hold time together without unifying it. By "quilting" time, a plurality of unforeseen and unheard-of events produces it. Countless deaths and countless births, generations to generations, from one to the other, from the unique to the unique. A myriad of glittering dots that give off an intermittent iridescence, in which the breath of time, unfinished, ever advances towards infinity. Thus, history is no longer the circular movement of course and recourse; it is not the eternal return of the same, or the anonymous succession of vicissitudes of peoples and sovereigns, but an infinite breath. As the generations pass ethically through time, they beat its hidden rhythm.

Notes

1. Cfr. §. 44 "The Problem of Justice Between Generations," 251–58.
2. See, on this point, key objections raised by Ricoeur: the French philosopher's different perspective on our duty to future generations rests on his critique of the notion of identity underlying Parfit's approach, which he views as neglecting the temporal dimension that constitutes identity as *ipseity*: "In this respect, the

shift in the discussion from problems of memory to problems of survival marks the appearance on the stage of a dimension of historicality which, it would seem, is quite difficult to describe in impersonal terms" (Ricoeur 1990, 136).

3. Jonas 1979, 2.IV "The Duty to Ensure a Future," 49–57.

4. Cfr, Ch. I "The Concept of Generations," 3–11.

5. Cfr. Rossignol (1993: 197–199) on the nexus between historical constitution via births and deaths and the concept of generation.

6. O'Byrne's interpretation, albeit with different nuances, follows in the same broad direction: a generation is not only a cohort of people who share a theme of interest that is at the center of their common existence, but also the process by which we come into being, the activities we engage in as creative beings, and the fact that, as a generation, we move on and leave room for the next. For this reason, we are "generational beings" (cfr., O'Byrne: 47–49).

7. II, V: "Temporality and Historicality," 424–55.

8. "The Succession of Generations. Contemporaries, Predecessors and Successors," 109–16; cfr. also Ricoeur 2000, "The Uncanniness of History," 393–411.

9. For these preliminary distinctions cfr. Liebsch 2016, 148–51. The *Zwischenzeit* is phenomenologically conceptualized as diachronic time *between* generations: "In a diachronical life, which spans from others who preceded us to others who will survive us, we may observe the opposite. This is the argument defended here from the outset: that we are, insofar as we potentially generate others, involved in their future lives, which are their own and [therefore] inaccessible to us" (33).

10. Cfr. Steinbock 1995, 3, especially *Critique and Responsivity*, 254–56; Waldenfels 1971, V. "Untergrund des Dialogs: bestehende Bindung aneinander," 318–67; "*Generativity* therefore means that I not only come into the world and am in the world with others, but also that I come from others and that I live again in others" 346; Housset 1997, ch. VI *L'héritier*, 179–205: "Even more so, for Husserl, the mortality of individual monads underpins the immortality of the *Monadenall*, thanks to the transmission, via death, of that which never dies. The mortality of the subject endows other subjects with a future. Vice versa, my immortality as a human person would suppress all future for humanity (. . .) it is not so much a spiritual legacy that is transmitted as a possibility to want to take care of the world" (230); cfr. Mouillé 1993, especially "L'unité universelle de la synthèse et la facticité transcendentale," 173–78, on the treatment of generativity in Husserl's *Krisis*. On genesis, phenomenological historicity, and generativity in Husserl, and the problems that arise in relation to Husserlian transcendentalism, see also Derrida 1990, "Preface to the 1953/54 Dissertation: The Theme of Genesis and the Genesis of a Theme," XVII–XLII.

11. See Menga 2016, especially VI. *Il futuro dell'altro*, 97–111. The author theoretically outlines the consequences and the advantages accruing from shifting to a phenomenological treatment of the theme of intergenerational justice. For a phenomenological and deconstructionist approach, cfr. also Fritsch 2018: "Questions

of justice ought to be understood as emerging with the time of birth and death, a social time that separates but also links generations" (7).

12. In §. 74. *The Basic Constitution of Historicality*, 434–39, Heidegger cites, in a footnote, Dilthey's idea of "generation," note 8, 436.

13. Derrida conceptually formulates this idea by way of a theoretical three-component device: conjunction (*conjonction*)/disjunction (*disjonction*) and injunction (*injonction*). See Derrida 1993, 3–76; cfr. De Roo 2013: Derrida identifies the three concepts of "absolutely future past," "generational politics," and "non-contemporaneity of the living present," cfr. *Tradition, Phenomenology, Responsibility*, 144–50.

14. A similar idea is expressed by Levinas: "This compensating time is not enough for hope. For it is not enough that tears be wiped away or death avenged; no tear is to be lost" (Levinas 1947, 91). Cfr. Caputo, 2002, 90–117. On this rift in the present and on the relationship with the future to which it opens up, see Severson 2013: 267–302; see also Vergani 2011, especially IX. *Fenomenologia del tempo*, 241–65; Vergani 2020, 217–52.

Bibliography

Caputo, John D. 2002. "No Tears Shall Be Lost: The History of Prayers and Tears." In *The Ethics of History*, edited by David Carr, Thomas R. Flynn, and Eudolf A. Makkreel, 90–117. Evanston: Northwestern University Press.
De Roo, Neal. 2013. *Futurity in Phenomenology: Promise and Method in Husserl, Levinas and Derrida*. New York: Fordham University Press.
Derrida, Jacques. 2003. *The Problem of Genesis in Husserl's Philosophy*. Translated by Marian Hobson. Chicago: University of Chicago Press. Originally published as *Le problème de la genèse dans la philosophie de Husserl*. Paris: P.U.F., 1990.
———. 1994. *Specters of Marx*. Translated by Peggy Kamuf. New York: Routledge. Originally published as *Spectres de Marx*. Paris: Galilée, 1993.
———. 2003. *Genèses, Généalogie, Genre et le Genie*: Les Secrets de l'Archive. Paris: Galilée.
Dilthey, Wilhelm. 1875 [1924]. "Über das Studium der Geschichte, der Wissenschaften, vom Menschen, der Gesellschaft und dem Staat." In GS V, *Die Geistige Welt* 31–73. Stuttgart: Vandenhoeck & Ruprecht.
Fritsch, Mathias. 2018. *Taking Turns with the Earth. Phenomenology, Deconstruction, and Intergenerational Justice*. Stanford: Stanford University Press.
Heidegger, Martin. 1962. *Being and Time*. Translated by John Macquarrie and Edward Robinson. Oxford: Blackwell. Originally published as *Sein und Zeit*. GA 2. Frankfurt: Vittorio Klostermann, 1927 [1977].
Housset, Emmanuel. 1997. *Personne et sujet selon Husserl*. Paris: P.U.F.

Husserl, Edmund. 1970. *The Crisis of European Sciences and Transcendental Phenomenology: An Introduction to Phenomenological Philosophy*. Translated by Davis Carr Evanston: Northwestern University Press. Originally published as *Die Krisis der Europäischen Wissenschaften und die Transzendentale Phänomenologie*. HUA VI. Den Haag: M. Nijhoff, 1937 [1954].

———. 1973. *Zur Phänomenologie der Intersubjektivität (1929–1935)*, HUA XV. Den Haag: M. Nijhoff.

———. 2006. *Späte Texte über Zeitkonstitution (1929–1934)*. *Die C-Manuskripten*, HUMA VIII. Dordrecht: Springer.

———. 2013. *Grenzprobleme der Phänomenologie (1908–1937)*, HUA XLII. Dordrecht: Springer.

Jonas, Hans. 1984. *The Imperative of Responsibility. In Search of an Ethics for the Technological Age*. Translated by David Herr. Chicago: University of Chicago Press. Originally published as *Das Prinzip Verantwortung. Versuch einer Ethik für die technologische Zivilisation*. Frankfurt: Insel Verlag, 1979.

Levinas, Emmanuel. 1978. *Existence and Existents*. Translated by Alphonso Lingis. Pittsburgh: Duquesne University Press. Originally published as *De l'existence à l'existant*. Paris: Vrin, 1974.

———. 1987. *Time and the Other*. Translated by Richard A. Cohen. Pittsburgh: Duquesne University Press. Originally published as *Le Temps et l'Autre*. Montpellier: Fata Morgana, 1948.

———. 1969. *Totality and Infinity*. Translated by Alphonso Lingis. Pittsburgh: Duquesne University Press. Originally published as *Totalité et infini*. La Haye: M. Nijhoff, 1961.

———. 2013. *Eros, Littérature et Philosophie (1921–1960)*. Oeuvres 3. Paris: Grasset/IMEC.

Liebsch, Burkhard. 2016. *In der Zwischenzeit. Spielräume menschlicher Generativität*. Ettingen: Ettingen.

Mannheim, Karl. 1952. *Essays on the Sociology of Knowledge 1893–1947*. London: Routledge.

Menga, Ferdinando G. 2016. *Lo scandalo del futuro. Per una giustizia intergenerazionale*. Roma: Edizioni di Storia e Letteratura.

Mouillé, Jean-Marc. 1993. "Naissance, Mort et Phénoménologie." *Alter*, no. 1: 149–93.

O'Byrne, Anne. 2010. *Natality and Finitude*. Bloomington: Indiana University Press.

Ortega y Gasset, José. 1961. *The Modern Theme*. Translated by James Cleugh. New York: Harper. Originally published as *El tema de nuestro tiempo*. Madrid: Revista de Occidente, 1923–38.

Parfit, Derek. *Reasons and Persons*. Oxford: Clarendon Press.

Rawls, John. 1999. *A Theory of Justice*. Cambridge: Harvard University Press.

Ricoeur, Paul. 1990. *Time and Narrative*. Translated by Kathleen Blamey and David Pellauer. Chicago: University of Chicago Press. Originally published as *Temps et recit III*. Paris: Seuil, 1983.

———. 1992. *Oneself as Another*. Translated by Kathleen Blamey Chicago: University of Chicago Press. Originally published as *Soi-même comme un autre*. Paris: Seuil, 1990.

———. 2004. *Memory, History, Forgetting*. Translated by Kathleen Blamey and David Pellauer. Chicago: University of Chicago Press. Originally published as *La Mémoire, l'Histoire, l'Oublie*. Paris: Seuil, 2000.

Rossignol, Stéphane. 1993. "*Zusammenhang*, Naissance et Mort: À propos de la "Philosophie de la Vie" de Dilthey." *Alter*, no. 1: 195–212.

Schütz, Alfred. 1967. *Phenomenology of the Social Word*. Translated by Fredrik Lehnert. Evanston: Northwestern University Press, 1967. Originally published as *Der sinnhafte Aufbau der Sozialen Welt*. Wien: Springer-Verlag, 1960.

Severson, Eric. 2013. *Levinas's Philosophy of Time: Gift, Responsibility, Diachrony, Hope*. Pittsburgh: Duquesne University Press.

Steinbock, Anthony. 1995. *Home and Beyond: Generative Phenomenology after Husserl* Evanston: Northwestern University Press.

Vergani, Mario. 2011. *Levinas fenomenologo. Umano senza condizioni*. Brescia: Morcelliana.

———. 2020. *Nascere: Una fenomenologia dell'esistenza*. Roma: Carocci.

Waldenfels, Bernhard. 1971. *Das Zwischenreich des Dialogs: Sozialphilosophische Untersuchungen in Anschluss an Edmund Husserl*. Den Haag: M. Nijhoff.

———. 2006. *Schattenrisse der Moral*. Frankfurt: Suhrkamp.

2

Responding to the Claims of Those Who Shall Come After Us

BERNHARD WALDENFELS,
TRANSLATED BY NICHOLAS WALKER

The Problematic Place of the Future

In its combination of uncertainty and inescapability the future resembles death, while in its continuous recurrence it resembles a perpetual birth. And it is no more possible to appropriate the future than it is to appropriate birth and death; a future that had nothing alien or strange about it would not be the future. This ineliminable strangeness touches and concerns me in my particularity, just as it touches and concerns others in theirs. If there is such a thing as an ethos of time, it manifests itself through the way in which we deal with time, the way in which we give shape to time, the way in which we find ourselves exposed to time. The ungraspability of the future has something deeply disturbing about it, something we seek to dispel wherever possible. One can invest the future in some enduring human goal; one can distance oneself from it through an artificially sustained kind of apathy; one can try and regulate it morally; one can calculate it technologically and exploit it economically; one can displace the future consequences of our own actions onto later generations in accordance with the famous motto "after us the deluge."[1] If individual self-assertion and self-preservation represent the first and last word, as they do in the political anthropology of Thomas Hobbes—in this regard a typical expression of early modern philosophy—then the question "How do you stand with the Other?" becomes the decisive modern question: "Am I my brother's keeper?" or "What is Hecuba to me?" Emmanuel Levinas, whose ethics of the Other invokes these questions that are both old and new, attempts to answer them with neither edifying talk, moralizing sermons, nebulous faith in progress, nor anxiety before the future, but with an essential phenomenological gesture that exposes what is ultimately at stake here. He points out that anyone who asks this question in the first place is guilty of a *principio principii* by merely presupposing "that the I cares only for itself, is nothing but care with regard to itself" (Levinas 1974, 150/1988). Care with regard to others, on the other hand—which Socratic *epimeleia* shows to be at once care for the soul and care for the *polis* (Plato 2002, 36c)—is grounded by Levinas in a twofold accord of time and the other.[2] Here we catch a distant echo of Zarathustra's discourse on "Love of the Neighbour," which instructs us: "Let the future and the farthest be for you cause of your today: in your friend you shall love the over-man as your cause" (Nietzsche 1980 4, 78/1968, 174). What is decisive, in both cases, is a movement of "going beyond" that arises in the present, in the today, but does not revolve around one's own present, one's own today.

The following reflections, essentially guided and prompted by what I call a "responsive" phenomenology, are principally focused on the relationship between alterity and temporality. They pick up from where my earlier discussion ended in *Schattenrisse der Moral*,[3] namely with the question concerning a genuine temporality of ethos that assumes its distinctive form through the way in which it responds to the claims of others. The emphasis here lies on what happens between the claim of the other and one's own response to that claim. This in turn raises the question as to how the singularity of the other is bound up with the sociality of "being-with." Thus the ethics *of the other* opens out into a politics *of others*, where "the third party" plays a crucial bridging role. For, as Levinas insists: "The epiphany of the face as a face discloses humanity"; through the face of the other we are addressed by the "whole of humanity," and the Thou commands us "against the background of a *We*" (1961, 188/1969, 213). The question, however, is whether the path that leads from the face-to-face encounter to this lateral being-with is not too reduced or diminished here; and whether the excessive dimension encountered in the extra-ordinary does not thereby run the risk of becoming entirely detached from the ordinary and enduring context of our life. Throughout what follows, we shall be addressing the future as a threshold phenomenon in this regard.

Responding to What Happens to Us

By the "response" that unfolds in the most varied registers of acting, speaking, handling, perceiving, moving, desiring, and so on, I specifically understand a mode of comportment that begins elsewhere, that is, begins from something that touches and concerns us, something that affects and calls on us in one way or another. All our doing and acting begins in the context of the pathic. This pathic dimension, which sustains and motivates our bodily comportment in a tacit or subterranean kind of way, is most explicitly revealed in particularly strong forms of pathos such as astonishment or terror, which unsettle or disturb the course of experience and may of course assume catastrophic or traumatic forms. In this context, I often use the Greek word *pathos*, which specifically captures the experience of "undergoing" or "suffering" something in the broadest sense, the experience of passivity and of passion. The things that happen to us or befall us only reveal themselves in the answer or response they call forth.

With respect to our specific question here we are principally concerned with the distinctive temporality that belongs to the double event of *pathos* and *response*, of claim and answer. The two terms involved in this double event do not succeed one another in the way they do in the relation of stimulus and response, where the two elements can be described independently of one another. On the contrary, the terms involved here relate to one another in an originary form of temporal displacement that I describe as *diastasis*, to use an expression that is already found in Plotinus and reappears in Levinas. This word literally signifies a kind of partition that connects and separates at the same time. If we leave aside the normal processes in which experience takes its accustomed and more or less regular course, we also encounter certain surprising things or events that, in relation to our usual expectations and anticipations, come too early or too soon; on the other hand, we also encounter answers or responses that, in relation to what disturbs, befalls, or terrifies us, come too late. This means that the memory through which we wrest from the past what has been forgotten touches upon something *immemorial*, which, like our own birth, belongs to a past that was never present; it also means that the expectations through which we anticipate things in the future touch upon something *un-expectable*, which, like our own death, will never be present. Here we encounter, therefore, not only a kind of primal past, something that psychoanalysis and phenomenology both strive to explore in their own way,[4] but we also discover a primal future that can only be disclosed for us in and through the other.

Words for the "future" such as the German *Zukunft* or the French *avenir* already suggest—precisely as *Zu-kunft* or *a-venir*—that something *comes* towards us even before we *go* towards it. The process of coming and going forfeits its equilibrium here, when something new breaks in and interrupts the normal give-and-take of experience with its symmetrical exchanges and alternating positions. This kind of un-everyday experience repeatedly finds its way into the course of everyday experience, when something "strikes" us or "occurs" to us without our really knowing how such a thing comes to pass. In *Beyond Good and Evil* we read: "A thought comes when 'it' will, not when 'I' will" (Nietzsche 1980 5, 31/ 2007, 23). Here we encounter a future that turns what is nearest into what is most remote, yet, as Nietzsche emphasizes, it springs forth in the today by exploding the core of the present. Even in the present we are not fully present-to-ourselves, are not fully at home or *chez nous*.

Delayed Responses

What comes to us from the future can come suddenly, out of the blue, but it can also seep into us or creep up on us in an imperceptible way. But the "now" in which something touches or affects us is never an extensionless now-point.[5] To put this in technological terms, we could say that this "coming" exhibits an analogical rather than a digital character, as all future technologies will have to acknowledge. But nor can the "now" be reduced, as Husserl thinks, to the inner core of a "living self-presence" (1950 1, 62), for the temporal displacement between pathos and response splits open the alleged core here. This displacement means that our answers or responses always arise with a certain delay. Something that belongs to the future announces itself in signs or *intimations* that await interpretation or even demand it, like the admonitory "Menetekel" that appears "as blazing letters on the wall" in Heine's *Balshazzar*. Here we find the traditional mantic practices that Freud still regarded as part of the prehistory that eventually led to the psychoanalytic interpretation of dreams.[6] This element of delay can also be observed in such transitional phenomena as the experience of awaiting, hesitating, experimenting, rehearsing, and so on, which all transpire at certain crucial junctures of experience; they belong to an initial or preparatory phase where that which is to come shows itself in the form of intimations and presentiments, in certain "initiatory acts" or "anticipatory actions" (see Waldenfels 1994, 460; 2015, 288). As far as grammatical expressions of these transitional phenomena are concerned, we would naturally think of gerundive or progressive linguistic forms such as "I am about to do" or "sto facendo," for example. We can only approach the "lived" future, which goes beyond any merely envisaged or imagined future, over "thresholds of unfamiliarity," which, like every threshold, we can be said to cross but never to overcome (Waldenfels 2015, ch. 7). This gives rise to a kind of affective disturbance that oscillates between anxiety and hope. Anxiety in the face of the future proves to be a specific form of anxiety-at-the-threshold; it calls for social rituals that allow us to invoke or "summon" the future.[7] Illusory conceptions of the future tempt us to assume that we could somehow find firm footing on one side or the other of this threshold. But we thereby simply find that the future gets overshadowed by the past or the past gets overshadowed by the future. What we might call future-ism or past-ism are just hostile brothers.

Temporal displacement, by contrast, implies that the past and the future are implicated or inflected with one another. This transpires in a form that, following Lacan and Merleau-Ponty, we can understand as a particular form of the second future (see Waldenfels 1994, 268, 623, and many other places). This differs from the first future, which refers to something that has not yet come to pass but that we hope or fear will happen, and in regard to which we actively try and intervene through our projects and intentions. We regard this normal future as our own future, even if it is shrouded in the darkness of the unforeseeable. But nor is the second future equivalent to the grammatical figure of the *futurum exactum*, which posits something future as if it has already happened. On the contrary, what the second future signifies is that the affect or the call of an Other "comes before" my own answer or response, but does so in such a way that I am compelled to come and meet it. The self that divides into a passive agent to whom something happens and a responsive agent who must answer the call both runs ahead of itself and lags behind itself. It is, as Plato says, both "older and younger than itself" (Plato 1999, 141a). This finds its corresponding grammatical form in the gerundive, where, for example, the statement *mihi faciendum est* indicates what I am to do or have to do, although the relevant act by no means simply springs from the initiative of the "I." When traditional grammar characterizes the pronoun *mihi* as a *dativus auctoris*, it specifically ascribes something to me that does not derive from me: the answer or response that is required of me is never simply or entirely my own. There is good reason why Bertolt Brecht in his *Legend of the Origin of the Book Tao-Te-Ching* has Laotse speak to the official as follows:

> For the wise man's wisdom needs to be extracted.
> So the customs man should be thanked.
> For it was he who called for it.

This little dialogue, in which the venerable sage engages at the border as he leaves his country behind, already brings us nearer to a kind of shared future, like that which is also evoked at the end of Brecht's poem "To Those Who Shall Come After Us," when the poet asks for our forbearance: "Gedenkt uns / Mit Nachsicht [Remember us / With leniency]."

But what has to be recognized first of all here is that no preestablished correspondence or consensus already prevails in this space between pathos and response. Pathos and response seek each other. In extreme situations, they can be almost entirely divorced from one another, specifically by resembling a *pathos without response* or a *response without pathos*. On one side, we have the kind of shock that leaves the shocked one in petrified speechlessness, throws him into a state of helpless lethargy, and weakens or deadens every living impulse. On the other side, we also recognize the kind of vacuous activity where stock responses are just automatically repeated. These extreme forms of behavior anticipate a pathology that, in the form of traumatization or repetition compulsion, can seriously and permanently impair the interplay of pathos and response. The polarized structure of such extreme formations also affects our experience of time—the suffering party may become fixated on past instances of hurt or pain as if they were still happening now, or may become impossible to reach and communicate with, producing nothing but stereotypical answers and responses that close off the dimension of the future. Hyperpathy and apathy alike generate an extreme form of imbalance. The pathology that afflicts the experience of time, as it appears here, also has specific sociopathological aspects, as we see, for example, in the form of collective mass psychosis and the type of morality that springs from resentment—phenomena that were expressly diagnosed by Nietzsche and Freud and were described in specifically phenomenological terms by Scheler.

The Inescapability of Responding

Here, once again, we are confronted with the crucial question that we raised at the outset. What is it that compels us to respond to the claims of others? The modern distinction between the "is" and the "ought" here springs into place and obscures what might rouse us from the slumbering egoism of our own being. Let us imagine that someone weak from thirst asks me for a glass of water, that someone completely lost asks you the way, or that a refugee wants to be allowed into our home, our city, our country. From the mere fact that someone requires something of us, it does not follow that we have to comply with the demand that this individual has made. The traditional virtue of hospitality does not help us much further here if the situation is a really challenging one and if our own interests are at stake. The claim of the other only appears to reveal and exert its binding power when the other in question is not a stranger, an alien, a foreigner, but is one of us, one who already belongs: in other words, when some collective claim of our own stands behind the claim of the other. And it is much the same when the claim of the other is reduced to a kind of universal juridical claim that places me on an equal footing with the other, or places the other on an equal footing with me. Through *incorporation* into a community that is already oriented towards the general good, or through *subordination* to a law that always holds for each and every one, we see that ethos and morality are here cut off from time. If there is temporality here, it is limited to actualizing some type of order or organization; there is nothing of that genuine time that belongs to ethos here; there is no *kairos*. The stipulation of a date for payment or the calculation of labor time for a specific task, for example, are matters that are legally defined or determined in advance. They do not bear on the issue of law as such.

It has to be said that teleologically or nomologically oriented solutions—theories that have found exemplary expression in the work of Aristotle and Kant, respectively—effectively fail us if all forms of order can be shown to exhibit a genealogy, if they can be traced back to *processes of instituting*: if, as we may put it with Foucault, *there is order but no such thing as the order*, or, in other words, if even morality has its blind spot (Cf. Waldenfels 1994, 584). If Hobbes derives the binding character of law from a mutual contract, this certainly leads towards an idea of time that does not simply unfold in a linear fashion, for any contractual agreement inevitably runs before or anticipates its own validity in the performative act of promising to abide by it. But such a contract is still fallible. It certainly makes use of individual self-interest but it is incapable of transforming this into a genuine interest in and for the other. A contract is not some kind of conversion, nor does it resemble the *periagōgē* that Plato envisages in his parable of the cave in the *Republic*. The claims of others are, and remain, competing claims; the other remains a potential enemy, a wolf in sheep's clothing.

Nietzsche plays with the thought of a certain animosity in friendship when he lets Zarathustra proclaim in his discourse *On the Friend* that one should wage war *for the friend*, that one should honor one's enemy *in the friend*, that one should be *closest to him* in one's heart precisely by resisting him (1980 4, 71f./1968, 168). This expresses an animosity that is not aimed at *the* destruction of the other, but directed towards a certain pathos of distance, towards a way of enduring and sustaining differences, towards a remoteness or otherness within what is also nearest and closest. Yet to play with the idea of animosity is also to play with fire, for the bloody wars that we know—in the meantime know all too well—not to mention the state-sanctioned and state-directed campaigns of genocide and destruction we have witnessed, cannot be regarded as honorable enterprises in any sense whatsoever. From where, then, are we to expect any source of resistance to this hostile impulse to destruction?

Levinas, who was compelled to experience this destruction of humanity firsthand in relation to his own family, recognizes the worst there can be when he has the other speak the words "Thou shalt not kill." Levinas is not appealing here to some feeling of benevolence that depends on propitious circumstances, nor is he declaring a universal law the validity of which could always be placed in doubt, like any other validity claim. He is giving expression to an immediate claim that we cannot possibly evade once we have heard it—a claim that generates ethical resistance. Our response to the claim of the other is not a matter of arbitrary choice on our part. It is submitted to the unavoidability or inescapability (*necessitudo*) of a practical necessity, to the impossibility of refusing to respond. In this predicament we cannot not answer, and failure to answer would also be an answer; a refusal to answer cannot un-hear the claim or undo its existence. This belongs to the rudiments of a logic of response this side of Good and Evil, prior to the distinction of "is" and "ought." How we respond falls to us, but not whether we respond. Freedom as responsive freedom emerges from the claim that the other lays upon us (Waldenfels 2011, 63–64).

Answering to the Claims of Future Generations

Yet the idea of responding to future claims clearly raises particular problems for us. How can we respond to the claims of those who are not yet living, not yet in a position to make any claims? Doesn't the idea of such future claims have something of "the message in a bottle" about it—a message that just floats around somewhere without any identifiable sender or recipient? Or is it that the claims of future others are not, strictly speaking, future claims at all, but present claims? These are questions we need to approach in a careful and tentative way in what follows.

This other future, this future of others, is certainly one that belongs emphatically to sites or places where we are not and cannot be present in person, even if we somehow try to imagine them for ourselves. We can only relate to these sites or places in a representative sort of way, insofar as we speak in place of the other, *au lieu de l'autre*. In Levinas, the process of substitution precedes any constitution of the other on our part. Yet here we must distinguish between an ordinary or secondary process of representation and an originary or primary process of representation (Waldenfels 2002, 447–50; and 2012, ch. 8). The former refers to cases where somebody stands in provisionally for someone else, such as the legal guardian who represents a person who has not yet come of age; or to cases where somebody represents the deceased, such as the executor of a will or bequest; or to cases where somebody has been chosen by due process to represent others, such as a parliamentary deputy or "representative of the people." This kind of representation is secondary in character since it is bound in an indirect way to the specific will of those who are supposed to be represented, even if examples of nepotism and corruption cannot always be excluded. Where those who will come after us are concerned, however, any representation could merely point anonymously to so many empty spaces to be filled with individual variables. For in the case that concerns us here there is, as yet, nobody who can actually be represented. In contrast to the various forms of ordinary representation, what I call originary representation is essentially characterized by the way that somebody speaks for himself and on his own part, yet *at the same time* speaks for the other and on the part of the other. In relation to one's own possibilities, what we have here is a lived impossibility—in the precise sense of a radical experience of alterity that is characterized by a certain "access to that which is in an original sense inaccessible" (Husserl 1950 I, 144).

Here we come upon the figure of *the third party* who places me alongside or on an equal level with the other, and who in "comparing the incomparable" transforms the singular claim of the other into a universal right, the excessive character of justice into a constituted legal order, and *the* other into *an* other, into "a member of society" among other such members (Levinas 1974, 202/1988).[8] Thus alterity and sociality intersect and involve one another in the way that we have described. The human sociability that unites and connects us contains a certain excess of unsociability; the other is a person as I myself am, yet at the same time is more than this. The "I" expands into "We"; something transpires between us, yet the I and the Thou are not simply terms or members of a "We," for this arises out of my response to your claims in the singular and the claims of you in the plural. It is not the "We" that says "we": it is I or someone else who says "we."[9] Even the inclusive "We" is never wholly inclusive as if it were some self-contained totality, whether this be family, community, people, culture, or an all-embracing humanity. This talk of "humanity" is particularly susceptible to ideology precisely because it runs the danger of overlooking and over-leaping the concrete demands of the experience we already share with one another. This is why Levinas postulates a "humanism of the other human being" that refuses to allow the relationship to the other to be absorbed or subsumed within some overarching structure of relationality in general. But does this really go far enough? Is the other human being as a human being of the future more than a projection of the present? The question remains as to whether or how those not yet born, the generations of the future, can even speak or announce themselves in this context.

The Generative Future

The predicative assertion that the future does not exist or does not yet exist makes things too easy for itself. For is there not an experience of the futural, is there not a sense of the future, which can be developed and cultivated in various ways? Do we not find that traces of the future already emerge in the present rather than only appearing later as something that follows afterward? As Merleau-Ponty emphasizes in his analysis of temporality in the *Phenomenology of Perception* (2002, 414f.), living time consists in the way that life is always in advance of itself and constantly surpasses itself. But this too can be conceived in a variety of ways.

Alfred Schütz, who analyzes Husserl's concept of the lifeworld in strictly social terms, devotes particular attention to the social *world around us* or *the world* of consociates (*Umwelt*) which emerges out of a we-relationship; this opens out into a closer or more distant *with-world or world of contemporaries* (*Mitwelt*) in which a certain simultaneity prevails, and this world, in turn, is embraced by an *antecedent world or world of predecessors* (*Vorwelt*) in the past and a *subsequent world* or *world of posterity* (*Nachwelt*) in the future. In the process of time there is a continuous transition from one world to the other. But what specifically characterizes the "world of successors" (*Folgewelt*) that belongs to the future is the way in which it is recognized as absolutely indeterminate and indeterminable. "It is only where the social world around us and our with-world can be interpreted as a world of successors because it will outlive us, in other words, where the future world of successors is in the process of emerging out of a genuine We-relationship or They-relationship, that we have a chance of applying to the world of successors as well the same interpretive principles that hold for the world of consociates and for the world of contemporaries" (Schütz 1974, 301/1976). These chances are reduced the further removed the world of successors proves to be. This construction of the social world encounters its own limits in the presuppositions of an interpretive sociology that is concerned exclusively with the meaning we attach to our own actions and the actions of others. Otherness in all its forms is always a relative otherness that manifests itself at the edges or frontiers of normality, which is grounded in an elementary sphere of familiarity, and which can be dealt with by means of recollections and expectations.[10]

Yet the otherness that inhabits the future, by contrast, assumes a weight and significance of its own when we turn our attention to the question of generativity. For Husserl, generativity is something that belongs, along with historicity, to the fundamental features and characteristics of human and interpersonal existence. Thus in *The Crisis of the European Sciences* Husserl writes: "I exist factically within a shared human present and within an open human horizon, I know myself factically in a generative context, in the unified stream of a historicity," and "this form of generativity and historicity is indissoluble" (1950 VI, 256).[11] While this certainly allows a place for the future at the heart of our experience, the resulting "community of intentionality" (1950 I, 157) here is still caught up in the limits of a phenomenology essentially oriented to intentionality: limits beyond which our own responsive phenomenology attempts to move by appealing expressly to the dimension of the pathic, to the dimension of responsiveness.

Two aspects of this generativity are of particular importance to us here: generation in the sense of procreation (*generatio*), which produces a connection between the procreators and the procreated, and the difference in age, which separates the procreators and the procreated from one another yet thereby allows a connection to arise between the members of a shared age group, which we describe as a particular "generation." When we speak of generation or procreation here we do not draw any explicit distinction between the masculine or feminine contribution to parenthood. What is more, we are not restricting the "generation" of new life simply to the corporeal reproduction and propagation of living beings. Thus Plato already employs a very broad conception of generation in the *Symposium* when he celebrates the works or achievements of eros. The generation or "begetting (*tokos*)[12] in the field of the beautiful" (Plato 1999, 205b) refers not only to the body and soul of the disciple who is receiving instruction, but also to the works and institutions of culture in general. In the context of wide cultural variation where the structure of the family is concerned, the concept of parenthood clearly also extends to adoptive parents and comparable carers, so that we should also think of relatives and members of extended families who participate in the process of rearing and upbringing. This generative nexus is not created and sustained solely through direct contact, but also through a processual *network* that allows nearer or more distant relationships to form and develop in various ways and through further processes of *interconnection*, since every "other" in turn has his or her own "others." In this way every relation and every acquaintance brings with it the possibility of yet further contacts in terms of their respective relations, relatives, and acquaintances, in a process of endless iteration (see Husserl 1950I, 158). If Levinas ascribes particular importance to the idea of fraternity in this context (see 1974, 20/1988), this is because it allows for a singularity in the plural—a singularity that goes beyond every "generic community" in the sense that it begins from the "familiar other" (Delhom 2000, 129). In this connection, I have spoken of a certain "intimate otherness" that embraces all significant others in the sense intended by G. H. Mead (Waldenfels 2015, 71). In Nietzsche "the friend" also occupies this place. "I and me are always too deep in conversation: how could one stand that if there were no friend? For the hermit, the friend is always the third person: the third is the cork that prevents the conversation of the two from sinking into the depths" (Nietzsche 1980 4, 71/1968, 167–68). The figure of Narcissus, who sinks into his own reflected image in the water, can also be understood as *aphilos*, the friendless one.

As far as the second aspect (i.e., the difference in age) is concerned, we can see that youth and age are not merely distinguished in accordance with the continually increasing number of years involved in a life. For generation and birth constitute a caesura that interrupts the "unified stream" of the story of a life. What arrives does not simply do away with what came before it. And this is not just because the children or offspring detach themselves qua generated products from the act of making—something that is true for every kind of *poiesis* according to Aristotle—but rather because the child, as an independent being, is not merely a product or made thing (*poema*), is not simply a "Gemächsel," as Kant puts it.[13] But how are we to grasp an act of generation that accomplishes the miracle of creating something externally, from without, that nonetheless lives internally, from within, on its own account? Can there be a "something" that is transformed into a "someone"? And what does this mean for a thinking that attempts to think futurity?

Levinas expressly asks himself this question, a question that threatens to disappear in the realistic everyday of birth and death, of "real birth" and "real death." In *Totality and Infinity*, Levinas focusses principally on the relationship of father and son and, specifically, in terms of the idea of fecundity (1961, 244–47; 267–69). The fact that he does not talk here about the relation between father and daughter, mother and son, or brother and sister belongs to a certain masculine tradition. The "feminine" comes into play in a different fashion in terms of a receptivity that first allows eros to prove fruitful. In the present context, I leave aside questions regarding the character and definition of sexual difference, although the process of carrying, bearing, and nourishing the child involves a particularly intimate corporeal relationship between the vital rhythms of mother and child. Levinas speaks of the child in terms of a "total transcendence," for "the I is, in the child, another. Paternity remains a self-identification, but also a distinction within identification—a structure unforeseeable in formal logic." And then he says, with explicit reference to the Jewish biblical tradition, "My child is a stranger, but a stranger who is not only mine, for he is me. He is me a stranger to myself (c'est moi étranger á soi)" (1961, 245/1969, 267). The otherness of the other rebounds upon one's own otherness when I, in a similar way that I am my body, am myself the other. This living on in the other as an other has absolutely nothing about it that can be appropriated without remainder.[14] Levinas specifically distances himself from a Hegelian conception of dialectic and particularly from the figure of Pygmalion who only encounters a fabricated alter ego in the image he has himself created. The classical form of dialectic that emerges out of the opposition of the self-same and the other plays out in the content of the said, not in the event of saying that comes, like the gaze, from elsewhere, from somewhere remote, and always exceeds the domain of the said. And something similar holds for the future that, in its arriving, also always signifies more than someone or something that just arrives. The eruptive event of arrival ultimately also signifies more than a possibility that just unfolds, as a possibility that I seize upon as my possibility. The relationship to the child is not subject to my powers. This relationship is itself, as Levinas puts it, fecundity.

Many things, it seems, could be expressed more simply and more clearly than through the biological metaphors of growth and fruitfulness. What does it mean to say that a child is "expected"? That something already lies hidden until it merely emerges into the light of day? Is the genesis involved here submitted to a half-natural, half-cultural process of pre-formation? Is it not that children also require us to wait with an expectation that is not entirely empty, yet does not expect something utterly determinate—as if we could simply anticipate what is awaited, plan it down to the last detail or artificially generate it to order? Would a medical strategy of reproduction that understands itself purely in terms of biotechnology not ultimately end up in the production of nothing but still births?[15] Consider the infant gaze that is evoked by Gottfried Keller:

> O suckling child
> Why do you behold me so?
> Whence the question
> Which lies in your eyes?

And the poem closes, without a trace of precocious arrogance, by hearkening to the barely perceptible reverberations within "a hollow shell." If we think of Virgil's *risu cognoscere matrem*, the smile by which the child's emerging self recognizes its mother, can this be anything but a kind of promise? And what happens if such a smile is absent? Traces of the future are not hard to discover in every comportment of the lived body, along with that "shifting dialogue" that is played out between claim and response, which can disturb the usual run of experience whenever we establish surprising new contacts or relationships of one kind or another (see Waldenfels 2002, 226).

Let us take a further step here. What are we to say of that shared character of the future without which there could be no "generations" in the sense of groups of people of a similar age? There are certain elementary forms of experience that are revealing here. If experience begins with what happens to me, with what is encountered by me, then right from the start this shows itself as something that does not happen to me alone, is not encountered by me alone, but as something that is encountered by *us*, that is to say, by all of us who share a certain situation. What I encounter is not something that simply flashes up or resounds within my own solitary soul, as the theory of individual impressions or sense data assumes; rather, what makes itself seen or heard in the here and in the now appears as if in search of someone to receive it. It presents itself in the context of a spatio-temporal field of indications and effects. Every affection in the phenomenological sense signifies an originary "co-affection" (see Waldenfels 1971, 154; 2015, ch. 2). To this co-affection there corresponds a co-response with moments of co-intention and co-affectivity, of co-belief and co-movement. Individuality does not consist in the fact that in the first instance each individual responds to something on his or her own. It consists, rather, in the fact that each of us responds in our own way. This holds for local events such as a heatwave or a detonation, but also for events on a greater scale such as an earthquake or a flood, which can affect the inhabitants of an entire city or an entire country. A war generation or a postwar generation is constituted by the community of those who have gone through something together, have suffered something together, or have helped to bring something upon one another. But something similar is also true for the awakening of new life in the spring or the experience of relief shared by those who have been spared something or saved from something. It is from such ubiquitous situations of rupture and transition that a future grows in the sense of the second future we have already mentioned, but this, too, grows precisely as a shared future. Events of this kind are celebrated when something that is exposed to danger or decay actually endures or survives. Those who have nothing to celebrate can be said to lack a future.

The age differences that pertain to different generations mean that various temporal fields affect and interact with one another in the form of *entwinement* and *intersection*. The experiences of the older generation mark, support, burden, and relieve those of the younger, while the relative freedom and spontaneity of the younger generation can animate and encourage the older. The younger and the older generation live in a time that they share between them, as Schütz rightly emphasizes, but they do not live through it *pari passu*. The children of emigrants experience indirectly what their parents have been through directly. Experiences of trauma may continue to exercise their effects in different levels and degrees. The experiences of others are internalized by those who are also involved and affected, in the way that the processes of speech get internalized. The temporal displacement between youth and age produces various ways of measuring or assessing time that do not simply follow one another in the way that different periods may be said to follow one another, for they present themselves in a "varying temporal fashion" (Husserl 1950, 205), namely in a way that is both simultaneous and non-simultaneous. Thus, generational conflicts emerge before they come to be verbally articulated and addressed as such. They arise on account of differing expectations, because what the younger generation does or fails to do disappoints the expectations of the older, or on the other hand because what the older generation has done or has failed to do contradicts the expectations of the younger. It can seem as if we were using an altogether different currency to pay for something here.

If there is such a thing as a contract between the generations, it is found in the unspoken expressive form of an implicit relation of give-and-take. To the original form of "tacit knowledge," in Polanyi's sense, there corresponds not only a *tacit sociality* (see Waldenfels 2015, 191) but also a *tacit future*. But then the explicit question regarding a just and appropriate distribution of rights and duties between different generations also directly presents us with the question of how we can treat "that which is not the same as the same"—the unequal as equal, the unlike as like—which is the question that inevitably confronts every kind of legal order. In Marx, Nietzsche, or Levinas, such a formula assumes a paradoxical form in view of the fact that what is *treated or posited* as the same *is* not thereby the same, which is why an element of injustice already clings to the domain of law and right itself (see Waldenfels 2006, ch. 5; 2015, ch. 6). Normative rulings and regulations must therefore be regarded as answers or responses that arise from a field of collective claims and demands and owe their motivational power precisely to situational claims of this kind. This is where we inevitably encounter what we can describe as a "co-claim of the law": "The law binds [*gilt*], though not without a voice of the law which *speaks*, or more precisely, *speaks too* when someone addresses me" (Waldenfels 1994, 308). A famous dictum of Kant's transcendental philosophy could thus be reformulated in terms of responsive thinking as the claim: claims of binding validity without claims of experience are empty. The originary conversion of singular claims of experience into rights and duties is therefore not to be identified or conflated with the application of universal laws or commands, as if the latter could even exist without such a genesis.

The Near Future and the Distant Future

One last question concerns the difference between the near future and the distant future. The future of those with whom we live as our contemporaries is described as the near future, whereas the future of those who are yet unborn or are born much later than we are, those we shall never personally come to experience, is described as the distant future. The relative anonymity of the world we share, the world of our contemporaries, thus seems to disappear from sight, to be lost in darkness, in the absolute anonymity of a world of posterity, of those who will come afterward. But this cannot mean that the world of those who succeed us are nothing but the blank pages of history. Personal and collective projects for the future—whether they are technological, economic, political, or aesthetic in character—produce their traces in the lifeworld: traces that far transcend the borders of the lives of those responsible for these projects. The works and achievements outlive us. They leave empty spaces of a kind behind them, but spaces that are not wholly indeterminate in character, spaces that, in their typical and structural character, can also serve as a model or basis for those who come afterward. They come to constitute individual and collective legacies with which material and cultural capital are build up. Goethe's saying "What from your fathers you inherit, make it yours in order to possess it" emphasizes the future promise of a possession that is literally *praegnans futuri*, heavy with what is to come, insofar as someone lives on in this and thereby gives shape to their own future. This giving on and taking over of what has been handed down to us renews the caesura that separates the encounter from the response. The imperative to "make it yours" demands a response that nonetheless may be withheld. That is why we cannot properly speak of "computer generations" in this regard.

Yet the question remains in what sense or how far a legacy can be regarded as binding or obligatory for us. Who obligates whom, and to what, in this connection? As we have seen, Levinas does not treat morality as something simply self-evident. He evokes the way the human future may be lost in a *faceless future*—may plunge into an utterly indeterminate "nothingness of the future" that is ruled by "gods who have no face" and yields nothing but the terrifying image of a "there is" that is appropriately captured in mythical terms (1961, 114f./1969, 142). It is obvious that no sense of binding obligation can possibly emerge from this abyss. Yet this shortcoming can also be expressed without recourse to such mythical symbolism. Thus, even in the midst of the optimistically minded nineteenth century, we also find the proverbial evocation of the great flood when Marx observes: "*Après moi le deluge!* is the watchword of every capitalist and of every capitalist nation. Capital therefore takes no account of the health and the length of life of the worker, unless society forces it to do so" (Marx 1970, 285/1976, 381). Money that obeys nothing other than its own laws not only treads on corpses but also "casts off the living"[16] once it sets to work (Marx 1970, 169/1976, 267). Symptoms of an "industrial pathology" (Marx 1970, 384/ 1976, 484) can also be identified with regard to the way we relate to the future. That the world of work is subject to a constant process of transformation does not rule out that the capitalizing of time also threatens to rob today's future of its full potential significance. When Marx assures us in volume 3 of *Capital* that human beings "are not owners of the earth. They are simply its possessors, its beneficiaries, and have to bequeath it in an improved state to succeeding generations, as *boni patres familias*" (Marx 1973, 784/1992), he appeals quite properly to a moral legacy, although he fails to reflect adequately on all the implications of this. If we leap forward to the bellicose twentieth century, we might consider a military memorial in Munich that was set up just after the Great War and projects its warlike sentiments into the indeterminate future with the elegant Latin phrase "Invictis victi future"——"To the unconquered the conquered who will conquer." Levinas knows what is at stake when he claims that the human face itself proclaims the commandment "Thou shalt not kill." This commandment does not simply bear on the immediate potential victim of violence, but speaks in the name of all those who are persecuted or endangered in any time or place.[17] This corresponds to the aforementioned co-claim of a law that is not faceless but shows a plurality of faces. Love of the neighbor is not extended or supplemented by love of those who are farther away, for love of those farther away is a form of the love of the nearest, of love of the neighbor.

But there are two critical aspects that need to be specifically brought out here. The realization of the ethical call requires a *responsive* politics that has to reckon with conflicting answers, with disagreement about various ways of answering the relevant questions (Waldenfels 1994, 358f.). Rights, duties, life chances are distributed in this way rather than that in any given case. Zarathustra warns us against the euphoria that can spring from love of the neighbor and declares: "It is those farther away who must pay for your love of your neighbour; and even if five of you are together, there is always a sixth who must die" (Nietzsche 1980 4, 78/1968, 174). Political answers that point towards the future, the consequences of which are only partially foreseeable and are more and more dependent on intervening technological factors, require a certain "morality-at-a-distance [*Tele-Moral*]" (Waldenfels 2006, 186). Political answers need to be discovered and developed, weighed against one another; they do not present themselves ready-made, nor can they simply be derived from the negativity of ethical resistance. Levinas draws too heavily on the account of humanity when he claims that "the whole of humanity" is suddenly disclosed or illuminated in the "epiphany of the face" and draws the conclusion that "Every social relation, as something derived, leads back to the presentation of the other to the same (*au Même*) [perhaps better: the self] without the intermediary of any image or sign, solely by the expression of the face" (1961, 188; 1969, 213).[18] Like every form of order, the social order too is selective and exclusive in some respect or other, just as everything can be said in every language, though only in a quite particular and specific way. When the Polish aphorist Stanisław Lec tells us: "Go out and learn languages. Including those that do not exist," he expresses a hyperbolic recommendation that discourages us from immediately measuring all claims in terms of possibilities we think we already understand. "Hyperbole" signifies something *more*, as Levinas often emphasizes: something over and above, an excessive claim or demand, rather than a superabundance of what we might wish for. The Overman who grows out beyond himself is not the "total human being" who appropriates his own essence and casts off all that is alien, as Marx puts it in his early writings (influenced in this regard by Ludwig Feuerbach [Marx 1968, 539/1975, 379–400]). It was Feuerbach who first gave ardent expression to the rhetoric of "the body," of "sensuousness," of "the relation of I and Thou," and so forth, and he begins his *Principles of the Philosophy of the Future* with an anthropological-theological drum roll in which we can hear the echo of Hegel's conception of mediation: "The task of these more recent times was the realization and humanization of God" (1966, 145). The farewell to previous philosophy, with which this text concludes, ends with an appeal to the future that is based on a "need of humanity" (1966, 219). The future remains caught up in an anthropological circle.

The second aspect concerns the question of the missing addressees and addressors of a still-distant future. Once again, this raises the question as to how far the claims of future generations can prove to be binding upon us. Are they really faceless and nameless? If the future has a face, it cannot lie solely in the person of the Other, as Levinas suggests, but it certainly cannot reveal itself without the Other in which the future assumes bodily form. It seems possible to calculate where the myriad distant dangers lie, what significant climate changes are to be expected, and how these things will directly impact upon the corporeal existence of the inhabitants of our earth. But why should this concern us if we do not know and cannot know anyone who could be fundamentally harmed by all this? Is there any bridge to the future that would be more secure than a bridge of snow that could melt away at any moment?[19]

Giving a Response, and Giving Time

Let us turn one last time to Nietzsche's *Thus Spoke Zarathustra*. This book opens with an enigmatic dedication to its readers—"A Book for All and None"—which admits everyone and names no one. This reserve reveals its true significance when we turn back once again to the issue of responding, when we strictly regard this as expressly *giving a response*, and indeed specifically as a "giving and receiving without measure": as a "giving à fonds perdu" (Waldenfels 1994, 609–526). A response that begins from elsewhere does not already have an addressee, as in an already established dialogue, for it discovers or fails to discover its addressee solely in the response itself. And does not something very similar hold for what we call the author? The question to which the author responds cannot be answered anywhere else than in the act of writing itself. Whether the act of writing has a future, as we say, depends on how far it dares to venture onto as yet uncultivated land, and thus runs the danger of ending in a no man's land. Yet something similar also holds for every act of radical giving that gives what it does not already possess. This also holds for a responsive politics that opens itself to the claims of others in organizing and incorporating itself in a responding "we."[20] Giving a response can only relate to that which belongs to the future by allowing it to arrive and allowing it to affect the response. In this sense, the future not merely *is*, but *gives itself*.

Thus Spoke Zarathustra contains a parting speech, "On the Gift-Giving Virtue." It evokes an ancient ethical tradition that exceeds the canon of rights and duties. The idea of "generosity"—and the word *generositas* points back to the *genus* or "kind"—is linguistically cognate with "generativity" as a productive event that is oriented towards the future, and substantively evokes the idea of a freely giving or spontaneous liberality (*Freigebigkeit*). This notion traditionally enjoys a certain aura of splendor, as with the Aristotelean virtue of magnanimity (μεγαλοψυχία), or of elevation and magnificence (μεγαλοπρέπεια).[21] If we take the German word for generosity or liberality, "Freigebigkeit"—which can be said to correspond to the Greek word for freedom, ἐλευθηρία—in a strong and literal sense, we arrive at the idea of "Freigeben" and "Freilassen," as a giving away and letting free that opens up an other future, a future for the other—we arrive at the idea of a given time that gives, as in Derrida's essay on "the gift." The "response of responsibility" (Levinas 1974, 180/1988) forms the core of an ethics of responsibility that not only answers for the consequences of what has been said and done, but begins and proceeds from what is to be said and done here and now.

Notes

1. For a critical survey of the field and a discussion of alternative views, see Ferdinando G. Menga, *Lo scandalo del futuro: Per una giustizia intergenerazionale* (2016).

2. I am alluding here to ideas that are already developed in the lectures that Levinas delivered in the period immediately after the war. See *Le temps et l'autre* (1947/1979); *Time and the Other*, trans. R. Cohen (Pittsburgh: Duquesne University Press, 1987).

3. See Bernhard Waldenfels, *Schattenrisse der Moral* (2006: SchM). I have already addressed some of the key issues and problems in the following texts: *Antwortregister* (1994: AR), *Bruchlinien der Erfahrung* (2002: BE), and, in a highly compressed form, *Grundmotive einer Phänomenologie des Fremden* (2006: GPF); I have also developed these reflections in relation to hyperbolic forms of experience in *Hyperphänomene* (2012: HYP) and in *Sozialität und Alterität* (2015: SA). In the present chapter I have briefly indicated a number of specific connections with these earlier discussions.

4. For a discussion of the affinity and the difference between phenomenology and psychoanalysis, and of the revisions to psychoanalysis that are required if it is to accord greater significance to the other and thus also to the future, see BE, ch. VII.

5. For Husserl's critique of the "punctual" conception of time, see Hua X 40: the pure now is "something abstract that cannot mean anything on its own," or is a purely "ideal limit"; thus the future, like the past, is harbored in the present in the form of implicit protentions and retentions.

6. S. Freud, *Die Traumdeutung* (1940 II/III, 3–5/ 1953 . . .). For a discussion of these particular connections, see Hogrebe 1992.

7. For more on the ambiguous character of the Greek word *elpis*, which can signify either neutral expectation or hopeful anticipation, see ch. 7 of my book on Plato (2017).

8. For the social role of "the third party," which has received considerable attention from phenomenonologists in particular, see AR 293–301, Delhom 2000, and Bedorf 2003, among others.

9. And we certainly cannot speak of a collective of human beings, things, and artefacts that could speak as a "we," as Bruno Latour has suggested in his recent piece *Cogitamus* (2010). In point of fact, the pluralization of the Cartesian ego is not particularly new; we occasionally come across the expression *nos cogitamus* in Husserl (1950 VIII, 316), and it occurs at significant points in my own contribution *Das Zwischenreich des Dialogs* (1971 = ZD, see 55 and 132) and in my *Spielraum des Verhaltens* (1980): "Vom Ich zum Wir," 191; I have subsequently avoided using this formula with good reason, however, since it still seems too Cartesian to me.

10. For a critical analysis of this approach, see my contribution in Srubar, Vaitkus 2013.

11. On this whole question of generativity, see ZD, 200–18 and 341–53: I examine the generativity that is built up on the basis of a "personal community of

effects" (Levinas 1950 VIII, 137) and place this in a dialogical context in relation to a future and generatively concatenated community of effects, an "inter-facticity" that participates in a "primordial facticity" (352). Anthony Steinbock has developed a veritable phenomenology of generativity on the basis of Husserl's approach to these issues (Steinbock 1995).

12. No strong distinction between procreation and birth itself is intended here.

13. See section 28 of Kant's "Doctrine of Right" in the *Metaphysics of Morals*, where he specifically discusses parenthood and the rights connected with it. We may note here that the Greek word for child, *teknon*, in the first instance generally signifies a "product" or "made thing," just as *teknopoia* signifies the production or generation of children. In this sense, the idea of biotechnology is not entirely new.

14. In a similar connection, Volkmar Mühleis speaks of parenthood as a "self-relativizing" process, as a form of "postponement" with respect to the other (2014, 225–27).

15. I refer the interested reader to my discussions of the technology of life and death in *Bruchlinien der Erfahrung*, 427–59.

16. Marx is playing on the ancient Greek word *tokos*, which can signify "interest" in the monetary sense as well as "offspring."

17. Compare the double dedication, in French and Hebrew, with which Levinas prefaces his book *Autrement qu'être* (*Otherwise than Being*, v). The first epigraph in French reads: "To the memory of those who were closest among the six million assassinated by the National Socialists, and of the millions of all confessions and all nations, victims of the same hatred of the other, the same antisemitism." The second one in Hebrew specifically remembers the victimized members of his own family.

18. For a critical discussion of a negative social ethics that in Levinas is merely presented in outline but in writers such as Bataille, Blanchot, Nancy, and Badiou derives from an evident overemphasis on the experience of the singular or the extraordinary, see Waldenfels 2015, 67–72; also Vanni 2009.

19. See Merleau-Ponty, *La prose du monde* (1969, 201; *The Prose of the World*, 145). The "happy writer and the speaking man [. . .] make themselves into another by saying what is most their own" and thereby "cross bridges of snow without seeing how fragile those are."

20. Here I would refer the reader to the book by Michel Vanni, *L'adresse du politique. Essai d'approche responsive* (2009). The author plays upon the double meaning of the French word "adresse," which signifies both the address to which something is despatched and the appropriate skill or ability with which someone is capable of responding to a task or challenge. He attempts to show that the response to the claim of another also always involves a moment of inappropriateness (*maladresse*), so that the response is never definitively accomplished and the future always remains open for further accomplishments.

21. In the New Testament, Paul also describes "love" in terms of a certain openness or greatness of mind (μακροθυμειν), which Luther aptly translates as *langmütig* (I Cor. 13, v. 4: the Authorized version has: "Charity suffereth long," while the Revised Standard Version reads "Love is patient").

Bibliography

Bedorf, Thomas. 2003. *Dimensionen des Dritten*. Munich: Fink.
Delhom, Pascal. 2000. *Der Dritte: Levinas' Philosophie zwischen Verantwortung und Gerechtigkeit*. Munich: Fink.
Derrida, Jacques. 1992. *Given Time: I. Counterfeit Money*. Translated by Peggy Kamuf. Chicago, IL: University of Chicago Press. Originally published as *Donner le temps I: La fausse monaie*. Paris: Éditions Galilée, 1991.
Feuerbach, Ludwig. 1986. *Principles of the Philosophy of the Future*. Translated by Manfred Vogel. Indianapolis: Hackett. Originally published as *Grundsätze der Philosophie der Zukunft*, in *Kleine Schriften*, Nachwort von K. Löwith. Frankfurt am Main: Suhrkamp, 1966.
Freud, Sigmund. 1953. "The Interpretation of Dreams." In *The Standard Edition of the Complete Psychological Works*, vols. IV–V. London: Hogarth Press. Originally published as *Die Traumdeutung* [GW X]. Frankfurt am Main: S. Fischer, 1940.
Hogrebe, Wolfram. 1992. *Metaphysik und Mantik: Die Deutungsnatur des Menschen*. Frankfurt am Main: Suhrkamp.
Husserl, Edmund. 1950. *Husserliana*. Den Haag bzw: Dordrecht.
———. 1970. *The Crisis of European Sciences*. Translated by David Carr. Evanston, IL: Northwestern University Press.
Latour, Bruno. 2010. *Cogitamus: Six Lettres sur les humanités scientifiques*. Paris: La Découverte.
Levinas, Emmanuel. 1969. *Totality and Infinity: An Essay on Exteriority*. Translated by Alphonso Lingis. Pittsburgh, PA: Duquesne University Press. Originally published as *Totalité et infini*. Den Haag, 1961.
———. 1988. *Otherwise than Being or Beyond Essence*. Translated by Alphonso Lingis. Pittsburgh, PA: Duquesne University Press. Originally published as *Autrement qu'être ou au-delà de l'essence*, Den Haag 1974.
———. 1987. *Time and the Other*. Translated by Richard A. Cohen. Pittsburgh, PA: Duquesne University Press. Originally published as *Le temps et l'autre*, Paris 1947, Montpellier 1979.
Marx, Karl. 1976. *Capital*. Vol. 1. Translated by Ben Fowkes. Harmondsworth: Penguin. Originally published as *Das Kapital*, Bd. I [MEW 23]. Berlin: Dietz, 1970.

———. 1992. *Capital*. Vol. 3. Translated by David Fernbach. Harmondsworth: Penguin. Originally published as Bd. III [MEW 25]. Berlin: Dietz, 1973.

———. 1975. *The Early Writings*. Translated by Rodney Livingstone and Gregor Benton. Harmondsworth: Penguin. Originally published as *Ergänzungsband*, 1. Teil. Berlin: Dietz, 1968.

Menga, Ferdinando G. 2016. *Lo scandalo del futuro: Per una giustizia intergenerazionale*. Rome: Edizioni di Storia e Letteratura.

Merleau-Ponty, Maurice. 2002. *Phenomenology of Perception*. Translated by Colin Smith. London: Routledge. Originally published as *Phénoménologie de la perception*. Paris: Gallimard, 1945.

———. 1973. *Prose of the World*. Translated by John O'Neill. Evanstan, IL: Northwestern University Press. Originally published as *La prose du monde*. Paris: Gallimard, 1969.

Mühleis, Volkmar. 2014. *Mädchen mit totem Vogel. Eine interkulturelle Bildbetrachtung*. Munich: Fink.

Nietzsche, Friedrich. 1980. *Kritische Studienausgabe*, hg. von G. Colli, M. Montinari. Munich: Deutscher Taschenbuch, 1980.

———. 1968. "Thus Spoke Zarathustra." In *The Portable Nietzsche*, translated by Walter Kaufmann, 103–439. New York, NY: Viking Press.

Plato. 1999. *Parmenides*. Translated by Benjamin Jowett. Champaigne, IL: Project Gutenberg.

———. 2002. "Apology." In *Plato: Five Dialogues*, translated by G. M. A. Grube. Indianapolis: Hackett.

———. 1999. *Symposium*. Translated by Benjamin Jowett. New Jersey: Prentice Hall.

Schütz, Alfred. 1976. *The Phenomenology of the Social World*. Translated by George Walsh and Frederick Lehnert. Evanstan, IL: Northwestern University Press. Originally published as *Der sinnhafte Aufbau der sozialen Welt*, Frankfurt/M. 1974.

Steinbock, Anthony J. 1995. *Home and Beyond: Generative Phenomenology after Husserl*. Evanston, IL: Northwestern University Press.

Vanni, Michel. 2009. *L'adresse du politique. Essai d'approche responsive*. Paris: Éditions du Cerf.

Waldenfels, Bernhard. 1971. *Das Zwischenreich des Dialogs. Sozialphilosophische Untersuchungen in Anschluß an Edmund Husserl*. Den Haag. [ZD]

———. 1980. *Der Spielraum des Verhaltens*. Frankfurt am Main: Suhrkamp.

———. 1994. *Antwortregister*. Frankfurt am Main: Suhrkamp. [AR]

———. 1996. *Order in the Twilight*. Translated by David J. Parent. Athens, OH: Ohio University Press. Originally published as *Ordnung im Zwielicht*, Neuauflage. Munich: Fink, 2014.

———. 2002. *Bruchlinien der Erfahrung: Phänomenologie, Psychoanalyse, Phänomenotechnik*. Frankfurt am Main: Suhrkamp. [BE]

———. 2003. "Der Fremde und der Heimkehrer. Fremdheitsfiguren bei Alfred Schütz." In *Phänomenologie und soziale Wirklichkeit*, edited by Ilja Srubar and Stephen Vaitkus. Opladen: Verlag für Sozialwissenschaft.

———. 2011. *Phenomenology of the Alien*. Translated by Alexander Kozin and Tania Stähler. Evanston, IL: Northwestern University Press. Originally published as *Grundmotive einer Phänomenologie des Fremden*, Frankfurt/Main. [GPF]

———. 2006. *Schattenrisse der Moral*. Frankfurt am Main: Suhrkamp. [SchM]

———. 2012. *Hyperphänomene*. Berlin: Suhrkamp. [HYP]

———. 2015. *Sozialität und Alterität*. Berlin: Suhrkamp, 2015. [SA]

———. 2017. *Platon. Zwischen Logos und Pathos*. Berlin: Suhrkamp.

3

Generativity, Generations, and Generative Intergenerational Solidarity

Untimely Reflections on the Way We Live
After One Another, With One Another,
and For One Another, in Its Unforeseeable Historicity

BURKHARD LIEBSCH,
TRANSLATED BY NICHOLAS WALKER

In Immanuel Kant's essay *Of the Different Races of Human Beings* (of 1795)—written partly in response to the French natural philosopher Georges-Louis Leclerc, Comte de Buffon (1797–88)—the philosopher observes that "all human beings on the wide earth belong to one and the same natural species because they generally produce [*zeugen*] fertile offspring with one another, no matter what great differences may otherwise be encountered in the forms which they assume" (Kant 1977a, 11; Ak. 2, 429–30; 2007, 84–85). This *generativity* produces the history of the human species "through an incalculable series of procreations [*Zeugungen*]"—something we could still describe today with the concept of *generation*. The generativity in question operates within the horizon of "ancestors" and "descendants" whose past and future generally fades into anonymity beyond a threshold of three generations or so. At the same time, however, they are all supposed to remain bound up with one another in the sense that each generation "transmits its enlightenment to the next" (Kant 1977b, 35; Ak. 8, 19; 2007, 110), and is also remembered in the process. This would surely seem to imply a certain world historical *solidarity* among all human beings.

Now this connection between generativity, generations, and the idea of generative and intergenerational solidarity—which at first seems merely to show up in Kant—appears to be utterly shattered today. In any event, it is certainly something that can no longer be assumed or presupposed. In what follows, without wishing to pursue any merely backward-looking intentions here, I would just like to raise the question of how, or whether, this connection can be genuinely rethought today. We shall see how the principal concepts that guide the following discussion stand in a subtle reciprocal relationship to one another: the solidarity in question presupposes the different generations, which themselves depend on human generativity; while the generative experience of time already opens up onto a life that depends on and stands in relation towards Others. Such a life immediately raises the question of whether it would not, itself, have to assume forms of solidarity in the horizons of an ultimately anonymous historicity that belongs to countless generations. Yet one hardly senses a trace of these concerns within the often rather polemical debate about the relations of current generations to one another. I begin by (1) taking a look at this debate before (2) inquiring into a generativity that (3) seems to require the kind of generative and intergenerational solidarity that alone can offer a truly human world.[1]

The Polemical Understanding of Current Relations between the Generations

"Once a human being comes to life, he is old enough to die" (Berndt and Burdach, 46). This is indeed true: anyone who is alive can "in principle" always die. And this late-medieval truism on the part of Johannes von Tepl, the author of *The Peasant from Bohemia* (written around 1400), has been adduced in support of the notion that death—understood as "being-towards-the-end"—is already present from the beginning as far as our human existence qua *Dasein* is concerned (Heidegger 1984, 245/1967, 289–90). Thus at least for all finitely "existing" beings, if not exactly for "all finite things," it certainly seems true to say that "the hour of their birth is the hour of their death" (Marcuse 1979, 197). Yet if birth and death do not simply or immediately coincide with one another, this implies that the latter always arrives later than the former—even if, of course, we cannot know *when* the end will arrive. Nonetheless, historically variable and contingent notions of "normal mortality rates" for human beings—where a relatively higher or lower infant mortality rate provide exceptions to the rule—still tell us that at any given time, the younger will generally die later than the older from whom they sprang. On the other hand, this also implies that the former in turn will not generally outlive their own descendants. As Hegel observes in the *Phenomenology of Spirit*, this accounts for the distinctive "feeling" experienced by "the parents towards their children" in recognizing their own being-for-self in the latter, in "witnessing the development in the children of an independent existence which the parents are unable to get back again" (Hegel, 1980, 336/1977, 273). For them this independent existence remains "an alien reality in its own right," whereas the children themselves, on the other hand, feel in relation to the parents that they "derive their existence from, or have their essential being in, what is other than themselves, and in what passes away." They realize that they are capable "of attaining independence and a self-consciousness of their own only by being separated from their source—a separation in which their source dries up" (ibid.).

The philosopher here brings out a generativity that does not merely imply that parents and children generally live out their lives before and after one another, but that the latter, the offspring, *arise precisely by separating themselves from the former* (Castoriadis 1984, 498, 515ff.). This process of mutual separation, inevitably realized as a kind of leave-taking, finally ratifies the disappearance of the corporeal source or origin of the children, whose memories increasingly slip away. Inevitably the children acknowledge too late their own more or less un-comprehended generative origin, which through them has always already receded from the life they can only live out diachronically. Thus, we come to "this alternation of successive generations" (Hegel 1980, 336/1977, 273), which, if we follow Hegel here, can only find its "enduring basis" in the ethical life of a people. Yet what ultimately counts in "the house of ethical life" is "not a question of *this* particular husband, *this* particular child, but simply of *husband and children generally*," or in other words, "the universal" on which "the relationships of the woman" are supposed to be grounded (Hegel 1980, 337/1977 274). This much would certainly then be clear if what was specifically required of women was to bear sufficiently numerous offspring fit and capable of serving in war, that is, as a biopolitical resource for the state (see Berghoff 1997).

In the horizon of the universal, as represented by the state, the singularity of each and every individual disappears from view precisely on account of the repeated acts of procreation through which men and women constantly bring forth the—seemingly ever replaceable—stock or supply of ever new fathers, mothers, and children. The fact that Kant rightly spoke of processes of procreation in this connection still serves to remind us that every group of human beings we term a "generation" in the broader sense can only exist on the basis of a generativity through which alone they come to be. Yet the general notion of a "change" or "alternation" of different generations expressly "abstracts" from all this.[2] This notion implies an anonymous plurality of older people and an anonymous plurality of younger people who live, or lived, at more or less the same time, and may also include all of those who are alive at any given time. It thus disregards precisely who descends from whom—in that "constant surplus of alterity" (Jonas 1987, 160) that is involved in the singularity of each and every irreplaceable and non-substitutable "successor"—and is concerned solely with the constant process of "replacement" or "substitution" (Derrida 2002, 413, 417)[3] of the older through those who come after. It introduces demarcations into historical time that not only separate questionably homogenized cohorts[4] of older and younger individuals from each other, but also efface the manifold forms of non-simultaneity (Pinder 1926/1961; Bloch 1984) as well as the various gradual transitional processes that arise from the intersection and interaction between the lifetimes of the younger and the older. (This is the only reason why David Hume and Auguste Comte could toy with the idea that one generation was capable of replacing the preceding one almost *at a stroke*; see Mannheim 1928.) The concept of generation needs to enrich the idea of generativity, which is still generally understood today in biological rather than in social and ethical terms, with a specifically historical dimension:[5] the younger generations emerge historically from the older generations by turning back to them in remembrance, whether it be to assume their legacy with gratitude, or to overcome the older generation, or indeed to try and forget them altogether. This latter is also still a way of relating to the older generation (Castoriadis 1983, 45; Ewald 1993, 474, 476; Derrida 1995).

Yet these alternative responses only become possible where this retrospective historical relationship is thematized in its own right. It is only through this relationship that later generations are able to establish a non-biological continuity with previous generations. That "series of generations [*Zeugungen*], each of which transmits its enlightenment to the next," as Kant put it in his *Idea for a Universal History from a Cosmopolitan Point of View* (Kant 1977b, 35; Ak 8, 19; 2007, 110), cannot establish any historical continuity if the successive generations do not also explicitly relate *historically* to those that have specifically preceded them.[6] From the hermeneutic point of view, the tradition handed down to us is always a kind of remembering "repetition" of the past: a past that in this way first becomes historically significant (Liebsch 2001). Indeed, it thereby becomes significant from a practical or pragmatic point of view, if Kant is right in claiming that "our later posterity [. . .] after a few centuries" will "naturally prize the history of the earliest times, the documents of which might long since have vanished, only from the viewpoint of what interests them, namely what nations and governments have done to achieve or to harm the goal of world citizenship" (Kant 1977b, 50; Ak 8, 30–31; 2007, 120). Yet it still remains strange and "disconcerting" that, from this perspective, "the older generations appear to carry on their toilsome labour only for the sake of the later ones"—and indeed have done so without this being their intention, as Kant expressly adds. It is only the later (or even the latest) generations that seem capable of profiting from what "a long series of their ancestors [. . .] had laboured upon, without themselves being able to partake of the good fortune which they prepared" (ibid., 37; Ak 8, 20; 2007, 110–11).

For Kant, from a cosmopolitan perspective, all those human beings who have already lived would ultimately have to be recognized as "ancestors" of those who live, or lived on, after them. Kant ascribes the "intention" of bringing about that "good fortune" or "happiness" [*Glück*] to be enjoyed by all those then living specifically to "nature." Thus nature's intention from the beginning with regard to the human race is to let what is rational to become actual, even if this is only possible through an antagonistic "unsocial sociability" that allows human beings to act irrationally *against* the ultimate vocation of their species, and even if this involves the "pitiless conclusion" that the life of those living earlier is thereby ultimately *sacrificed* for that of those living later, as some interpreters have supposed (Miklós 2016, 63, 116, 133; Blumenberg 1986b, 215f., 241).

Yet later generations have also repudiated this very idea, and for their part specifically reproached the generations before them, to dispense with the whole burden of a historical legacy that seemed to condemn them to a merely instrumental role for the sake of something better that would only be actualized, if at all, after their own death. The most blatant but by no means the only example in this regard (Mommsen 1985) is surely the Futurist movement, which at times was very closely allied to Italian fascism (Schmidt-Bergmann 2009). The programme endorsed by Futurism challenged all attempts to establish new binding forms of connection between or over and beyond the generations, binding forms of connection that were being increasingly put into question by the constantly accelerating and increasingly discontinuous historicity that is characteristic of modernity. This modernity ultimately no longer allows anything really solid or substantial to endure, as

The Communist Manifesto (1847–48) had indeed prophesied (Marx 1971, 529/1968, 38; Berman 1988; Koselleck 2003, section 2). A history subject to such constant dynamic change would inevitably raise the much-discussed "social question," with its resulting biopolitical concerns for entire populations and their future (Donzelot 1980; Foucault 1991). Yet this future was conceived in terms of generations of people whose unparalleled capacity for exploitation seemed readily acceptable to many in the context of the ruthless process of advancing industrialization. Thus in 1914 the Irish socialist George Bernard Shaw, in an essay on the redistribution of wealth, explicitly criticized the "Manchester tradition," which was prepared to consume nine generations in the space of one (Shaw 2017). In this context, one could no longer argue that all generations would at least contribute something of their own to the advantage of later generations within a broader history of progress. For the generative connection now threatened to disintegrate entirely in a violent kind of way, if not in biological terms then certainly from a hermeneutic-historical point of view.

This may explain why people started to explore quite new structures of intergenerational connection and solidarity: structures that were no longer thought of as operating in a basically organic "nature-like" way. The most significant example of this new approach is undoubtedly the concept of a "generational contract," already formulated in 1928 and often reinterpreted since (H. Imbusch; see Ritter 1989, 135). This concept presupposes an "economy of material and symbolic processes of exchange between the generations" (Bourdieu 1993, 289). As certain social critics have observed, this idea of "generational justice"—which is cited so often it can easily sound like an empty formula—has come in the meantime to exercise an almost hegemonic influence.[7] Yet for all this, it is still clear that we can hardly speak of a normatively clarified or well-governed relationship between the generations. Nor does it change the fact that some people do not find it inappropriate to invoke the prospect of an effective "war between the generations" that supposedly threatens to develop precisely because the older generations now increasingly live (want to live or indeed have to live) a long—or rather all-too long—life at the expense of the younger generations who succeed them. Thus, according to Francis Fukuyama (1992), the worst thing of all is that they are unwilling to make way for their children, or even their grandchildren or great-grandchildren. Here we may remember the remarks of Peter Kropotkin (2017), who observed that the Russian peasants once seemed to have shared his view when they said: "I am living away the life of others—it is time for me to go."

If the former American political adviser Fukuyama is right, then the issue that lies behind the now increasingly polemical relationship between the generations has long since ceased to be merely that the younger generation, in the natural order of things belonging to generative life, generally reach the end of their lives, according to their date of birth, after those who are older; or no longer simply concerns the ethical notion that children owe their parents something out of filial piety (or even thankfulness for the life they have received as a gift), as many people still believe (Marion 2008). For now, by contrast, it seems as if the older generation owes the younger generation a death *in good time*, a death that is economically defensible rather than drawn out beyond measure—in other words, a death that is no longer harboured *as such* in the act of birth. This is something that is not remotely acknowledged in all the popular appeals to von Tepl's dictum.

It is of course hardly an original thought that "we owe God a death," as William Shakespeare says (Henry IV, Part II, Act 3, scene 2, line 250), or "owe nature a death," as Sigmund Freud rephrased it after him (1962, 237). Yet this thought takes on a quite different significance once it is turned into a (quite unrealizable) demand raised by the younger generation against the older—with the predictable consequence that the concern for one's own death in each particular case (an essential theme of reflection from the ancient Stoics through Martin Heidegger up to Michel Foucault) is transformed into the fear of living *too long* in the eyes of others. It is certainly plausible to suggest that an increasingly diminished regard for the life of those who are older may result all too easily from the tendency to evaluate that life primarily or exclusively as a massive cost factor in terms of the virtual economic balance to be struck between the relevant generations. The situation we have just outlined in a very compressed and undoubtedly somewhat simplified way in relation to the polemical discussion surrounding the concept of a "generation" can easily lead one to forget one thing: that there is a human generativity that does not produce any generations inasmuch as it does not relate to experiences that are actually specific to generations.[8] But there is no generation (and no problematic or distorted relationship between different generations) without a prior generativity that can assume a historically differentiated profile in relation to different generations. If we entirely lose sight of this connection, then it can seem as if human life in a historical perspective amounts to nothing more than an "alternation of successive generations" that push onwards into being and then, in turn, relinquish it—if need be with a moralizing-eugenic attitude on the part of the younger generation who otherwise see their own life chances diminished, even though they too must expect to be charged, in due course, with leading an overlong and "unproductive life" (Lessenich 2008, 110ff.).

This is how the relationship between the generations is polemically framed today, where those who live earlier can always be reproached for living "at the cost" of those who have sprung, or will spring, from them. They can reduce these costs, however, by consuming less, above all in relation to the irreplaceable but diminishing source of energy from fossil fuels; and also by lessening the burdens on the future of those who live after them, burdens they will never themselves have to meet; and last but not least, by not living too long and thereby making excessive demands on the social finances. Reproaches of this kind have already been interpreted as something like a racism directed against the process of aging itself: an attitude that is then inevitably countered with a kind of *Methuselah conspiracy*, as it has been called, if we follow the line of certain (clearly very successful) contemporary writers who can see only one thing here: an intensely polemical competition for dominance. Then the only remaining question is who will win out over whom: whether the "fervor" of the young will lead to the subordination of the older generation, or whether some kind of gerontocracy will triumph instead.

Whichever way we look at it, such reproaches show one thing above all, namely just how far we are prepared to regard the respective generations as divorced or disengaged from one another, even to the point where we can only imagine the relation between them as a struggle wherein each advances solely at the expense of the other. And this just seems to be another sign, among many others, indicating a substantial weakening of solidarity in the social realm: a realm that ultimately seems to manifest our being-with-one-another only in the mode of being-against-one-another. Yet generations can only exist on the ground of a prior generativity by virtue of which each one of us lives *on the basis of others and in relation towards others*, whether in the context of a widely ramifying physical-corporeal genealogy or in the sense of a shared and historically mediated cultural heritage. In this regard, generative life is always and inevitably a form of *inter-temporal* life that opens out beyond our own birth and our own death onto the life of others who have preceded us and of others who will succeed us, every one of whom must also be recognized as irreducibly "singular" and "non-substitutable." It is questionable, however, whether in itself such an approach already provides sufficient support for the sort of *diachronic solidarity* that could prevent the generations that emerge from that broader human generativity from absurdly attempting to realize and assert themselves against one another in terms of polemical relations; absurdly, because they seem to ignore entirely the fact that the different generations can only emerge out of each other. And, in point of fact, the different generations are never really just historical "subjects" that stand in such polemical relations. The contrary impression is only produced by those descriptions of generational relations that effectively allow us to forget that these relations are grounded in a prior generativity (Husserl 1962; 1973, 171f.) and cannot exist unless this generative solidarity has some political form in which to express itself. Thus, instead of continuing with such polemically framed descriptions, which serve to completely obscure or misrepresent the inner connection between generativity and generations, I would like in what follows to inquire how far, within the context of human generativity, we can discover traces of an intergenerational solidarity that essentially resists all merely polemical generational relations.

From Generation to Human Generativity

The concept of "generation" is derived from the Latin *generatio*, etymologically traceable to the Greek word *genesis*, which, significantly enough, encompasses a great range of meanings including "origin," "production," "procreation," and "creation" (Weigl 2006, 11). The basic thought here—if we ignore the unintelligible notion of *creatio ex nihilo*—usually suggests the following sort of schema: x through G becomes z. In terms of the ontology that occidental thought has inherited from the ancient Greeks, in the case of x and z we have to be talking about "something." Thus z must be "something else" or "something other" in comparison to x, and possibly even something "wholly other"—at least in morphological or phenomenalistic terms. Through G, x is led to z, or in other words transformed or transmuted, even though x and z need not exhibit any external similarity to one another. (In this connection we only have to think of DNA, of the various stages of embryogenesis, of the child that finally emerges from the process.) Thus, it may appear as if what has arisen, what has been produced, generated, and/or created, has nothing in common with what it has emerged from. We have a radical example of this when we are confronted with a veritable case of creation that produces z from x *as if from nothing*. It doesn't really matter whether we are talking about a trick, about a striking piece of magic or apparent sorcery, or about a seeming miracle that we are as yet unable to understand. (Even the causal unfolding of a preconstituted genetic program can easily appear as an astonishing miracle.) In every case, the process of genesis or generation brings forth something else or something different; and, indeed, brings it forth out of something else or something different, which in turn raises the question of how the latter, apparently by virtue of its own power (given the appropriate circumstances, etc.), is capable, *in itself*, of letting something emerge that, in the end, is not at all similar to it: something that can only provoke astonishment on our part. It is in this sense that the French molecular biologist François Jacob, in his report on the current state of research in genetics, can write: "Sexual reproduction is ultimately a mechanism for the production of otherness. Something other than the parents. Something other than all the existing individuals of the species" (Jacob 1998, 136).

But is it true that human generativity only brings forth *something* that is other? Is it not rather that the substrate identified in the mid-1950s as DNA, in and through various highly complicated epigenetic processes on the part of a living being—which, corporeally speaking, is fully developed or, in other words, is "something"—also brings forth *someone*: an Other who cannot ontologically be grasped (or certainly not adequately grasped) as "something"? When we ask about someone—about someone Other—we are not primarily asking *what* they are, or *what* this individual is; we are asking about *who* they are, about *who* this is. And this question is concerned with the Other qua Self, not with the selfsameness of something. But can the selfhood of someone exist solely on the basis of the selfsameness of a biological substrate that must at the least allow that *someone* should develop from *something* (from DNA, from a collection of cells, from a preembryonic state)? Precisely how this comes about still remains an enigma. Yet often enough we come across the idea that one day it will be possible to intervene in our biology in such a way that we shall be able to pre-program other human beings—assuming that precisely what and who is already inscribed in the biological substrate from which it is to emerge from it, almost as if it were a book (Blumenberg 1986a; Kay 2005).

Now objections have often been raised against this idea. Thus, it is pointed out that each of us is a personal being, a psychologically constituted individual, a unique self that cannot possibly be understood on the model of the selfsameness, the reproduction, or the reidentification *of something*. For on the basis of something, namely our body, we have become not only *something else*, or *something other*, but have become *someone else*, and *someone other*. And this otherness, which itself can only be understood in relation to Others, cannot be reduced to what we are and what we have biologically emerged from. Thus, in such ontogenetic processes, something (x) gives rise to something radically different (z), namely to someone who cannot (at least not "adequately") simply be grasped *as something*. What is more, each of us is not only "another" or "someone else" in a merely indeterminate sense, but an Other in the strong sense that the twentieth-century philosophy of alterity has attached to this concept. Each one of us, therefore, is not only somehow relatively or comparatively "other," but is irreducibly an Other—even in relation to ourselves (Liebsch 2015a/b). In this way, every self is, as Paul Ricoeur puts it (1990), an Other (*autre*). And no one is simply the Other of *others*, as Derrida also insists with an anti-dialectical emphasis (2002, 362).

Many writers have attempted to show and explore why this should be so—why someone to whom we relate through a who-question is a person, a self, an Other who lives in terms of and out of their own self and, moreover, exists historically in a self-like fashion, that is, without simply being reidentifiable like things that remain identical to themselves and can be compared with one another as various items or instances. How a biological substrate is able to bring forth something that is so different—a human self that exists in a historical way, not some merely selfsame entity that can be recognized and reidentified through external criteria, and so forth—will long remain a mystery, an enigma. Thus, while we can certainly say that something else or something other arises out of a biological substrate, we do not really have any idea *how someone other, or an Other, can come to be out of something*—"an other that is not mine, my hôte, my other, not even my neighbor or my brother" (Derrida 2002, 363), or "my/our" child, "my/our" son, "my/our" daughter. . . . Thus the coming to be (*genesis, generatio*) of Others has always seemed like a kind of miracle, even if we are not prepared to speak at this point of some kind of creation (*ex nihilo*).

The question is even more astounding when we consider that the biological substrate for its part has emerged in turn from Others, namely from the normally heterosexual union of the parents. As Others who stand in a particular relationship to one another, they beget something that in an utterly enigmatic and mysterious way can also bring about someone else, bring forth an Other. It is not exactly right to say, as has been said so often by appeal to Aristotle, that "a human being produces a human being" (Oehler 1963). It is rather that two individuals who are Others for each other produce a third individual by means of a biological substrate, that is merely *something*, but allows *someone* to emerge out of itself in an unforeseeable way (though by no means simply out of itself, but also by virtue of the care and attention provided by others). Thus, future Others "arise" *indirectly* from Others who have preceded them and whom they are bound to outlive, unless violence, disease, or unexpected death intervene to disturb the normal process, so that, as Petrarch says, "the one who arrived last is the first to depart" (Petrarch 2009). It is in this sense that we can understand what Alfred Schütz wrote in a note from 1958: "The phenomenological clarification of the generational problem will surely have to be sought in the problematic surrounding the subsequent living on [. . .] of the other" (Schütz 1984, 343).

But what precisely does this "problem" or "problematic" consist in? Certainly not simply in the question of whether the other lives on beyond other people (survives longer, overcomes disease or other violent threats of one kind or another, and in this sense somehow manages *to get away* for some time at least). If the question of survival or living on were simply reduced to this, it would be quite sufficient to answer it by reference to the differing lengths and only partially parallel lifetimes of individuals who have been generated out of one another and therefore inevitably live their lives *after one another*. In this regard, a linear and chronological concept of time would be entirely sufficient, one that would help us to coordinate the relevant points of time (birth and death) and relevant stretches of time with one another (Kaempfer 1991, 83) to determine who outlives whom and for how long.

But such a concept of time is precisely incapable of explaining the significance of the fact that the beings in question have emerged from out of one another—whether physically, socially, or culturally through (a) a reproduction that simply repeats something that was there before; or (b) an *évolution créatrice* that reveals what has arisen from what existed before as something that is irreducible to the conditions of its emergence and, therefore, as something significantly new; or (c) a kind of *generative filiation* on the basis of others[9] who can only realize in a historical way—that is, only after the event—who (not what) they are in relation to Others who have preceded them and brought them into the world in the first place. In contrast to the reproduction and evolution of something that is to be located or identified as "the same thing" coming before or after something else in a straightforward chronological sense, the significance of such filiation can only manifest itself in the historical life of Others who will have to look back and ask how it was possible, and who was responsible, for the circumstance that (and means by which) they were able to come into the world at all.

Emmanuel Levinas has described the fact "que nous n'avons pas choisi notre naissance" as the "grand scandale de la condition humaine" (Levinas

2009b, 109, 15.6), and connects this experience with Martin Heidegger's concept of thrownness or "*Geworfenheit*" (Levinas 1969). Yet we are not "thrown" into the world, but are rather "born" into it, as has often been argued against Heidegger by appealing, among others, to Hannah Arendt in this regard. In the light of this utterly elemental circumstance, which all of our subsequent life presupposes, the experience of the contingency of one's own existence as *Dasein* intrinsically raises questions directed towards Others, for it is the generativity of Others that is responsible for the life that will spring from it. However much we may experience our individual life as contingent, ungrounded, or baseless, or even as arbitrarily and thus capriciously "thrown" into the world, the causal and ethical responsibility for one's existence lies directly with those without whose generativity no one would be "there" at all. There is no one else "to thank" for one's life but, precisely, those from whom it has sprung, although there can be no sufficient grounds or reasons for this life. The existence of what we call descendants cannot seamlessly be derived causally from the life of what we call progenitors, and nor does this existence find its sufficient grounds, at least subsequently, in that life. Insufficiently "grounded" (Musil 1983, 233ff.) as the existence of the human being inevitably is, the individual cannot at some later stage of their own life help but raise the question as to why, how, and with what consequences they have been brought into the world unasked. This is precisely what led Kant directly to the demand that we should try to make (our) children "content with this condition" as far as possible (Kant 1977c, 394/1996 Part I, §28, 430). The British utilitarian John Stuart Mill went a step further, describing it as a "moral crime" to "bring a child into existence without a fair prospect of being able, not only to provide food for its body, but instruction and training for its mind." Thus "if the parent does not fulfil this obligation, the State ought to see it fulfilled, at the charge, so far as possible, of the parent" (Mill 1962, 239).

It was clear to Kant that a certain duty sprang directly from the contingent character of the life of our offspring—a life that is not grounded in sufficient reason, namely the duty to care for that life appropriately. We owe them this, especially when we are directly responsible for the existence of the offspring in question. And the relevant responsibility extends far beyond the early years of care for them, extends into the very life of these future Others, a life in which the question of whether they can be reconciled or "content" with their contingent or non-necessary existence will continue to remain for an unforeseeable length of time. Up to the point of death and its attendant circumstances, the offspring or descendants will never be able to answer this question in a final or definitive way. No one can "definitively" be called happy before their death, as Aristotle said, repeating a dictum of Solon. So, too, no one before their death is able to say "in the final analysis" whether he or she would not retrospectively reject or repudiate the life accorded to them. War, genocide, violence, and torture in so many places remain a threat until the end. Up until death, everyone is, in principle, exposed to the possibility of some act of violence that can make all attempts or promises on the part of others to make their offspring content with their existence in the world appear exaggerated, negligent, or intrinsically implausible. From this point of view, "the problematic of outliving" or surviving (Schütz) certainly does not simply lie in the question of whether others actually outlive us or instead, perhaps, come to an early end; for it also involves the question of whether or how they can experience their life, the life they owe to others, as "livable," "acceptable," or "affirmable." None of this lies in the power of those who must in some sense take responsibility for the life they have brought about. Whether their original promise to their offspring can be regarded as remotely plausible, or, indeed, as being subsequently fulfilled is something that may only be answered by those whose "insufficiently" grounded existence can be experienced as livable, acceptable, and affirmable, however, *only* by virtue of this promise and the intrinsically precarious realization that it implies.

Those responsible for the existence of their offspring must always, at least implicitly, make this promise. All those who accept and receive the newborn, brought unasked into the world, are intrinsically obliged to vouch for this promise, and they cannot "blame" or hold anyone else responsible in this regard. Rather, the newborn child itself, the "infant" who is as yet literally unable to speak, calls Others to a life that must promise to act appropriately for and do justice to the child. It is not as if we first encounter the child as some kind of empty ethical space, as something that would only subsequently provoke the question of whether one "has" any particular duties or a certain responsibility towards it. Nor is it clearly set out from the start what exactly we owe the child. But generative life, as we know it, cannot be thought at all without regard to the minimal question as to what we owe Others who have been "already brought into the world" without their consent (Liebsch 2016b). Unless we *already feel obliged to respond to this question*, no moral deontology or ethic of responsibility could move us to acknowledge generative life as *something more than simply indifferent* in relation to Others who come into the world.

In the light of what has been said, "the problematic of outliving" lies initially in this non-indifferent character that leads from the very start to the question of how we reconcile Others to their notoriously "insufficiently grounded" life, and as to what we owe them, that is, what we must promise them if their life is later to appear to them as truly livable, acceptable, and affirmable. In this sense, every promise to care for them and about them must open out onto an unforeseeable future, one where it essentially depends on third parties, so to speak, to determine whether that promise will be fulfillable. This promise ultimately points back to the context of a liberal and democratic form of life that provides the institutional framework and conditions for living a free life among equals, a life that is organized as justly as possible. These are demanding conditions, which no one on their own is in a position to guarantee or simply re-create anew, and we must acknowledge the historical presuppositions that allow us to institutionalize such a form of life—one that can certainly be destroyed very quickly, but can only be rebuilt with considerable effort over several generations.

In this sense, it is clear that the human generativity from which different generations emerge is certainly not exhausted by the familial relations of fatherhood, motherhood, and childhood. What the Czech phenomenologist Jan Patočka (1988, 44) called the "generational relationship of filiation" cannot be reduced to the mere reproductive life of the parents via their offspring. This is so whether we are considering a repetition of the same (of the genotype, for example) or some sort of transubstantiation that, according to Levinas (2009b, 317), allows Others to emerge directly from Others without recourse to the selfsameness of a substrate or to the form of self-identity that can be recounted narratively and grasped as a form of self-production capable of relating to others in a historical way.[10] Nor, in and of itself, can such a "generational relationship" simply give rise, in some *acontextual and ahistorical* fashion, to future Others (sons and daughters) out of already existing Others (the parents)—an impression that we frequently receive from Levinas, who never specifically employs a concept like that of "a form of life."[11] But a generative relationship between parents and children must assume a familial or quasi-familial form of communally shared life if it is to prove resilient and dependable, that is, if it is to accomplish what such a relationship has to "promise": the opening and preservation of spaces for offspring who did not ask or consent to be born, spaces in which they are able to lead a genuinely livable, acceptable, and affirmable life. This promise can only be kept (if it is to be kept at all) if familial and quasi-familial forms of life are structurally supported or embedded in a freedom-oriented democratic form of life whose fundamental public and institutional structure they cannot themselves create, but on which they must rely for the existence of such spaces.

But this is hardly what Levinas has in mind when he tries to express a familial generational relationship of filiation in terms of the idea of *fecondité* (1969, 267ff.). It is only *en passant* that he connects this idea with specific reflections on the political and historical structure of human forms of life. Levinas shows himself to be far more interested in grounding human generativity by recourse to "the erotic." It is this dimension that inevitably opens up the non-anticipatable diachronic character of a time of the Other who emerges in this connection. In this diachrony the parents are "capable of another fate" (ibid., 270ff.), which they cannot anticipate and which, in the normal course of things, is only completely fulfilled when they no longer exist, that is, when their own life has ebbed away. In this way, the *sexual alterity* of mothers and fathers in their relation to one another[12] is inextricably bound up with the ineliminable *historical alterity* that delivers them over to a diachrony in which the life of a third party, namely their children, unfolds; and the children, for their part, spring from the parents in *generative alterity* as Others in a radical sense and not merely as living reproductions of those who "beget" them. In this connection, Levinas (ibid., 394; 1971, 301) speaks of a distinctive process of "alter-ation" (*altération*), which expressly issues "through the discontinuity of generations," as he puts it, into an "infinite time," into "the time of the absolutely Other." In this way, his phenomenological social philosophy, which can address the idea of the *radically* Other but never that of the absolutely or "wholly Other," does not just run the threat of reverting to theology. It also threatens to overleap the *historical concept of a generation* that cannot be dispensed with if we wish to understand how the promise that is harbored in social filiation and fecundity implies the horizons of future time in which "those who come after us," as we say, will have to discover the conditions of a life that can be truly lived, accepted, and affirmed by them.

However, when it comes to the question of precisely how this whole complex of factors should be understood, there is a great deal of sharp disagreement. What is surely the undeniable and direct dependence on such conditions of life of those who will exist in the future demands, at the very least, that these lives will not be placed in immediate jeopardy or devastated from the outset. But are we talking of a deontological "ought," that is, a duty, here? If so, then who "has" this duty in relation to whom?

And why precisely does it exist? And how far does it extend? Does human generativity already imply some fundamental responsibility or obligation to future generations, as we so often put it with such telling vagueness? Is the universality of this frequently invoked connection actually capable of being expressed in more concrete form?[13] If the range of this concept of responsibility or obligation is not determined more precisely, does not this talk of "future generations" ultimately just imply all human beings (and even posthuman beings, living beings that have been produced by human beings themselves and that may perhaps one day surpass their makers) that will ever come to live on earth? Can a responsibility or obligation that "we" are supposed to have in the present towards all human beings as yet unborn really extend that far? How can we already owe some kind of obligation to those who do not yet exist? And who are "we" here? Are we talking without qualification about all those who exist at the current time, including those who have no offspring at all? Or do not wish to have any, perhaps because the prospect of a history for the human species that continues to unfold as before fills them with a dread they would certainly not want to pass on to their offspring or descendants? (Horstmann 1983). And how can they be directly concerned with the fate of those who one day will themselves be prepared to bring others into the world unasked, regardless of how poor their prospects of survival may turn out to be?

The social-phenomenological approach that has drawn on the work of Levinas in particular has essentially focused on the internal sexual and generative "alter-ation" involved in intergenerational relations on the basis of human generativity itself. But the way in which it has done so risks depriving the concept of a generation of its historical features, with the result that this approach barely recognizes, and has little to say about, the problem of future generations. Here it is worth noting that the Latin concept of *generatio*, taken over into German as *Generation* in the eighteenth century, began to be used in a specifically historical sense rather early on. Thus, we already find Friedrich Schleiermacher, the pedagogue and philosopher of religion, expressly asking how one "generation" is supposed to relate to the next one. In the fields of art history (Wilhelm Pinder), sociology (Karl Mannheim), and finally social phenomenology (Alfred Schütz), the concept of "a generation" came to be firmly established in the thought of the early twentieth century. This concept was employed to explicate *the fundamental structures of the particular historical times that countless individuals live through together*; and it also included those who paradoxically, like the generation of the "Futurists," wished to throw off the authority of inherited tradition as an oppressive burden and thus proclaim and embrace a model of freedom that no longer recognized any historical limits or parameters. The excesses of a freedom conceived in such terms did not, however, bring about the progress envisaged by the Futurists but instead, and inevitably, turned against those who were to come afterward. We can see the unmistakable effects of this mentality in, for example, the processes of atomic and chemical contamination and pollution that, over many years, have rendered entire ecologies and habitats effectively inhabitable, places in which those who are unable to leave on account of poverty or the lack of practical alternatives are condemned, indefinitely, to live and suffer.

We have seen examples of such things in the case of Hiroshima and Nagasaki, in the regions of Vietnam laid waste to this day by the militarized use of defoliants such as Agent Orange, in the radioactive contamination of sites such as Chernobyl in the Ukraine or Fukushima in Japan. Hence, we cannot avoid this question: how are we to judge a life, a way of living, that has or can have such predictable consequences for Others—for those who are living at the present time or who will live in the future—and that with a greater or lesser degree of probability will indeed have such consequences in the future? When we consider the relevant technological inventions and developments and their ensuing practical application with or without explicit reflection on their consequences or close analysis of the attendant risks and dangers; and when we consider the probable worldwide—and possibly irreversible—effects of all these things, then we find ourselves confronted with horizons of human responsibility that are spatially and temporally immeasurable and wherein any notion of providing more concrete or specific form to these issues must, sooner or later, fall away. Thus, the enormous radioactive half-life of nuclear waste—and the hundreds of nuclear reactors remaining throughout the world, despite the question of how to dispose of them being, as yet, more or less unaddressed—will remain a massive problem for humanity (if indeed humanity still exists) for centuries to come, when all those most immediately responsible have long since departed this world. Thus, the responsibility in question stretches out into temporal horizons completely unpopulated by those who could be held responsible for the problems therein. Every later attempt to ascribe responsibility will prove futile: those once responsible will no longer have to answer *to* anyone or stand *before* anyone for what they have done or not done. And the subsequent question of whether they ever previously felt responsible *for* something or someone will no longer have an addressee, so that every concrete structure for determining responsibility will evaporate.[14] Thus it seems reasonable to pose the question of our relationship to the future in terms of where this relationship comes into play in the most originary and concrete way. And even for philosophers such as Hans Jonas, who are convinced of our responsibility for the future existence of the human race even with regard to the very distant future, this place is none other than the experience of parenthood or human generativity (Jonas 1982, 88ff., 234–41).

Human Generativity as Archetype for a Generational Relationship that Expresses Responsibility and Solidarity?

Hans Jonas appeals to the paradigm of parental responsibility in the context of an ontological responsibility for future human existence in order to elucidate how this responsibility stretches out into the future. But we have no obligation with regard to future members of the human race in the sense of securing *their* particular existence in all cases. On the other hand: if they are already there or will be there in the future, it appears irresponsible not to care whether they will encounter conditions of a life that is genuinely livable for them. Not to care about this is to believe we have no obligation in relation to them, that we owe them nothing, not even the elementary conditions of a life that is "acceptable" to them or "livable" for them, indeed not even the question of *whether* we owe them anything and, if so, precisely what we owe them.

But Jonas does not regard parental responsibility merely as an example. He is essentially concerned with it as an authentic archetype or "eternal paradigm." It is, thus, a matter of "immediate evidence" in the phenomenological sense that the child, in its very being, makes an immanent claim that places its addressee into an "incontrovertible" relationship that demands a response. According to Jonas, this claim implies an "Ought," namely the obligation to care for the existence of the child in a responsible way. The responsibility assumed here is the practical response demanded by that claim that Jonas understands, in turn, as "the inner right of the object" of responsibility (ibid., 234). Here "Being" and "Ought" coincide for Jonas insofar as one only needs to look to know that one specifically ought to accept and take on the newborn child. Allegedly, this demand or summons already lies in the sheer existence of the child, even though it is not directed at anyone in particular and does not indicate in concrete terms precisely what is to be done to "take on" the newborn in question. The questions of *who* it is that believes he or she is "intended" or addressed by the claim of child—which thereby becomes a binding demand—and of *what* is to be done in appropriate response are entirely secondary in relation to the claim itself. For the latter may, as Jonas admits, "fall on deaf ears," be simply ignored, or even emphatically rejected, as we see in cases of infanticide or deliberate exposure to the elements. But "that changes nothing with regard to the incontrovertible character of the claim as such and the immediate evidence belonging to it" (ibid., 235). Nor, as Jonas tells us, are we talking here of a "'request' directed at the surrounding world ('Accept me and take me on'), for the newborn cannot yet speak," or, again, of a question of either familial love or love on the part of relatives.[15] In itself, the sheer existence of this being that depends on the responsibility of Others implies that these Others, whoever they may be, find themselves claimed or called upon to take on the newborn child. For this, they do not need to have produced the child, to be related to the child, or even to love the child, whatever the reasons in this regard might be (Marion 2008, §39).

This ontologically immanent imperative, which is how Jonas understands the claim of the newborn, signifies the ethical demand: Accept me and take me on.[16] It is obvious that in the usual course of things this claim is primarily directed at the parents. Yet in principle this claim is also encountered if we should happen to come upon an exposed or abandoned child (or perhaps an unaccompanied child attempting to escape a place of danger or insecurity) and then give the child over into the care of some third party, who must in turn also recognize this claim upon themselves. (Here we might think of so-called "baby-hatches" where infants can be handed over anonymously to others or, again, in the contemporary context of reception centers for "minors" who have fled to Europe from Africa or the Middle East.) Jonas specifically avoids basing his argument on some given norm of universal responsibility, derived from who knows where, that requires concrete application only in the "particular case." Nor does he speak of any "judgment of worthiness" with regard to the newborn—a judgment that would first have to justify the decision of whether or not to accept and take care of the child. On the contrary, what is at stake here is this child "in its absolutely contingent uniqueness." That alone is supposed to suffice, prior to any judgment of value, prior to any comparison with the fate of others, and independently of any contractual relation; that alone suffices to determine the responsibility of others for a being that is encountered in all its present facticity and uttermost fragility. Here, fragility means that the child is not just entirely exposed to the reality of transience, but is also intrinsically "a being under threat of destruction." For it ineluctably demands both immediate and long-term reliable care. In the absence of such assumed responsibility over time, the child is unable to survive at all. Yet the responsibility in question goes far beyond the securing of physical survival alone. It must promise to protect the child from harm or violence as far as this is possible, to facilitate and promote the overall socialization of the child, and thus help in opening up possibilities of an individual path for the child to pursue in its subsequent life. And that life will show that the child cannot be understood as a case of mere reproduction, as simply the production of another being, as just a repetition of the existence of substitutable progenitors. For the child must be understood precisely as *an Other being that steps out onto other roads*, whatever they may be.

The archetypal responsibility involved here is not taken as a selfsame *something* that can then be reidentified or reproduced. Rather, it must be assumed or taken over for the sake of a *future* self, that is, for the life of an Other, for one who must discover for him- or herself how this life in this particular case can be *"livable."* The responsibility that the newborn child *gives* us, and that requires us to accept it and take it on, can miscarry so that we fail to fulfill that "promise" to do all we can do (in the context of the relevant social, economic, and political conditions) to let the child begin and continue a life of its own. Yet that promise not only risks being broken from the start on account of its excessive character (and thereby appearing, subsequently, to be implausible, since it depends on a reliable political and institutional framework of a shared life, which is something no one can ever adequately guarantee); the promise also relates to the future of an Other that it is quite unable to anticipate. This amounts to more than the obvious point that the future cannot be foreseen in detail, for it also involves the fact that the child, for its part, is a "generative" being from which there may in turn spring "Others" who will be caught up in this same "intrigue" of responsibility and who will therefore also raise the question of whether the promise harbored within this assumed responsibility can be kept. Itself a generative being, the child is one from whom there can in turn emerge future Others who also bring with them a generative and un-anticipatable future. What is at issue here is by no means simply a cognitive iteration of generative relations that theoretically could in principle extend endlessly into the future. Rather, in and through the presence of children, their own generative future, and the future of their children and their children's children, is already co-present in a bodily sense—though it is precisely one that, as the future of future Others, cannot be specifically anticipated. Thus, the responsibility one must assume or take over for them reaches unavoidably and indirectly far beyond the horizon of the lives of those who are in existence at the present time.

It may seem very doubtful as to how on earth such a promise can be kept, but it is quite clear that it requires, at the very least, that we do nothing that would already and inevitably undermine what it means to accept and take on a child as a being that is itself generative—starting with issues of obvious physical and psychological neglect, but including any attitude of indifference with regard to violent or oppressive circumstances and living conditions; and in relation to the generative future of the child itself, this also extends to situations in which the child would be condemned from early on to endure the destructive consequences of the lives of others—things that can damage the prospects and possibilities of his or her own life, or even prevent such prospects and possibilities altogether.

And finally, we might consider the effects of the international debt crisis that has not just left its mark on the countries of southern Europe such as Greece, Italy, Spain, and Portugal, but has long since affected the world economy as a whole; or again the far-reaching effects of global climate change that clearly show that the responsibility inherent in human generativity cannot be reduced to the relations between parents and children (Liebsch 2016b). A host of different lateral social, political, and economic factors stretching way back into the past continue to shape current conditions of life, which may be seen as reliable and beneficial to a greater or lesser degree and are conditions for which the older generations, in the first instance, must bear responsibility. But, although they are certainly relevant to their own generative responsibility, the older generations cannot be held directly and causally responsible for these factors—or can be held responsible for them only in part. This becomes clear when we are forced to anticipate the radical retrospective question posed by our offspring and descendants as to how we let them come into the world under conditions that may prove to be entirely unacceptable or unbearable. Was it not already quite foreseeable that they would encounter conditions entirely unsuitable for any life they could find truly acceptable, or that the conditions for any such life would be violently disrupted or distorted? No assumed responsibility for caring and assisting those we bring into the world is, in principle, shielded from such reproach.

We now know that it was partly due to a variety of contingencies—such as the fortunate fact that during the Cuban missile crisis and during the large-scale NATO maneuvers (dubbed Able Archer) in the autumn of 1983, there were some Russian officers who were not prepared to follow orders unquestioningly—that humanity was not plunged on those occasions into a Third World War that readily could have led to a drastic atomic confrontation between the superpowers of the time. Since then we have innumerable examples of how the literary and visual media have explored apocalyptic scenarios of catastrophe where those who survived in spite of everything were forced to ask how those whom they survived could possibly justify bringing offspring into the world. Even without the horizon of expectations that have been so drastically depicted in fictional terms, it is clear that it is no longer possible simply to deny or ignore problems that, in many ways, have not even begun to be resolved or adequately addressed, such as the storage of atomic waste in the context of its radioactive lifetime (around a million years), the issue of nuclear disarmament, the global pollution of the ecosphere, the question of increasing global warming as a result of dramatically intensified processes of combustion, and the potential biological manipulation of the existing stock of vegetable, animal, and human life. This is precisely why Hans Jonas's reflections on the future "relationship between humanity and nature" were already presented under the telling title of *Dem bösen Ende näher*, namely: Nearer to the Evil End. Whether (or when) this end will actually arrive as a result of deadly weapons of one kind or another, or of technological, ecological, and biological disaster, and how "near" to this end we already are, may remain an open question for now. What is decisive here is that the *direct* "archetypal" responsibility—which already seems "excessive" or immeasurable in view of the diachronic future of an Other—is ineluctably entangled with an *indirect* responsibility to promote broadly advantageous conditions of life and to reflect, in view of the prospects for the future, on the full reach and import of this responsibility. Thus, in a rather paradoxical way, we have to situate a diachrony of responsibility in the face of an authentic and *non-anticipatable* future of each and every singular and unique Other *within the historical horizon* of such prospects for the future. On the other hand, we have also to consider that the demonstrably critical contemporary ecological and political prospects for a truly livable life relate specifically to Others who will live their *own* life in a completely unforeseeable way—and indeed have an original claim to be able to do so.

If we do not avoid doing everything that would already and effectively restrict, violently distort, or even destroy the possibilities of life that would otherwise be open to these Others, they will, later and inevitably, question this and raise the problem of an inadequately discharged responsibility on account of which they will have to suffer, even though they can receive no recompense from those who are directly responsible. In the face of those who will live after us—namely the "future generations," as we typically like to put it—those now living can only take responsibility in a virtual sense, insofar as they anticipate being called to account at some later point—something that, as a rule, they will manage to evade. Being called to account in this way is not something that merely comes into play as a contingent expression of "bad conscience" on the part of those who know very well, or should have known very well, how they have shown themselves to be wanting with regard to the life possibilities of future generations. Rather, this calling to account rests essentially on the responsibility always already given to us by and from the Other. For the responsibility, which everyone assumes when they accept and take on a child, cannot avoid relating in this way or that to a future Other: an Other who, in turn, will have a generative future of their own in which their offspring or descendants (the "grandchildren" and "great grandchildren" etc.) will be able to ask the same question of their progenitors. To take on a child (of one's own in a biological sense, or by fostering or adoption) is to say in and through this very act (which needs no explicit further planation): "I shall be responsible for you; and indeed for the horizon of a subsequent future responsibility in which you, and in time your children, your grandchildren, and others in turn, will be able in retrospect to ask how it was possible that we ourselves lived as well or as best we could by accepting or countenancing the damage to the life possibilities of those who will only have to suffer those possibilities as a result of our own generativity." Thus our present generative responsibility *for* a single Other already harbors in itself the significance of subsequent responsibility *before* a plurality of quite unknown and indefinite Others who, as a rule, will no longer be able to touch or concern those who preceded them. In this way, the "before whom" of responsibility (the anticipatable retrospective question of those who live after us) and the present "for whom" of responsibility inevitably fall apart or fail to coincide.

Every generative being inevitably lives *from and through* Others—whose physical, social, political, economic, cultural, and historical heritage this particular human being assumes and takes up in its own way, without ever being able *to do without* the past—a past that, for good or ill, they owe ambivalently to those they know or have known personally, but also of course to countless unknown Others. But so too does every generative being live *in relation towards* Others: not only on the basis of a physical or biological relatedness that allows us in some way to recognize ourselves in our own offspring or descendants, but also by virtue of a nonbiological fecundity or fruitfulness that, in the best case, serves to open up new paths of their own for those who live after us, and to save them from a mere repetition of the same.

Thus writers such as Jonas, Derrida, and Levinas undertake to reveal a "creative temporality" that opens up a space and creates a leeway for future ways and possibilities of exploring otherness or of "becoming-other." Levinas himself, however, fears nothing so much as the notion of any individual or community being consigned to the so-called "judgement of history" (Levinas 1969, 241, 242, 243) that leaves behind nothing but a kind of necrologue for the lives of others. This is why he restricts himself to describing a diachronic inter-time that is supposedly grounded in an erotic sociality. According to this account, human beings engender Others whose "authentic" future is said to be irreducible to what has preceded them and made them possible. *What is "made possible" through generativity is precisely a future life that escapes any intended process of "making possible" and can therefore never be produced or brought forth in a technological fashion.* Yet, as far I am aware, when Levinas talks about "human generativity" in this way and describes it in terms of "fecundity," he never explores its relevant historical horizons beyond a process of filiation that embraces merely a couple of generations. As a result, he overlooks the fact that, and the way in which—within the horizon of a future that poses significant threats to a greater or lesser degree—we are already economically, ecologically, and politically confronted with questions that concern our capacity to survive at all. From the generative perspective, he overlooks the essential role that inevitably falls to the question of whether the generative responsibility for Others can be connected to the promise to fulfill this responsibility not just once (on the occasion of their birth) but in an ongoing and lasting manner in the context of more complex forms of coexistence with countless Others and their own generative future: a task that is fulfilled by recognizing how we can relate to them in a responsible way, even if we can *no longer* later be "held responsible" in the sense of being "called to account."

The line of thought we have explored here thus would imply something like a generative solidarity, understood not just as a generous "readiness [. . .] to share the fate of the other,"[17] which is by no means necessarily restricted to those alive today, but in the stronger sense of an openness to the fate of future Others, which those who are live today can essentially no longer "share." This openness, which nonetheless participates in an expressly un-shareable future "beyond the possible,"[18] cannot be seen merely as an expression of a solidarity towards others that is built up in any old way we like. For we must recognize precisely where its roots lie, namely in the generative experience of time that already allows the authentic future of Others and their descendants to be co-present in our own life here in the present, whether we want this to be so or not. Insofar as this future is always already opened up by virtue of Others, of those who follow on after us, we cannot but relate to it in a paradoxically subsequent fashion, for this co-presence of a future that escapes those who are alive now can be glimpsed in human generativity from the beginning. Yet it gets forgotten in the notion of a simple sequence of generations that brings about later generations at whose expense the present ones seem to exist until they are banished from the scene of history by the latter. But this notion only serves to obscure the question of whether or how generations not only appear *after one another* in historical time, but emerge *from one another*, and can therefore also be there *for one another* in the horizon of an unforeseeable future—in the generative asymmetry of their staggered and intersecting lifetimes that never allow the births of one generation to coincide with the deaths of another.

    The diachrony of this generative inter-temporal life—a life "between times" in which we live at once from Others and in relation towards Others—means that it cannot be restricted to the birth "that is in each case mine" and the death "that is in each case mine" so that the life in question can be understood exclusively in terms of its own finitude. For this life reaches out into the open horizons of past and future, into the anonymous mortality and natality of Others, including even those who remain entirely alien or unknown to it. But if we think that all we can see in these endless historical horizons is just so many generations succeeding one another—generations that produce tens of thousands, and millions, and eventually billions of beings, before consigning them once more to non-being, beings whose willingness to contribute to this "alternation of successive generations" cannot possibly be presumed—then we lose sight of that precarious "ground of meaning" (Husserl), which, ultimately, can be discovered only in human generativity.

    But expecting this generativity to vouchsafe a solidarity that extends in principle to all future generations—a solidarity that would, in advance and without exception, burden those living now with an immeasurable responsibility for the future of those generations—surely seems to involve an excessive and exaggerated claim. It is not for nothing that Kant alludes in the *Metaphysics of Morals* to the presumption of deciding "on our own initiative" to bring a person into the world without any corresponding "consent" on their part (1977c, §28f.; 1996, 430): a world, moreover, for whose violence and injustice no newborn child can bear any blame or responsibility, and the demands of which are necessarily quite beyond it. This event of coming-into-the-world unasked involves an unavoidable yet always enduringly problematic process of opening up the generative experience of time in relation to previous and subsequent generations. But this certainly does not mean that the question of how intergenerational solidarity can become factically possible and how it can assume concrete form is already thereby answered by, for example, simply asserting an unlimited responsibility in this regard—an idea that has clearly often appealed to many of those who have been quite ready to announce the future of the human race. It is only this *question* that unavoidably presents itself in and through human generativity from the beginning. But we have good reason *at the very least* to call attention back to this question, if the suspicion is correct that the semantic-genetic connection between the concept of generativity and the concept of generations has been so widely neglected or forgotten that it now looks as if the idea of just living after one another in a purely serial and indifferent sense without any trace of solidarity whatsoever has come to represent the standard view: a view now increasingly combined with the notion that all too many people wish to live all too long and thereby enjoy their inter-temporal existence at the cost of others. The negativity of this kind of thinking surely offers an excellent reason for going back to reflect once again on the "forgotten" internal connection between generativity, generations, and intergenerational solidarity.

Notes

1. A concrete elaboration of such a notion of solidarity would far exceed the limits of a contribution such as the present one. Here I must simply restrict myself to an attempt to clarify some of the fundamental concepts involved and the cultural-intellectual historical background of these concepts. I draw on certain preliminary studies that specifically avoid reducing human generativity to the biology of "procreation" (as the Kantian remarks cited at the beginning of this chapter might, at least at first, strongly seem to suggest). In this regard, see Liebsch 2016a.

2. In German, it is possible to speak of both *Geschlechter* and *Generationen* in this particular context, where both terms would be rendered as "generations." In the standard German Duden Dictionary (vol. 7: *Etymologie*, 210 and 215), both German terms are sometimes treated as synonyms for "the totality of all those human beings who are born at roughly the same time," or again for "the totality of human

beings who are alive at the same time as one another." In this connection, it has often been presupposed without further discussion that such a simultaneity, in a more than merely chronological sense, can only exist if it relates to a synchronic experiential space. In Rousseau (1997) we read the following: "It might appear that life were a good that we enjoy solely on condition of handing it on, as representatives of something that must continue from generation to generation" (the word "generation" serves in the English translation to render the French *race*, which could be translated in German as *Geschlecht*, a word that can also refer to the human race or species itself, as well as specifically to gender and sexuality).

3. Here I cannot discuss the important question that is also crucial to the work of Levinas, namely whether such non-substitutable "Others" do not expressly require a particular kind of "representation" on their behalf.

4. Wilhelm Dilthey specifically spoke of a "generation" as a "homogenous whole" (see Riedel 1974).

5. This point is particularly emphasized by Ricoeur (1988).

6. Koselleck (1989) has shown very convincingly how this became possible.

7. Lessenich 2012, 123, and 126. Butterwegge has pointed out how the seemingly moral-sounding rhetoric that readily adopts this concept can be appropriated in support of a more or less neoliberal programme for reducing or dismantling structures of the modern welfare state (see Butterwegge 2014, 350f.; also Butterwegge, B. Lösch, and R. Ptak 2017, 275). It is also clear in this case just how *detrimental* this rhetoric can be as far as coming generations are concerned.

8. It would certainly be going too far to assume that what we are talking about here is a historical perspective that could only really develop in the context of a modern understanding of history. At the same time, it can hardly be denied that certain particularly modern experiences of accelerated change have been readily interpreted in relation to the historical temporal differences between successive generations. Koselleck in particular has drawn attention to this specific aspect (2003, 107, 195, 268).

9. It was by pursuing certain suggestions of Henri Bergson that the early Levinas attempted to interpret the temporality of filiation as a specific form of duration (*durée*). See Levinas 2009a, 218f., and 265. This idea of duration is later replaced by that of diachrony, something that cannot be conceptualized without recourse to the interruption provided by generative temporality. See Levinas 1987, 414.

10. For further discussion of these two forms of selfsameness (as a kind of selfhood), see Liebsch 2012.

11. Although we should certainly not overlook Levinas's reflections on the economy of lodging (*demeure*) in this connection.

12. Levinas does not merely describe these relations as reciprocally asymmetrical; he also characterizes them in such a way that the alterity already presupposed here always appears to be that which belongs to "the feminine." Thus he begins by saying: "The absolutely Other is the Other" without any reference to sex or gen-

der, but then he claims that "the Other" is "the woman" (1969, 25 and 265). Yet generativity is actually only interpreted by Levinas in terms of "paternity," where again only "the son" is expressly invoked (ibid., 268–69 or 277). But as a result, it seems that Levinas cannot make any use of the alterity of the (feminine) Other to elucidate the generativity that he repeatedly illustrates with reference to the father-son relationship. The question of how the husband or the father can be the (masculine) Other for the (feminine) Other, the woman or mother, thus remains entirely unanswered, as does the question of the connection between sexual difference and generative difference (father: daughter; mother: son).

13. For an exemplary discussion of this issue, see Birnbacher 1988.

14. Although we can surely anticipate the enormous difficulty that members of future generations will experience in trying to comprehend this situation when they realize how they must face the concretely foreseeable consequences of ecologically ruinous social and economic policies for which there is no one to take responsibility.

15. Thus, it is not because we are generative beings or because we can produce offspring that we are responsible in the close-knit generational context of a literal bodily filiation. It is rather the other way round: in this kind of context, responsibility intrinsically calls us to exercise care and concern, even if there is no direct or more distant biological relatedness in question.

16. In *Dem bösen Ende näher* (1993, 73), Jonas also speaks of a kind of "original obligation or indebtedness" (*Urschuld*) in this connection.

17. In the words of Jean Cohen and Andrew Arato (cited in Zoll 2000, 199).

18. This is specifically how Levinas characterizes human fecundity (1969, 267).

Bibliography

Berghoff, Peter. 1997. *Der Tod des politischen Kollektivs*. Berlin: Akademie.
Berman, Marshall. 1988. *All That Is Solid Melts into Air: The Experience of Modernity*. Harmondsworth: Penguin.
Bernt, Alois, and Konrad Burdach (Hg.) 1917. *Der Ackermann aus Böhmen*. Berlin.
Birnbacher, Dieter. 1988. *Verantwortung für künftige Generationen*. Stuttgart: Reclam.
Bloch, Ernst. 1984. "Der Faschismus als Erscheinungsform der Ungleichzeitigkeit." In *Theorien über den Faschismus*, edited by Ernst Nolte, 182–204. Königstein: Athenäum.
Blumenberg, Hans. 1986a. *Die Lesbarkeit der Welt*. Frankfurt/M.: Suhrkamp.
———. 1986b. *Lebenszeit und Weltzeit*. Frankfurt/M.: Suhrkamp.
Bourdieu, Pierre. 1977. *The Outline of a Theory of Practice*. Translated by Richard Nice. Cambridge: Cambridge University Press.
Butterwegge, Christoph. 2014. *Krise und Zukunft des Sozialstaats*. Wiesbaden: Springer VS.

Butterwegge, Christoph, Bettina Lösch, and Ralph Ptak. 2017. *Kritik des Neoliberalismus*. Wiesbaden: Springer VS.
Castoriadis, Cornelius. 1983. *Durchs Labyrinth*, Frankfurt/M: Suhrkamp [*Crossroads in the Labyrinth*. Translated by Kate Soper and Martin H. Ryle. Cambridge, MA: MIT Press. 1984].
———. 1984. *Gesellschaft als imaginäre Institution* [*The Imaginary Institution of Society*, Cambridge: Polity Press 1997].
Derrida, Jacques. 1994. *Specters of Marx: The State of the Debt, the Work of Mourning, and the New International*. Translated by Peggy Kamuf. London: Routledge.
———. 2002. "Hospitality." In *Jacques Derrida: Acts of Religion*, edited by Gil Anidjar, 356–420. New York: Routledge.
Donzelot, Jacques. 1980. *Die Ordnung der Familie*. Frankfurt/M.: Suhrkamp.
Duden. 1963. Bd. 7. Etymologie. Mannheim: Duden.
Ewald, François. 1993. *Der Vorsorgestaat*. Frankfurt/M.: Suhrkamp.
Foucault, Michel. 1991. "Govermentality." In *The Foucault Effect*, edited by Graham Burchell, Colin Gordon, and Peter Miller. Hemel Hempstead: Harvester Wheatsheaf.
Freud, Sigmund. 1962. *Aus den Anfängen der Psychoanalyse*. Hamburg: Fischer.
Fukuyama, Francis. 1992. *The End of History and the Last Man*. Glencoe, IL: The Free Press.
Hegel, Georg W. F. 1980. *Phänomenologie des Geistes*. Frankfurt/M.: Suhrkamp [*Phenomenology of Spirit*. Translated by A. V. Miller. Oxford: Oxford University Press, 1977].
Heidegger, Martin. 1984. *Sein und Zeit*. Tübingen: Niemeyer [*Being and Time*]. Translated by John Macquarrie and Edward Robinson. Oxford: Blackwell, 1967).
Horstmann, Ulrich. 1983. *Das Untier: Konturen einer Philosophie der Menschenflucht*. Wien, Berlin: Medusa.
Husserl, Edmund. 1962. *Die Krisis der europäischen Wissenschaften und die transzendentale Phänomenologie. Husserliana VI*. Den Haag: Nijhoff [*The Crisis of European Sciences*. Translated by David Carr. Northwestern University Press: Evanston, 1970].
———. 1973. *Zur Phänomenologie der Intersubjektivität. Husserliana XIV*. Den Haag: Nijhoff.
Jacob, François. 1998. *Die Maus, die Fliege und der Mensch*. Berlin: Berlin Verlag.
Jonas, Hans. 1982. *Das Prinzip Verantwortung*. Frankfurt/M.: Suhrkamp [*The Imperative of Responsibility*. Chicago: University of Chicago Press, 1985].
———. 1987. *Medizin, Technik und Ethik*. Frankfurt/M.: Suhrkamp.
———. 1993. *Dem bösen Ende näher*. Frankfurt/M.: Suhrkamp.
Kaempfer, Wolfgang. 1991. *Die Zeit und die Uhren*. Frankfurt/M.: Suhrkamp.
Kant, Immanuel. 1977a. "Von den verschiedenen Rassen der Menschen." In *Werkausgabe, Bd. XI*, Hg. Wilhelm Weischedel, 9–30. Frankfurt/M.: Suhrkamp ["Of the Different Races of Human Beings." In *Anthropology, History, and*

Education, translated by Holly L. Wilson and Günter Zöller, 84–97. Cambridge Edition of the Works of Immanuel Kant, Cambridge: Cambridge University Press, 2007].

———. 1977b. "Idee zu einer allgemeinen Geschichte in weltbürgerlicher Absicht." In *Werkausgabe, Bd. XI*, Hg. Wilhelm Weischedel, 31–50. Frankfurt/M.: Suhrkamp ["Idea for a Universal History with a Cosmopolitan Aim." In *Anthropology, History, and Education*, translated by A. Wood, 109–20. Cambridge: Cambridge University Press, 2007].

———. 1977c. *Die Metaphysik der Sitten. Werkausgabe, Bd. VIII*, Hg. Wilhelm Weischedel. Frankfurt/M.: Suhrkamp. ["*The Metaphysics of Morals.*" In *Practical Philosophy*, translated by Mary J. Gregor, 363–603. Cambridge: Cambridge University Press, 1996].

Kay, Lily E. 2005. *Das Buch des Lebens. Wer schrieb den genetischen Code?* Frankfurt/M.: Suhrkamp.

Koselleck, Reinhart. 1989. *Vergangene Zukunft*. Frankfurt/M.: Suhrkamp.

———. 2003. *Zeitschichten*. Frankfurt/M: Suhrkamp [*Sediments of Time*. Translated by Sean Franzel and Stefan-Ludwig Hoffmann. Redwood City, CA: Stanford University Press, 2018].

Kropotkin, Peter. 2017 [1902]. *Mutual Aid: A Factor in Evolution*. Independently published.

Lessenich, Stephan. 2008. *Die Neuerfindung des Sozialen*. Bielefeld: Transcript.

———. 2012. *Theorien des Sozialstaats zur Einführung*. Hamburg: Junius.

Levinas, Emmanuel. 1971. *Totalité et infini. Essai sur l'extériorité*. Haag: Nijhoff [*Totality and Infinity: An Essay on Exteriority*. Translated by Alphonso Lingis. Pittsburgh: Duquesne University Press, 1969].

———. 2009a. *Carnets de captivité. Œuvres 1*. Paris: Imec, Grasset.

———. 2009b. *Parole et silence. Œuvres 2*. Paris: Imec, Grasset.

Liebsch, Burkhard. 2001. "Überlieferung als Versprechen." In *Vernunft im Zeichen des Frem den: Zur Philosophie von Bernhard Waldenfels*, edited by Matthias Fischer, Hans-Dieter Gondek, and Burkhard Liebsch, 304–44. Frankfurt/M.: Suhrkamp.

———. 2012. *Prekäre Selbst-Bezeugung: Die erschütterte Wer-Frage im Horizont der Moderne*. Weilers wist: Velbrück Wissenschaft.

———. 2015a. "Anders (als) anders—ein Adverb auf Irrwegen? Zum Verhältnis zwischen Emmanuel Levinas und Paul Ricœur." In *Anders: Eine Lektüre von Jenseits des Seins oder anders als Sein geschieht von Emmanuel Levinas*, by Paul Ricoeur, 59–110. Wien, Berlin: Turia + Kant.

———. 2015b. "Von der Angst, ›anders‹ zu sein, zur normalisierten Verschiedenheit? *Disability and Diversity Studies* im Kontext einer Kultur der Differenzsensibilität." *Soziale Welt* 66 (4): 351–70.

———. 2016a. *In der Zwischenzeit: Spielräume menschlicher Generativität*. Zug: Die Graue Edition.

———. 2016b. "Schuld—Schulden—Verdanken: Ein Beitrag zur Revision des Verhältnisses von Moral und Öko nomie." *Archiv für Rechts- und Sozialphilosophie* 102 (4): 508–31.

———, ed. 2016c. *Der Andere in der Geschichte. Sozialphilosophie im Zeichen des Krieges: Ein ko op e rativer Kommentar zu Em manuel Levinas'* Totalität und Unendlichkeit. Freiburg: Alber.

———. 2016d. "Schwerpunktbeitrag: De-moralisierte Gesellschaften—Zwischen Schuld und Schulden." http://philosophie-indebate.de/wp-content/up loads/2016/12/Burkhard-Liebsch-De-moralisier te-Gesellschaften-1.pdf.

Mannheim, Karl. 1928. "Das Problem der Generationen." *Kölner Vierteljahreshefte für Soziologie VII*, 157–85, 309–30.

Marcuse, Herbert. 1979. *Triebstruktur und Gesellschaft*. Frankfurt/M.: Suhrkamp [*Eros and Civilization: A Philosophical Inquiry into Freud*. Boston: Beacon Press, 1972].

Marion, Jean-Luc. 2008. *The Erotic Phenomenon*. Translated by Stephen E. Lewis. Chicago: University of Chicago Press.

Marx, Karl. 1971. "Manifest der Kommunistischen Partei." In *Die Frühschriften*, 525–60. Stuttgart: Kröner ["*Manifesto of the Communist Party*." In *Karl Marx and Friedrich Engels: Selected Works*, 35–63. London: Lawrence and Wishart].

Miklós, Tamás. 2016. *Der kalte Dämon: Versuche zur Domestizierung des Wissens*. München: Beck.

Mill, John Stuart. 1962. "On Liberty." In *Utilitarianism*, by J. S. Mill, edited by Mary Warnock, 126–250. London: Collins.

Mommsen, Hand. 1985. "Generationskonflikt und Jugendrevolte in der Weimarer Zeit." In *"Mit uns zieht die neue Zeit." Der Mythos Jugend*, edited by Thomas Kroebner, Rolf-Peter Janz, and Frank Trommler, 50–67. Frankfurt/M.: Suhrkamp.

Musil, Robert. 1983. *Der Mann ohne Eigenschaften, Bd. 1*. Reinbek: Rowohlt [*The Man without Qualities*. Translated by Sophie Wilkins. London: Picador, 1997].

Oehler, Klaus. 1963. *Ein Mensch zeugt einen Menschen*. Frankfurt/M.: Klostermann.

Patočka, Jan. 1988. *Ketzerische Essays zur Philosophie der Geschichte*. Stuttgart: Klett-Cotta.

Petrarch, Francesco. 2009. *Letters on Familiar Matters*, vol. 1. Translated by Aldo S. Bernardo. New York: Italica Press.

Pinder, Wilhelm. 1961 [1926]. *Das Problem der Generation in der Kunstgeschichte Europas*. München: Bruckmann.

Ricœur, Paul. 2004. *The Conflict of Interpretations*. Edited by Don Ihde. London: Continuum.

———. 1988. *Time and Narrative*. Vol. 3. Translated by Kathleen Blamey and David Pellauer. Chicago: Chicago University Press.

———. 1992. *Oneself as Another*. Translated by Kathleen Blamey. Chicago: University of Chicago Press.

Riedel, Manfred. 1974. "Gene Ration." In *Historisches Wörterbuch der Philosophie, Bd. 3*, 274–77. Basel: WBG.
Ritter, Gerhard A. 1989. *Der Sozialstaat*. München: Beck.
Rousseau, Jean-Jacques. 1997. *Julie, or the New Heloise*. Translated by Philip Stewart and Jean Vaché. Hanover, NH: Dartmouth College Press.
Schmidt-Bergmann, Hansgeorg. 2009. *Futurismus*. Reinbek: Rowohlt.
Schütz, Alfred. 1984. "Viertes Notizbuch aus Minnewaska–New York, 26.10.–9.11.1958." In *Strukturen der Lebenswelt, Bd. 2*, by Alfred Schütz and Thomas Luckmann, 343–81. Frankfurt/M.: Suhrkamp.
Shaw, George Bernard. 2017. *Fabian Essays in Socialism*. Andesite Press.
Weigel, Sigrid. 2006. *Genea-Logik*. München: Fink.
Zoll, Rainer. 2000. *Was ist Solidarität heute?* Frankfurt/M.: Suhrkamp.

Section 2
The Politics of Human Generations

4

Absences that Matter

Phenomenological Insights into (the Predicaments of) Intergenerational Justice

FERDINANDO G. MENGA

Within at least some fields of the current scholarly debate concerning the question of "Who can enter—or be recognized as part of—the democratic space?," there is a general consensus that political membership is the result of a boundary politics, that is, a politics of inclusion and exclusion. Membership, in other words, cannot avoid being the product of a process—never warranted and always, therefore, contingent—that renders *present* in the public realm what is potentially absent and can possibly remain so.

Furthermore, since a human rights–based politics has become, in principle, the primary yardstick for the democratic soundness of polities, the issue of an incrementally inclusive membership inevitably becomes more complex, as it is intertwined with the question of "who can be considered human?" and thus reaches into a significantly more radical politico-ontological dimension.

As a consequence, because such a transition from absence to presence—from invisibility to visibility—is the only dynamic constituting the humanity of the human, this brings to the fore the ethico-political, but also legal, stake embedded within any act of representation that produces a determined framework for the appearance of the human.

Importantly, this stake runs into its own further radicalization as soon as one maintains, in line with Judith Butler's position, that the issue of "Who counts as human?" (2004, 20) is not only a matter of how an absence is rendered (or represented as) present, but also—and much more—a matter of how such an absence can be granted pride of place as an absence in the public realm. Only those who can be considered "grievable" (ibid.), so Butler argues, are, in fact, fully human: that is, only those whose absence or loss is capable of leaving a trace in the public sphere by means of representative instantiations. The politics of the obituary, so perceptively analyzed in her investigations (ibid., 32f.), tells no different a story than that of *absences that matter*.[1] Only by counting as absent, by having a space of representation as absent, do subjects acquire the status afforded to those fully recognized as being human. To the contrary, ungrievable lives—absences that do not matter—are not even regarded as forgotten humans, but, more precisely—and rather worse—as "de-realized" individuals who have never crossed the basic threshold of humanity itself. These absences float, as it were, as unperceived beings in a nowhere, so that it is precisely in their being unperceived that the violence perpetrated on them is so effectively reinforced.[2] Indeed, who could ever imagine questioning or challenging a violence that is presumed to be exerted nowhere and on nobody?

I do not further develop this line of thought here. But I touch on the issue of absences that matter to point out that it carries a *temporal*, as well as a spatial-topological, relevance. This is especially true when we consider absent individuals in terms of remote future subjects, whose transcending absence should matter *as absence*.

As one may well imagine, this is far from being a merely speculative concern, as it immediately speaks to the very factual problem of how one must think—in ethical, political, and also legal terms—of a responsibility for future generations, a responsibility for individuals whose absence should properly count.

Yet if we ask what avenue of thought is required for absent future people to be adequately rendered present within the realm of democratic polities, then it soon becomes apparent that our current ethical, political, and legal orientations are entirely dominated by a counter-dynamic of presentism. Consequently, what I would like to submit in this investigation is that a true and proper responsibility for the future demands no less than an ethico-anthropological revolution: a revolution such that a new configuration of ethical subjectivity and moral motivation arises that is radically oriented to the future itself and, as such, is able to give sustenance to politics and law—although I do not, in principle, exclude the reverse, that is, that some trajectories of politics and legal praxis, in being already nourished by such an ethico-anthropological reconfiguration, might trigger the required revolution.

Having set out an introductory frame, I want to use this chapter to touch on two main areas: in the first place, I want to outline the central features I have in mind for an "ethico-anthropological revolution" within the realm of intergenerational justice. In the second place, I aim to describe how a certain phenomenological approach based on the primacy of alterity can deliver an interesting contribution in terms of the new configuration of the ethical motivation and attendant ethical and political subject that would be required.

Future Generations and the Problem of Ethical Presentism

We hear it everywhere as a sort of ecological mantra: urgent action and robust rescheduling of the priorities in the agendas of international environmental policies has become a task that can no longer be deferred. This demand is all the more urgent when extended to the ambit of intergenerational ethics and politics, since climate change not only affects current generations or generations in a near future, but also carries the potential to inflict irreversible harm on remote future generations. *Pace* the negationist theories on climate change, if we do not rapidly reverse the trend in our environmental policies, the risk we are facing and are perhaps, even, barely able to avoid is that we condemn future generations—in the best-case scenario—to life conditions that are greatly impoverished compared with those enjoyed by current generations.[3]

However, on closer inspection, the sense of an obligation to avoid harm to future generations and even to foster their prosperity, broadly perceived, runs into a central predicament. In his important book devoted to the ethical tragedy of climate change, Stephen Gardiner defines this predicament in terms of a "perfect moral storm" (2011) bearing down on the environmental and intergenerational issue, arising, in his view, through the convergence of several interrelated elements on a single point, namely, the defense of the priority of present interests. More precisely, we are dealing with a presentism in moral motivation and power relations that is accompanied by a fatal lack of robust theoretical guidance adequate to the task of tackling the "many problems characteristic of the long-term future" (ibid., 41), thereby leaving us without resources with which to challenge the preeminence of the contemporary. Compounding this picture is a further and problematic factor, in that the current framing of the theoretical debate on the intergenerational issue has the effect of delivering theories that are well equipped to support presentism, thereby legitimizing the "intergenerational buck-passing" (ibid., 35) and the exploitation of the future by the present. And, thus, the moral storm reaches its climax. Gardiner calls it a true and proper "moral corruption" (ibid., 46) motivated by, and further accentuating, the "tyranny of the contemporary" (ibid., 36, 143).

Therefore, drawing on Gardiner's account, what is called for is an even stronger commitment to the theoretical side of the problem: an engagement that, through a thoroughgoing establishment of the ethico-anthropological resources to challenge the moral corruption and tyranny of the contemporary, establishes its ability to respond to a genuinely future-oriented ethics. In the absence of a robust effort with which, on the one hand, to ground the radical motivational platform (cfr. ibid., 68) for a genuine response to future nonexistent beings and, on the other hand, to elucidate the ethical and political subjectivities able to give sustenance to it, the chance of being able to challenge the aforementioned perfect storm remains extremely low. For the dynamic inhering in the storm is exactly such that presentism in power relations, presentism in moral motivations, and presentism in theoretical underpinning reinforce one another in an alliance that verges on the indefeasible. Simply put, if the main interest is such that, in Gardiner's words, "the current generation favors buck-passing, but does not want to face up to what it is doing, it is likely to welcome any rationale that appears to justify its behavior" (ibid., 45). Importantly, this intertwinement of motivational and theoretical presentism underlying moral corruption is, then, further supported by a presentism in power relations, since it is characteristic of the intergenerational context that "the victims are not yet around to defend" themselves (ibid., 46).

Since this alliance underpins the prevailing trend, one searches the political and legal practices and institutions in vain for some way out of this storm: practices and institutions that in fact seem only to accentuate and amplify the logic of presentism. For one thing, in the ambit of the political, and as many have pointed out (Thompson 2005 and 2010; Tremmel 2006, 187; Gardiner 2011, 143ff.; Jenkins 2013, 290; Fritsch 2015, 27ff.), the current democratic institutions exhibit the structural, and traditional, problem of being "systematically biased in favor of the present" (Thompson 2005, 246). Furthermore, enmeshed as they are in the primary pursuit of their own reelection, governments habitually base their decisions on an "extraordinarily narrow temporality" (Jenkins 2013, 290). In the realm of law, despite much that has been accomplished lately in light of a more future-adaptive reconsideration of legal mechanisms and institutions,[4] the traditional and prevailing view in theory and practice remains more or less unchanged, inasmuch as it is still the case that future people, as unidentifiable persons, are not properly held to have rights (Macklin 1981, 152) and, as indeterminate persons, are not properly held to have interests (De George 1981, 160). Highly representative of this is De George's position, namely that "future generations or future individuals or groups should collectively be said to have a right only to what is available when they come into existence, and hence when their possible future rights become actual and present" (ibid.).[5] From this, the legal conclusion one can directly draw is no more and no less than that mercilessly summarized by the Italian constitutional theorist, Gustavo Zagrebelsky, when he finds that the issue of "rights of future generations" is one that "breaks contemporaneity [as] the very basis upon which the validity of norms [. . .] and law has presented itself so far" (2016, 85). Legally speaking, this can lead to only one consequence, namely, that "if law [. . .] presupposes a present holder" of rights in order to function, this properly means that "future generations, as such, have no subjective rights whatsoever they can claim in front of previous generations. All the harm that they can suffer, even the deprivation of the minimal conditions of life, cannot be understood in terms of a violation of some kind of 'right' in legal terms" (ibid., 86).

Presentism and Moral Intuition

These consequences of presentism in the ambits of ethics, politics, and law give me the opportunity to raise my first main question: why is the theoretical terrain ill equipped to deliver a strong motivational justification for intergenerational duties and, most importantly, for obligations to remote future generations, in such a way as to nourish the viability of its ethical, political, and legal implementation?

It would be impossible to engage in great detail with this question in the space of one short chapter. But the issue at stake can be summarized, albeit with some simplification, in the following way: a genuine future-oriented ethics is confronted with a foundational resistance in the realm of traditional ethical theories because, despite explicit dedication to the problem of futurity, these theories are sustained, nonetheless, by the very presentistic semantic they should instead contrast. As Janna Thompson rightly recalls, "intergenerational justice makes its appearance as an addendum to theories of synchronic justice" (Thompson 2009, 3). Accordingly, a foundational predicament arises in that, when called to deliver the radical motivation for a responsibility towards future nonexistent persons, these present-based theories are thus compelled to draw upon external sources that are incompatible with what their present-centered construction has on offer.[6] This external source is typically raised, when the available rational strategies run short of arguments, in terms of a moral intuition that imposes an immediate obligation towards the future.[7] Traditional theories thus face a disquieting situation in that, to adequately address the deep motivational impulse for a future-oriented responsibility, they are forced, in one way or another, to relax those main foundational precepts that reflect a present-centered stance and commit themselves to an intuition that displays no proper location—or coherent justification—within the traditional theoretical structure (Auerbach 1995, 209).

This is the case, for instance, in the context of contractualist and contractarian theories that are the most widely deployed theories in the intergenerational justice debate. The founding condition of these theories is the existence of co-present individuals who, in their capacity for mutual cooperation, are able to enter into a contract. Individuals in a contract situation "concentrate on determining the bargains or agreements" that they would endorse, on "the rights that they can claim or on the responsibilities that arise from their collective [. . .] actions" (Thompson 2009, 3). However, the problem then arises that we lack the means by which to make a contract, bargain, or agreement with future persons, with persons who are not yet born. Future individuals "are unable to claim their rights, negotiate or agree" (Kobayashi 1999, 14). Not only is there no mutual cooperation between present and future persons, but there is also an absolute asymmetry, since contemporaries can affect the circumstances and destiny of the future ones, while the latter cannot influence those of the former at all (Gardiner 2011, 37–38).

My main concern here is not so much to discuss the various arguments and attendant shortcomings of these theories with regard to the problem of (remote and radically absent) future generations.[8] Rather, it is to show how, when addressing the justificatory source of intergenerational duties, contractualist and contractarian theories eventually find the need to draw upon a moral intuition that is external and troubling to their own structural prerequisites.[9]

This is true in the case of John Rawls, who, in adapting his principle of justice to the intergenerational ambit (1971, §§ 24, 44), finds it necessary to modify precisely the fundamental and characteristic "motivation assumption" of those subjects, in the original position, committing to the preliminary conditions entailed by the veil of ignorance. As is well addressed within the literature, it is only thanks to such a modification that the theory renders itself able to respond to the necessity of a "just savings principle" for the benefit of future generations. The modification operates in such a way that the subjects involved in the ideal choice scenario are no longer regarded as "self-interested" and "mutually disinterested" individuals but rather as those "representing family lines": in other words, as "fathers [sic]" who "care for their sons [sic]." What is decisive about this modification for the economy of my analysis is not to do with its successes or failures in fulfilling the scope of an adequate justification for intergenerational justice, but to do with two important things that it lays bare: first, this change of motivation shows that Rawls's theory *as it stands* is unable to derive a motivation for intergenerational justice without recourse to a moral intuition (1971, 139, 292);[10] second, it shows that, in contrast to anything that Rawls maintains, such a theoretical twist is by no means coherent with the fundamental preconditions set by the veil of ignorance. On the contrary, as Brian Barry aptly points out, Rawls's modification can be understood as an "entirely *ad hoc*" (Barry 1989, 191) insertion into the theory, since there is no compelling reason for relaxing the original postulate of self-interest other than that "it enables Rawls to derive obligations to future generations" (Barry 1977, 279).[11]

Even more telling is the case of David Gauthier's contractarian theory based on the explicit refusal of any basic moral intuition and its consequent adherence to the sole device of rationally justified choices (1986, 148, 269, 298).[12] What is, however, extremely problematic in Gauthier's theory is the fact that the banished moral intuition *volens nolens* strikes back again in terms of an ultimate justification of obligations towards future generations by means of the extension of the Locke's proviso (ibid., 16). In fact, according to Vallentyne's reading (1986, 82), if one closely inspects Gauthier's foundational assumptions, one finds no real rationale but only a "moral" imperative "to refrain from violating the proviso (bettering one's position by worsening the position of others)." As a consequence, an intuitive moral foundation for intergenerational obligations ends up being operative even in the very theory that explicitly attempts to discard any such moral foundation.

A predicament that is different in form but similar in substance is also detectable in the contractual theories that, instead of obeying the logic of a strict mutuality, derive obligations towards future generations from that of an "indirect reciprocity"[13] that boils down to this formulation: since a generation has received benefits from past generations, it has an obligation to transmit these benefits to future generations. There are a number of problems here, but the main one to preoccupy my analysis is, again, the unavoidable recourse to an external foundation in moral intuition, since what is presupposed by any such theory, but cannot be explained in terms of its own structural resources, is the validity of the gift/obligation relation on which it rests. In other words, it does not clarify, but only draws on, the notion that I am obligated to give to others because I have myself received from others (Barry 1991, 232).[14]

The consequentialist position developed by Derek Parfit displays perhaps one of the most telling instantiations of the way in which moral intuition intervenes from without and by necessity. As we know, Parfit's Non-Identity Problem (1984, 351–79) delivers one of the most cogent arguments for denying any kind of moral obligation towards future generations. He rejects the notion of any obligation in the present to prevent or minimize harm to future generations, because the very actions that seem to provoke harm to future individuals are also those responsible for producing their existence. Hence, if the current generation opts for an austere climate policy for the sake of avoiding harm to future persons, those measures would, by affecting reproductive conditions and decisions, also affect the number and identity of future subjects. If, on the other hand, the current generation chooses to adopt other policies, including resource-depleting ones, those measures would lead to a different number and identity of future persons. The conclusion? Even if the persons of the latter group were to inhabit a world with worse conditions than that of the former group, as long as they declared a preference to live such a life rather than not to have lived at all, then they could not claim to have been harmed by the world-worsening conditions of which their own existence was a consequence. The conclusion Parfit draws from this line of reasoning is that a strict consequentialist theory based on a person-affecting principle cannot legitimate intergenerational obligations. What is interesting, however, for my own analysis is that, notwithstanding this conclusion, Parfit does not advance a coherent counter-position to intergenerational justice. On the contrary, surprisingly, he argues for the necessity of finding a better theory—as he calls it, the "x theory" (ibid., 364, 378)—that is able to overcome his own negating argument (ibid., 443, 451). It goes without saying that it is precisely this compulsion to find some such theory, even despite the negative findings of his own argument, that further underscores the primordial force of a moral intuition commanding responsibility (ibid., 447, 451f.).[15]

All of this gives us at least a general picture of how mainstream theories feel a certain discomfort with the admission of a moral intuition while at the same time finding the need to adopt it as their ultimate foundation. Perhaps this disquieting state of affairs can best be summarized by the very embarrassment shown by Barry—as a notorious and vehement defender of strict rationalism—in closing one of his important essays devoted to the problematic character of intergenerational justice. On the one hand, he seems all too clearly to discard the idea that we ought "to fall back on an appeal to moral intuitions" (1977, 276). On the other hand, however, he holds open the possibility "that it may come to that" (ibid.)—a possibility that then becomes a pressing urgency when he concludes as follows:

> I must confess to feeling great intellectual discomfort in moving outside a framework in which ethical principles are related to human interests, but if I am right then these are the terms in which we have to start thinking. I conclude that those who say we need a "new ethic" are in fact right. It should [. . .] as a minimum include the notion that those alive at any time are custodians rather than owners of the planet, and ought to pass it on in at least no worse shape that they found it in. (Barry 1997, 284)

Future Ethics in Light of a Phenomenology of Alterity

All of this leads to the second question I want to address: if a presence-based perspective fails to deliver a radical moral motivation for a future-oriented responsibility, what ought an adequate moral paradigm look like if it is genuinely to "welcome the future"? (Muers 2008, ch. 1). The answer I submit is the following: to engage radically with a responsibility for the future, one needs to transgress the ethical perspective that responds to the future problem only by extending the semantic of the present. We are, rather, I suggest, called to deal with a radical reorientation of moral thought, such that one no longer adheres to the paradigmatic character of an ethics founded on the "here and now" of present time and present subjects. One should instead begin to consider an ethics for the future that draws its motivational force directly from a futuric transgression of ethical presentism.

However speculative such a futuric perspective might appear, I maintain it is concrete and effectively perceptible once one begins to consider alternative ways of depicting the very emergence of moral obligation; and it is here, precisely, that a phenomenological perspective can make a fertile contribution. In different ways, authors such as Emmanuel Levinas, Jacques

Derrida, and Bernhard Waldenfels (to name just a few) have insisted that that which primarily determines the moral subject, ties subjects together, and motivates moral obligations in intersubjective realms, is prior to anything to do with the acquisition and defense of interests and the concomitant sets of rights and duties arising within the space or semantic of presence and symmetric co-presence of cooperating individuals. As we have seen, the classical liberal-contractual stance continues to dominate the formulation of the intergenerational issue and the way in which it is then approached. Contractual perspectives, despite their various modulations and differentiations, are based on the foundation of a moral subject determined by a primordial presence to itself that is by way of an atomistic self-appropriation and the related fostering and defense of its own self-interests. The definition of the intersubjective relationship that follows from this is shaped in terms of the co-presence of reciprocally self-interested individuals who cooperate in view of fulfilling their interests within a corresponding regulatory framework of rights and duties, responsibility, and justice.

The phenomenological perspectives I have just mentioned by no means challenge the contractual frame as a whole. Rather, they claim a more originary layer underlying the emergence of moral obligations (Levinas 1979, Derrida 1992 and 2001, Waldenfels 2006 and 2011). According to these perspectives, in fact, what constitutes the primordial feature of the moral subject and simultaneously represents the very source of moral obligations is not the atomistic self-centeredness of the subject claiming interests and committing to the intersubjective relationship on the basis of a connected set of rights and duties in view of their fulfillment and protection. What makes the subject in the first place is, reversely, its primordial decenteredness and exposure to the other, prior to any scenario emerging from contractual prerequisites.

To speak, especially, with Levinas: before the subject can settle in its enclosed space of self-presence, and before it can transpose an intersubjective engagement into the play or battlefield of converging/diverging interests and the formulation of good reasons for interacting, it is haunted by the call of the other. In other words, the subject is haunted by the other *prior* to the conditions of symmetry, cooperation, and, thereby, contract. And if *presence* and co-*presence* regulated by a contract are what normally mark the *condition* of interaction, then this explains why Levinas insists so vehemently that the relation with the other forces the subject into an experience of an *unconditional* demand, or, more precisely, a demand that comes from "a past [that has] never been present" (Levinas 1987b, 68).

Conclusively, according to Levinas, it is the very appearance of the other within the sphere of the subject prior to the possibility of claiming interests, delivering reasons for interacting or non-interacting, that constitutes the subject as not only decentered, but also *ethically* so. Indeed, if the other calls the subject into constitution by the very demand to be responsive to it, then the decentering of the subject by the other and the decentering through an irreducible call to responsibility for the other coincide (Levinas 1987a, 57ff.).

In an extremely insightful passage from *Otherwise than Being*, Levinas writes: "Responsibility for the Other is not an accident that happens to a subject, but precedes essence in it, has not awaited freedom, in which a commitment to another would have been made. I have not done anything and I have always been under accusation—persecuted. The ipseity, in the passivity without arche characteristic of identity, is hostage. The word *I* means *here I am*, answering for everything and for everyone" (Levinas 1991, 114).

Leaving aside the hyperbolic emphasis on some elements of this passage that I cannot engage with here, what I would like to retain from this insight is a core element that is of relevance within the context of my investigation. Using Robert Bernasconi's words, as he comments on Levinas's position on the subject, this element can be described as the essential fact that "I am radically responsible for the other prior to any contract, prior to having chosen or acted, indeed prior to my taking up a subject position in relation to an other" (Bernasconi 2002, 67). In the *Introduction* to their coedited book on Levinas and environmental ethics, William Edelglass, James Hatley, and Christian Diehm (2012) also convey the same message in their own comparative analysis: "Unlike Kant, who founds his proto-ethics upon the human capacity to reason coherently, Levinas turns directly to that dimension of my social existence in which I am called to be attentive to and responsible for another, that subtle yet profound feature of sociality in which I (the first person pronoun is important here) find myself being 'for the other' and not simply 'for myself' " (ibid., 7).

Given these general features of a phenomenologically intended structuring of the subject, and of the emergence of the ethical experience out of the motive of alterity, it is now possible to see how they can function as generative elements for a more comprehensive foundational strategy for fostering intergenerational duties.

Remarks on a Fruitful Reshaping of Intergenerational Ethics from a Phenomenological Perspective

Yet an expansion of a phenomenology of otherness in the light of a more comprehensive legitimation of a responsibility for future generations is possible only if a preliminary and troubling point is addressed: on the one hand, it is relatively easy to imagine the terms in which the diachronic break of a present-centered ethics can arise as a demand that haunts the subject from "a past which has never been present"; on the other, it is not as easy to picture the sense in which a comparable diachronic break of a present-centered ethics may irrupt from the future. The first instance can be depicted in the emergence of the call of a singular other that always anticipates the subject's strategies of calculation, reasoning, and contractual taming of the intersubjective relationship. Yet how might one imagine a *future* nonexisting other enacting something like a demand, such that this claim decenters the subject and, simultaneously, calls upon it for an unconditional responsive/responsible behavior?

Answering this pivotal question is no easy task. And perhaps much of the unease it engenders stems not so much from the apparent theoretical predicament it produces but rather from the demanding ethical reorientation or revolution that—as mentioned at the beginning—it requires. Generally speaking, my contention is that a radical call from a future-connoted other, which commands responsibility prior to any contractual codification, imparts no suggestion of an otherworldly or speculative exercise. Rather, this demand from the future already takes place on a concrete ethical basis, as Levinas perceptively recalls, most especially in his early lectures *Time and the Other* (1987c, 74ff.) and later essays (ibid., 114ff.), but also as Waldenfels highlights in his contribution to this volume. What is also important is that this demand arises in no instances other than those speaking to the unconditional concern to care for future generations: a concern that mainstream theories in intergenerational justice do also maintain and grasp when forced to call upon an irreducible moral intuition as their justification of last resort. Thus, a Levinas-inspired view focusing on the perception of a moral interpellation by the future causes no real theoretical predicament. Rather, it builds a direct connection to, and convergence with, the traditional debate concerning intergenerational duties in its adherence to the moral intuition as a strategy.

This convergence, in turn, tells us two important things. First, as moral subjects we are, in the end, neither primarily atomistic nor constituted in such a way as to be centered in the present, but are decentered by means of a primordial intersubjective relatedness. Second, as decentered subjects, we are not only ethically decentered in being haunted by an unconditional past, but also in being called upon by a future-commanding responsibility.[16]

In my view, the unsettling predicament that is part and parcel of this issue lies in what such an assumption demands of us. But to engage with this further, I want first to emphasize some of the features that a phenomenological position advocating subject-decenteredness can bring to a future ethics.

In the first place, unlike the present-centered or synchronic theories of intergenerational obligations, a phenomenological view based on the unconditional demand of responsibility stemming from otherness and implying decenteredness of the moral subject is better placed to circumscribe appropriately the very site from which the moral intuition to care for future generations emanates. Indeed, as we saw in the earlier quotation from Barry, a present-centered theory can, at most, concede the use of the moral intuition as an external force and, last, as an *extrema ratio*. The consequence of this theoretical attitude, however, is that it produces a disquieting situation in that such an allegedly *externa* and *extrema* ratio eventually shows itself to be unavoidable, despite other starting assumptions. By contrast, the phenomenological position I have outlined draws explicitly on this unconditional motivating force as a primordial motive. In addition, it furnishes a structural explanation for its emergence and constitutive role within ethical experience.

In the second place, the prior exposure to alterity and the decentered constitution of the moral subject make possible a more open structure of subjectivity itself. A subject constitutively exposed to alterity implies, in fact, an ontological non-fixity and, subsequently, a radical self-transformativity and self-questioning that are directly responsive to whatever concrete obligations may open up; or better, are directly responsive to whatever moral emergences alterity puts into being through its command. As a consequence, the alterity-exposed subject advanced by Levinas does not imply merely an anthropocentric self-alterability limited to a "disruption of egoism" (Edelglass/Hatley/Diehm 2012, 5). A more fundamental sense of self-alteration is here entailed: the transformativity of a constitutively alterity-exposed subject includes the possibility to welcome genuine instantiations of non-anthropocentric otherness within its ethical realm. Drawing again from Edelglass, Hatley, and Diehm: "if Levinas is correct to say that it is morally naïve for me to place myself at the center of things, we might begin to wonder if it is not equally naïve for humanity to do likewise, to center its vision of ethical life upon itself" (ibid., 5). The benefit of this view for the intergenerational ethical issue is clear: if we accept the radical interpellation of future others that disrupts our egoism and present-centered interests, then this disruption is such that we have to be ready to embrace the need to consider the command to take responsibility not only for future human others, but also for future nonhuman forms of alterity.[17]

Precisely here, a theory fostering the notion of a subject who radically opens up to the ethical alterity of the future provokes a sort of moral revolution or, at least, strong reorientation. In fact, as already Karl Jaspers ([1958] 1963) and Günther Anders (1956) have noticed in their books written at the aftermath of the devastating nuclear events of Hiroshima and Nagasaki, a serious concern for the harm that future persons might undergo requires a strong anthropological turn in the ethical life of present generations. This turn, inspired by the urgency to act for the benefit of future beings, demands that we start exploring the opportunity to break with the traditional logic of duties counterbalanced by the fulfillment of interests, and to accept instead the logic of sacrifice.[18] Even before Jaspers and Anders, thinkers such as Friedrich Nietzsche ([1885] 2006, 44) and Nicolai Hartmann ([1925] 2014, ch. XXX) have also theorized that to advocate, fully, for a *Fernstenliebe*, a love of the farthest or the remote, an inevitable "injustice" (Hartmann [1925] 2014, 321) towards the present is required, if justice is defined in terms of obligations in correspondence to the fulfillment of interests.

In this respect, I maintain that the strategy of overextending the ambit of interest to include features otherwise pertaining to the semantic of sacrifice is a dubious tactic. This is the strategy deployed, for instance, by Janna Thompson in her nonetheless insightful book on *Intergenerational Justice* based on "lifetime-transcending interests" (Thompson 2009, 39ff.). I can only praise this book for the author's effort in attempting to overcome synchronic-based theories of intergenerational justice by making clear that it is part and parcel of political constituencies to be founded on transcendence-oriented and purely "diachronic" intergenerational aspirations (ibid., 45). Nevertheless, I submit that in reducing all motivating impulse for ethical action to only that which can be comprehended in terms of interests, she displays a set of phenomenological flaws. It not only forces an enlargement of the realm of interest to such an extent that the pertinence of its meaning loses all clear contours, but it also, and more importantly, imposes an indirect construction of motivation for phenomena that are in fact much more direct and possessed of an underlying "straightforwardness."[19]

To be sure, Thompson is right in saying that interests motivate (ibid., 41). Yet what troubles me is the other feature entailed by her account of interests: that they are to be considered as *owned/possessed* by the corresponding interested subject (ibid., 40). The insertion of this feature comes as no surprise since it reflects the cardinal precept of the classical liberal tradition out of which the relation obtaining between property, subject, and interests emerges. As Macpherson (1962) reminds us, interest is the very engine of the expanding dynamic of appropriation exerted by the one who is primordially defined as the very *locus* of self-ownership: the possessive individual.[20] In line with this, my overall concern with Thompson is that, despite her effort to break with polities based on synchronic interest, she nevertheless falls back on the liberally construed semantic of the present in her very faithful and unquestioning adherence to the preeminence of what is implied by the possession of interest. It is precisely here that I diverge from her position: I find it unconvincing that we experience the motivating force to act for the benefit of future others or for the environment either in terms of the ownership of interests or in terms of moral conduct indirectly linking us to a source of interest. On this point, harking back to Levinas's theory of an alterity-exposed subject, my contention is that we experience much of the motivating impulse as a true and proper instantiation of dispossession and passivity rather than as active ownership, or in other words, as an immediate command to be responsible, prior to any delayed conceptual assimilation into a sphere of interest. For what, in fact, is the interest we possess when striving for the intergenerational aspiration of defeating diseases in which we are not directly involved and from which not even our immediate successors will benefit? What kind of possessor is one—and what kind of interest has one—when reaching out one's hand to the fugitive who is about to drown in the Mediterranean? Furthermore, what kind of interest attaches to what kind of possessor when, confronted by a polluted environment, one feels a disquieting unease? All these experiences engender a sense of guilt and accusation even if we know we are not the immediate perpetrators of this state of affairs. Here I believe that Levinas's explanatory strategy of a decentered subject who is immediately constituted by the command to responsibility arising from its exposition to alterity, his idea that this command intervenes within the subject's sphere provoking an experience of passivity and substitution (Levinas 1991, 113ff.)—an unconditional experience of feeling accused and guilty for something I have not done and yet I have to expiate (ibid., 118f.)—all of this delivers a much closer phenomenological explanation than that seeking to derive the motivating impulse from the indirect conceptualization according to which we would act for the sake of general interest in the well-being of humankind that we *possess*. It is worth keeping in mind that even Kant, one of the greatest supporters of the transition through the generality of the moral maxims, shows us all too well—as Waldenfels (2006, 44) reminds us—that the very motivating impulse to act morally ultimately stems from a "voice of the conscience" that calls upon us unconditionally and prior to any possibility of our giving reasons for it. It is, as Kant himself defines it, a *Faktum der Vernunft* without itself being a rationally derivable fact (Kant [1797] 1956, 352 [A 38–39]).

Nevertheless, this kind of reorientation in moral thinking represents a difficult task because it requires the exertion of a moral sensitivity that must be always on the alert. More precisely, it engenders an ongoing practice of attestation, since it does not have any final conceptual or ontological sustenance (Levinas 1987b, 70f.). This idea represents, in my opinion, the greatest difficulty and the greatest source of unease. Yet there is also some comfort to be derived from the fact that often, in history, it is not fully fledged theories, but the very iterative practice of attestation carried out by the exercise of moral sensitivity and imagination, that has been the engine for those transformative demands that have impelled the conceptual and politico-legal reframing of crucial issues.[21]

Concluding with Some Political-Phenomenological Remarks

As the last step of this investigation, let me conclude with some political-phenomenological remarks. The ethical approach I have been advancing, which draws on the subject's decenteredness and on the sematic of sacrifice, gives me the opportunity to explain why it is, in the realm of a possible corresponding political theory, that one cannot so easily build on constituencies motivated only by "lifetime-transcending interests." As I have just shown, even though they may be open to otherness itself, as well as to caring for the other, interests are not consonant with the required passivity and dispossession of the subject. As a consequence, instead of pursuing Thompson's solution of establishing a future-oriented polity predicated on generation-transcending aspirations, I submit that Arendt's theory of plurality is far better placed to deliver the kind of a political design that is fit to respond to the call or claim of the future.

As we know from *The Human Condition*, it is Arendt's view that one of the core tasks that plural action realizes is that of giving appearance to public arenas and, consequently, of granting permanence to a world otherwise condemned to its own, overly rapid, disappearance (1958, 197ff.). As Arendt further specifies, the goal of securing any such enduring framework is made possible only on the condition that any imaginable plural polity recognizes itself as being constituted by an intergenerational polis as the space in which, on the one hand, present individuals find the very possibility to immortalize themselves and, on the other, future individuals can build on the past (ibid., 55–56). To be sure, in this regard, Janna Thompson is absolutely right in criticizing Arendt for giving sustenance to the idea of a generation-transcending polity by enlisting an overly elitist Athenian model of the polis, according to which "citizens competed with each other to be immortalized by their deeds and left labour of reproducing life to servants and women" (Thompson 2009, 47).

My counterpoint to this, however, is that this is not the whole story—and, more importantly, not the most relevant story—that Arendt can impart on the intergenerational structure of polities. For, I submit, the intergenerational nature of any imaginable plural polity in Arendt's theory cuts rather deeper, and aligns more precisely with the idea of a communitarian subject characterized by a radical exposure to otherness, passivity, transformativity, and futurity. This vision comes into the picture as soon as one takes on board the fact that, for Arendt, if plural interaction aims to achieve the durability of the political world, it is simultaneously, and more fundamentally, meant to realize this dimension under the condition of securing *plural participation*. It is in fact the fostering of plurality for the avoidance of any degeneration into monolithic forms of polities that primarily animates Arendt's political discourse. And it is precisely the imperative of protecting the plurality of participation that, in Arendt's view, demands the articulation of a simultaneously decentered, passive, and future-exposed political subject. Arendt unites all these features in one sole constitutive condition for the plural political space: this condition is natality (cf. Arendt 1958, 175ff.).

Natality sets a sort of connected co-implication that can be described as follows: the plurality of polities is enforced and maintained only under the condition that diverging forces and unanticipated transformative claims be raised within a public sphere that otherwise would be condemned to totalizing uniformity. The unexpected and transformative nature of plurality lies, in turn, in the possibility of novelty. Radical novelty comes into the political world only through natality: that is, by means of the unexpected coming-into-being of the newborn with her/his capacity to begin and alter present states of affairs. The newborn as futurity-instantiation, in other words, materializes as the very altering and at the same time alterity-exposed condition of the polity's present. The conclusion to be drawn from this is that natality, as the very embodiment of plurality and alterability in polities, implies that the future is not the mere prosecution or projection of the present and of present interests, but rather represents the very disruption of the community's present as the being haunted by a responsivity to—and responsibility for—a transcendence that is to come.

Exactly here, political transcendence displays not only its topological but also its chronological dimension. Accordingly, if, in reference to the spatial dimension, one does well to speak with Claude Lefort of a transcendence at the very core of democratic collectives in terms of "*an empty place*" of power (1988: 17, 225ff.) that can never be incorporated into the body politic, then, in reference to the temporal dimension, one might equally speak of a future transcendence as a "void time" of responsibility, which spectrally haunts the present polities and can never be saturated by their claims or demands.[22]

The theologian Karl Rahner once wrote in an eschatological *Fragment* that "future is not that which we are heading to, such that we can make a construction thereof out of our present, but rather future is that which is coming to us from its end" (1971, 178). Dietrich Bonhoeffer goes even further in granting this eschatological dynamic a more overtly ethical character when he writes that "the penultimate is really nothing in itself [. . .] Something becomes penultimate only through the ultimate. Therefore, the penultimate is not a condition of the ultimate, rather the ultimate conditions the penultimate. The penultimate is [. . .] a *judgment* which the ultimate passes on that which has preceded it" ([1940–41] 1998, 151, my emphasis).

Once viewed from the genuine perspective of natality, then so too, perhaps, does political responsibility show, in a similar vein, its genuine eschatological reach as a responsibility perpetually haunted by what Derrida would call a judgment to-come (1992: 27). At its core, in fact, natality speaks to a political judgment that pronounces not only on what we have done, but also and much more primarily on what we *will* have done.

Notes

1. Here the twist of Butler's famous book title: *Bodies That Matter* (1993).
2. To deepen Butler's analysis on the issue of the "violence of derealiziation," see at least Butler 2004, 33ff.
3. To this point it suffices to refer to the IPCC Sixth Assessment Report (2002).
4. Cf. Brown Weiss 1989; Tremmel 2006; Westra 2006; Gosseries 2014; Lindahl 2021.
5. In similar vein, cf. Beckerman and Pasek 2001, 14.

6. The indication of the necessity to transgress the foundational mechanisms of the traditional theories as a reaction to their incapacity to aptly tackle a radically future-oriented responsibility is an issue brought about by several critics, who indeed concomitantly advocate the need for a "paradigm shift" or even true and proper "new ethic." Such an issue is thematized by authors—just to name a few—as diverse as Jonas (1973, 44–45), Barry (1973, 284), Baier (1981, 178), Auerbach (1995, 217), and Douglas McNeill (2010, 197).

7. I further deepen my investigation on moral intuition in the realm of intergenerational justice theories throughout my volume: Menga 2016.

8. I discuss this point in detail in Menga 2021, ch. 1–3.

9. For a thorough investigation of such a predicament as regards the contractualist and contractarian strategies in motivating intergenerational duties, see my article: Menga 2023, 198–204.

10. On this point, see Barry 1989, 202f.

11. To be sure, a thorough discussion of this largely debated point would exceed the economy of the present investigation. Let me, however, articulate here two further aspects as relevant to my reading. In the first place, it is important, in my view, to stress how Rawls's *ad hoc* argument—as a necessary accommodation to his theory—is intimately connected to the tenet of a moral intuition to care for future generations. For, otherwise, one could wonder why Rawls does not more coherently adhere, at the end of the day, to the precepts dictated by the veil of ignorance, thereby concluding that the defense of intergenerational obligations is simply impossible. Second, I wish to point out that Rawls's later modification of his argument on the matter (see Rawls 1993, 271–75) does not really solve the predicament. As I have pointed out elsewhere (Menga 2021, 74), while such a change might well respond to the critiques against his *ad hoc* solution, it only dislocates the problem, as this new version of the argument falls prey to recurring to the functioning of an intergenerational cooperation, which is however never compellingly demonstrated. Hence, what ultimately happens in Rawls's modified argument is a mere transposition of the problem regarding the motivational assumption. Conclusively, regardless of the Rawlsian version one adopts, the moral motivation to care for future generations remains unexplained in its radical provenance. For a further critical reading of Rawls's later version of his intergenerational argument, see also Thompson 2009: 22ff.

12. Such a postulate in Gauthier's theory is perceptively underlined by Vallentyne 1986, 92f.

13. For an analysis of such an approach, see Gosseries 2001, 297ff.; Gardiner 2011, 106.

14. While the connection gift-obligation rests, in my view, on an unsatisfying explanatory strategy if viewed from the perspective of "indirect reciprocity," it gains a much clearer and more solid substantiation once depicted from the phenomenological stance recently deployed by Matthias Fritsch in his "asymmetrical reciprocity"

approach (2018: 107ff.). Fritsch's strategy, however, should not be understood as a merely slight modification of the indirect reciprocity stance, but rather as a true and proper substantial revision thereof. I maintain, in fact, that Fritsch's anthropological and social philosophical tenets (Arendt's natality, Levinas's phenomenology of alterity, Marcel Mauss's and Derrida's analyses on the gift) should be interpreted as irreducible to the ones underlying indirect reciprocity. For a closer reading in accordance—but also in discordance—to Fritsch's phenomenological investigation, see Menga 2021, 147–69. As regards a closer discussion devoted to the several arguments entailed in the "indirect reciprocity" approach, which would exceed the economy of this investigation, see Gosseries 2004, 148–83 and Menga 2021, 137–47.

15. On this point, see Auerbach 1995, 148–54; Kobayashi 1999, 139, 145.

16. I further develop the analysis of this motive, which I trace in Derrida's, Rosenzweig's, and Waldenfels's thought, just to name few other authors, in my book, Menga 2021.

17. Such a phenomenological decentering of anthropocentric subjectivity—"anthropodecentrism," so we may also define it—could have as an attendant consequence the building of a fecund intersection with stances that are of great importance for posthuman perspectives. It is not by chance, in effect, that María Puig de la Bellacasa, in her recent research on a posthuman view of care, stresses so strongly the need of a dynamic that "decenters the human subject" (2017, 141).

18. Cf. on this also Levinas 1987b, 72.

19. By recurring to the semantic of "straightforwardness," I am explicitly referring here to the English rendering of the Levinasian term *droiture*. Such a concept is widely adopted by Levinas throughout his oeuvre in view of displaying the radicality of the relation with alterity, which is to be understood as never indirectly derived from a previous (rational and neutralizing) mediation. Exactly in line with such a *droiture*, Levinas intends the relation with the other and the language of the other as a straightforward demand/ingness. More precisely, to put it with the words of a beautiful passage in *Totality and Infinity*: "Language, which does not touch the other even tangentially, reaches the other by calling upon him or by commanding him or by obeying him, with all the straightforwardness [*droiture*] of these relations" (1969, 62).

20. To be sure, tracing the logic of a possessive individuality of liberal provenance in Thompson's communitarian approach might appear as surprising. Yet it could be interpreted as less disquieting if one follows, for instance, Hans Lindahl's perceptive legal-phenomenological investigations (2013, 227–34) when showing how the same basic precept of self-reference is at work in both approaches, although such a self-reference is deployed at a different amplitude: while the liberal approach draws on an atomistic self-ownership (self-identity), the communitarian harks back to the precondition of a macro-subjective self-reference (say, cultural identity).

21. This is at least true, for instance, for the case of the emergence of animal ethics and its implementation and enforcement in legal systems.

22. On the theme of a spectrality of the future that can be adopted for the scope of genuinely intended intergenerational polities, see the insightful analysis by Matthias Fritsch (2018, 52).

Bibliography

Anders, Günther. 1956. *Die Antiquiertheit des Menschen*. Vol. 1: *Über die Seele im Zeitalter der zweiten industriellen Revolution*. München: Beck.
Arendt, Hannah. 1958. *The Human Condition*. Chicago: University of Chicago Press.
Auerbach, Erich. 1995. *Unto the Thousandth Generation: Conceptualizing Intergenerational Justice*. New York: Peter Lang.
Baier, Annette. 1981. "The Rights of Past and Future Persons." In *Responsibilities to Future Generations: Environmental Ethics*, edited by E. Partridge, 171–89. Buffalo, NY: Prometheus Books.
Barry, Brian. 1977. "Justice Between Generations." In *Law, Morality, and Society*, edited by P. M. S. Hacker, J. Raz, 268–84. Oxford: Clarendon Press.
———. 1989. *Theories of Justice*. Berkeley: University of California Press.
———. 1991. "Justice as Reciprocity." In *Liberty as Justice: Essays in Political Theory 2*, by Brian Barry, 211–41. Oxford: Clarendon Press.
Beckerman, Wilfred, and Joanna Pasek. 2001. *Justice, Posterity, and the Environment*. Oxford. Oxford University Press.
Bernasconi, Robert. 2002. "What Is the Question to Which 'Substitution' Is the Answer?" In *The Cambridge Companion to Levinas*, edited by Simon Critchley and Robert Bernasconi, 234–51. Cambridge: Cambridge University Press.
Bonhoeffer, Dietrich. [1940–41] 1998. "Die letzten und vorletzen Dinge." In *Werke*, VI: *Ethik*, by Dietrich Bonhoeffer, 137–62. Gütersloh: Chr. Kaiser-Gütersloher Verlagshaus.
Brown Weiss, Edith. 1989. *In Fairness to Future Generations: International Law, Common Patrimony, and Intergenerational Equity*. Tokyo: United Nation University Transnational Publishers.
Butler, Judith. 1993. *Bodies That Matter: On the Discursive Limits of "Sex."* London: Routledge.
———. 2004. *Precarious Life: The Powers of Mourning and Violence*. London: Verso.
De George, Richard T. 1981. "The Environment, Rights, and Future Generations." In *Responsibilities to Future Generations: Environmental Ethics*, edited by E. Partridge, 157–65. Buffalo, NY: Prometheus Books.
Derrida, Jacques. 1992. "Force of Law: The 'Mystical Foundation of Authority.'" In *Deconstruction and the Possibility of Justice*, edited by Drucilla Cornell, Michael Rosenfel, and David G. Carlson, 3–67. London, New York: Routledge.
———. 2001. "I Have a Taste for the Secret." In *A Taste for the Secret*, by Jacques Derrida and Maurizio Ferraris, 1–92. Cambridge: Polity Press.

Douglas, McNeill, Richard. 2010. "The Ultimate Paradigm Shift: Environmentalism as Antithesis to the Modern Paradigm of Progress." In *Future Ethics: Climate Change and Apocalyptic Imagination*, edited by S. Skrimshire, 197–215. London: Continuum.

Edelglass, William, James Hatley, and Christian Diehm 2012. "Introduction: Facing Nature after Levinas." In *Facing Nature: Levinas and Environmental Thought*, edited by William Edelglass, James Hatley, and Christian Diehm, 1–10. Pittsburgh, PA: Duquesne University Press.

Fritsch, Matthias. 2015. "Democracy, Climate Change, and Environmental Justice." *Mosaic* 48 (3): 27–45.

———. 2018. *Taking Turns with the Earth: Phenomenology, Deconstruction, and Intergenerational Justice*. Stanford, CA: Stanford University Press.

Gardiner, Stephen. 2011. *A Perfect Moral Storm: The Ethical Tragedy of Climate Change*. Oxford: Oxford University Press.

Gauthier, David. 1986. *Morals by Agreement*. Oxford: Clarendon Press.

Gosseries, Axel. 2001. "What Do We Owe the Next Generation(s)?" *Loyola of Los Angeles Law Review* 35: 293–354.

Gosseries, A. 2004. *Penser la justice entre les générations: De l'affaire Perruche à la réforme des retraites*. Paris: Flammarion.

———. 2014. "The Intergenerational Case for Constitutional Rigidity." *Ratio Juris* 27 (4): 528–539.

Hartmann, Nicolai. [1925] 2014. *Ethics*. Vol. 2: *The Realm of Ethical Values*. Translated by Stanton Coit. New York: Routledge.

IPCC Sixth Assessment Report 2022. *Climate Change 2022: Impacts, Adaptation and Vulnerability*. https://www.ipcc.ch/report/ar6/wg2/.

Jaspers, Karl. [1958] 1963. *The Atom Bomb and the Future of Man*. Translated by E. B. Ashton. Chicago: University of Chicago Press.

Jenkins, Willis. 2013. *The Future of Ethics: Sustainability, Social Justice, and Religious Creativity*. Washington, DC: Georgetown University Press.

Jonas, Hans. 1973. "Technology and Responsibility: Reflections on the New Tasks of Ethics." *Social Research* 40 (1): 31–54.

Lefort, Claude. 1988. *Democracy and Political Theory*. Translated by D. Macey. Cambridge, UK: Polity Press.

Levinas, Emmanuel. 1979. *Totality and Infinity: An Essay on Exteriority*. Translated by Alphonso Lingis. Dordrecht: Kluwer Academic Publishers.

———. 1987a. "Philosophy and the Idea of Infinity." In *Collected Philosophical Papers*, by Emmanuel Levinas, translated by Alphonso Lingis, 47–60. Dordrecht: Kluwer Academic Publishers.

———. 1987b. "Phenomenon and Enigma." In *Collected Philosophical Papers*, by Emmanuel Levinas, translated by Alphonso Lingis, 61–74. Dordrecht: Kluwer Academic Publishers.

———. 1987c. *Time and the Other [and other Essays]*. Translated by R. A. Cohen. Pittsburgh, PA: Duquesne University Press.
———. 1991. *Otherwise than Being or Beyond Essence*. Translated by Alphonso Lingis. Dordrecht: Kluwer Academic Publishers.
Lindahl, Hans. 2013: *Fault Lines of Globalization. Legal Order and the Politics of A-Legality*. Oxford: Oxford University Press.
———. 2021. "Place-Holding the Future: Legal Ordering and Intergenerational Justice for More-Than-Human Collectives." *Rivista di filosofia del diritto / Journal of Legal Philosophy* 10 (2): 313–29.
Kant, Immanuel. [1797] 1956. *Die Metaphysik der Sitten. Tugendlehre*. In *Werke* (in sechs Bänden). Vol. 4, edited by W. Weischedel. Darmstadt: WBG.
Kobayashi, M. 1999. "Atomistic Self and Future Generations: A Critical Review from an Eastern Perspective." In *Self and Future Generations: An Intercultural Conversation*, edited by Tae-Chang Kim and R. Harrison, 7–61. Cambridge, UK: The White Horse Press.
Macklin, Ruth. 1981. "Can Future Generations Correctly Be Said to Have Rights?" In *Responsibilities to Future Generations: Environmental Ethics*, edited by E. Partridge, 151–55. Buffalo, NY: Prometheus Books.
Macpherson, C. B. 1962. *The Political Theory of Possessive Individualism*. Oxford: Clarendon Press.
Menga, Ferdinando G. 2016. *Lo scandalo del futuro: Per una giustizia intergenerazionale*. Roma: Edizioni di Storia e Letteratura.
———. 2021. *Etica intergenerazionale*. Brescia: Morcelliana.
———. 2023. "When the Generational Overlap Is the Challenge Rather Than the Solution: On Some Problematic Versions of Transgenerational Justice." *The Monist* 106 (2): 194–208.
Muers, Rachel. 2008. *Living for the Future: Theological Ethics for Coming Generations*. London: T&T Clark.
Nietzsche, Friedrich. [1885] 2006. *Thus Spoke Zarathustra. A Book for All and None*. Edited by A. Del Caro and R. B. Pippin. Cambridge: Cambridge University Press.
Parfit, Derek. 1984. *Reasons and Persons*. Oxford: Clarendon Press.
Puig de la Bellacasa, Maria. 2017. *Matters of Care: Speculative Ethics in a More Than Human World*. Minneapolis: The University of Minnesota Press.
Rahner, Karl. 1971. "Fragment aus einer theologischen Besinnung auf den Begriff der Zukunft." In *Zur Theologie der Zukunft*, by Karl Rahner, 177–82. München: dtv.
Rawls, John. 1971. *A Theory of Justice*. Cambridge, MA: The Belknap Press of Harvard University Press.
———. 2009. *Political Liberalism*. New York: Columbia University Press.
Thompson, Dennis F. 2005. "Democracy in Time: Popular Sovereignty and Temporal Representation." *Constellations* 12 (2): 245–61.

———. 2010. "Representing Future Generations: Political Presentism and Democratic Trusteeship." *Critical Review of International Social and Political Philosophy* 13 (1): 17–37.
Thompson, Janna. 2009. *Intergenerational Justice: Rights and Responsibilities in an Intergenerational Polity*. New York: Routledge.
Tremmel, Joerg. 2006. "Establishing Intergenerational Justice in National Constitutions." In *Handbook of Intergenerational Justice*, edited by Joerg Tremmel, 187–214. Cheltenham: Elgar.
Vallentyne, Peter. 1986. "Gauthier on Rationality and Morality." *Eidos* 5 (1): 79–95.
Waldenfels, Bernhard. 2006. *Schattenrisse der Moral*. Frankfurt a.M.: Suhrkamp.
———. 2011. *Phenomenology of the Alien: Basic Concepts*. Translated by A. Kozin and T. Stähler. Evanston: Northwestern University Press.
Westra, Laura. 2006. *Environmental Justice and the Rights of Unborn and Future Generations: Law, Environmental Harm and the Right to Health*. London: Earthscan.
Zagrebelsky, Gustavo. 2016. *Senza adulti*. Torino: Einaudi.

5

How Can We Take Claims of Future Generations Seriously?

Combining Different Perspectives in Our Action

Eva Buddeberg

The increasing scope and complexity of human action necessitates a moral theory that is not limited to the close range.[1] In his famous *Imperative of Responsibility*, Hans Jonas even calls for "a new ethics of long range responsibility."[2] But might it not be enough simply to apply existing approaches more consistently and comprehensively? I would like to explore and defend this latter position in light of Emmanuel Levinas's ethical theory, which centers around the immediate encounter with the other, to whom we *need* to respond and to whom we are responsible even before we are present to ourselves as subjects. But it also goes further in that, by taking "the other of the other" into consideration, the ethical perspective is expanded so as to encompass, without concrete predetermined limitations, all those who could possibly be affected by our actions and to whom we must also, therefore, do justice. In this way, Levinas's ethics of the other human being includes all future other human beings within its scope. Yet questions linger to do with *how* justice can be done to all these others who may be affected by our actions. As I see it, an institutional and legal framework is required that could facilitate, and ultimately guarantee, a broadening of the scope of our considerations to include all those affected—within both the present and the future—by our actions.

I elucidate these theses by outlining the basic concept of Levinas's ethics against the backdrop of various competing theories and by explaining the strengths of his first-person-based description of an unconditional obligation towards the other human being as the basis of all ethical theory. In a second step, I work out to what extent this conception already goes beyond face-to-face situations. Finally, in a third step and with reference to Karl-Otto Apel and Jürgen Habermas's discourse ethical approach, I examine what kind of further, basic framework is appropriate—and perhaps necessary—for this broader perspective to be able to accommodate our responsibility towards future generations.

1.

Why start with Levinas? Perhaps the most important reason to examine whether a moral theory that follows from Levinas's can account for the claims of future others is that Levinas—rightly, in my view—placed the encounter with the concrete other at the center of moral philosophy and characterized the first-person perspective as that which, from the outset, falls under the prior claim to respond to the other human being. Nonetheless, *prima facie*, and with reference to the standpoint from which a universally valid morality should be described, a variety of different positions have been adopted by other thinkers in this regard. Roughly speaking, we can distinguish at least three different approaches. For example, some philosophers, in their search for a claim of absolute and universal validity, conclude that an external, impersonal, and impartial or neutral third-person perspective, devoid of particularizing qualities or characteristics, is required for the conceptualization of ethical concerns. Other philosophers, such as Christine Korsgaard, draw on Kant's deontological ethics to highlight the idea that in following the categorical imperative, we constitute ourselves as agents and persons (see above all Korsgaard 2009). Here the relation of the subject to itself comes to the fore.

But, in ways that challenge the emphasis placed on the impartial observer and the tendency to prioritize the relation to one's own self, various other philosophers show that the pursuit of moral norms, duties, or virtues is fundamentally oriented by the claims and needs of other people—or, at least, of those who are concerned about or affected by our actions. The specific nature of these claims, they argue, cannot be understood by assuming an external and impartial point of view or by conceptualizing morality primarily as a self-relation. Instead, we have to consider the "other" or "others" who are *addressing us*.

Stephen Darwall, for example, considers morality as being essentially based on our capacity to address others and to be addressed by others as beings of reason(s) whereby we implicitly acknowledge the other's dignity. This dignity consists, in his view, of a "second-personal authority of an equal: the standing to make claims and demands of one another as equal, free, and rational agents, including as a member of a community of mutually accountable equals" (Darwall 2006, 121). The "recognition respect" by which we acknowledge this dignity is further characterized by Darwall as "acknowledgement of this authority that is also second-personal." As he continues, "it is always implicitly reciprocal, if only in imagination" (Darwall 2006, 121). On the one hand, this kind of respect is taken to be "second-personal," in that we encounter them personally and so *address* and acknowledge *other human beings as "you."* On the other hand, it is also "second-personal" in that we express this form of respect precisely in the encounter with the other in the course of which he or she is *addressing us as "you"* (cf. Darwall 2006, 40). Thus, Darwall underlines that it is "our equal second-personal authority [. . .] that is most fundamental" (Darwall 2006, 121).

For Darwall, this authority and the respect by which we respond to it are fundamental, neither implying, nor predicated upon, any "revaluation or appraisal of excellence, even of someone's merits as a person" (Darwall 2006, 126). Nor is it a question of acknowledging "personhood" as an "admirable quality" (all this still falls within what Darwall calls "appraisal respect" [cf. Darwall 2006]), but one of "how our relations to [the other person] are to be regulated or governed" (Darwall 2006, 123). Hence, what Darwall seems to have in mind resembles what Axel Honneth, following Stanley Cavell, takes to be the basis of morality: a form of "non-epistemic affirmation of the other person's human personality" that can also appear as "mere indifference" or "negative feelings" (Honneth, 2008, 51).

I generally agree with Darwall's approach to conceptualizing our moral obligation in terms of our relation to others as concrete individuals: the basis of morality is neither an abstract law nor our self-relation, but arises from the fact that others address us with demands that we need to take into account in our own actions. I also concur that the ethical necessity to respond to their claim upon us cannot be derived from the specific nature of their relation to us or the respect we might have for their particular qualities or capacities, neither of which has bearing on morality even if they may furnish reasons for other forms of esteem or obligation.

However, Darwall's approach seems to me problematic in at least the following three ways:

(1) It remains unclear to me whether and to what extent we can actually take up a "*second-person standpoint.*" In our relation with other acting and perceiving human beings, we are always in a *first*-person position, for only in this way we do perceive the world and "the others" and experience ourselves as the free authors of our actions. Moreover, it is from our position as an "I" or "we" that we address as "you" those others who, crucially, are in the "second-person" only from our own vantage point. However, this "other" or these "others" can obviously address us—from their point of view once again, in the first person—as "you." Strictly speaking, nobody really takes up or inhabits a *second*-person standpoint: I am always in the first person addressing the other in the second person, who, in turn, is addressing me in the second person. In my understanding, this is what Darwall must have in mind when he emphasizes the "second personal" character of moral reasons, authority, and standpoint. In other words, for Darwall there is something distinctive about the way in which human beings relate to each other, and that distinguishes this from their relations to all other *objects* in the world: they can address each other as a *you*. Thus the "second-person standpoint" never really abandons the first person (as Darwall admits) and is not strictly speaking a "standpoint" but a hypothesis, which refers to the specific way *we relate to other human* beings and are *concerned by them*.

(2) I fail to grasp fully the type of validity Darwall can actually claim for his thesis. A large proportion of the examples he gives to illustrate his point are based on relations of authority that pertain to particular and concrete situations in which someone explicitly and voluntarily utters such demands. But *if,* as it seems, he does not want to relinquish the claim of universal validity of morality that we are committed to all other human beings independently of authority relations and particular situations, then clearly his position must necessarily be that as human beings we are not only related in this way to some specific "others" in specific relations or particular situations,[3] but, more generally, to *everybody*. Thus, as Korsgaard sees it, the "apparently optional character of the second-person standpoint" raises the possibility that "someone who does not engage in second-personal address fails to see reasons that she has" (Korsgaard, 2007, 20 and 21). Thus, her insight that for Darwall the second-person standpoint differs from the first-person perspective in that it does not seem to be unavoidable seems to be correct, as does her conclusion that "unless [someone] has a reason to take up the second-person standpoint and its presuppositions, it is possible that he will never know" (22). In that case, the very reason for our moral

obligation would not lie in the other human being's authority but in *our decision* to take it into account.

(3) Finally, I doubt that Darwall is right in rejecting the perspective of a third person in what he describes as "second-person standpoint." However, we need to take into consideration the many passages where he argues that we acknowledge, for example, the second-person authority of other persons in considering them and ourselves "as equal free and rational agents, including as a member of a community of mutually accountable equals" (Darwall 2006, 121), for we thereby attribute qualities *to* and make a judgment *about* ourselves and *about* others in a perspective in which we do not address the other as "you" and do not experience ourselves as "I" or "we," but describe and assess the other and ourselves as third persons.[4] Thus, while it is correct to question whether or not morality can be described *solely* from the perspective of the third person, since this as a "pure observer perspective" fails to recognize the normative claim under which we experience ourselves when we encounter other people, this does not mean that it is altogether superfluous with regard to morality.

A more promising alternative, in my view, seems to be Levinas's quasi-phenomenological[5] description of the *encounter with the other who is revealed to the subject most especially by their face*. I highlight just a few of its main characteristics.[6] It is important to bear in mind that the face is not limited to its sense-perceptible form, but differs, Levinas emphasizes, "from every represented content" (Levinas 1969, 177), for its nature precisely does *not* consist in "figuring as a theme under my gaze, in spreading itself forth as a set of qualities forming an image" (Levinas 1969, 50). Without identifying any concrete content, Levinas describes the face as something that "signifies by itself" (Levinas 1969, 261), "speaks," and "is already discourse" (Levinas 1969, 66). He thereby impugns the exclusivity of the transcendental subject as sense-giver: the face of the other is not reliant on sense being given to it by the subject perceiving it.[7] Hence, in the encounter with the face of the other, the subject—the sole sense-giver within the phenomenological tradition—"is experiencing," in what is initially a nonobjectifying manner, that there is a meaning, a sense, that cannot be realized by their own cognitive or mental efforts but can only be received. The subject is "addressed," since the impression that the other "speaks" or "expresses [themselves]" remains the experience—albeit not an intentional experience—of the subject. It is a feature of every act of expression (or speech) that it must have (at least potentially) an addressee. If this addressee is not explicitly determined, then potentially *everyone* who is experiencing the other expressing themselves is in fact being addressed (cf. Levinas 1969, 278).

Just as the source of our moral obligation can be found in the other, Levinas describes the perspective in which this obligation is experienced as that of the perceiving (albeit a mode of perceiving that is not intentional) and acting subject. This subjective perception is more consistent with a *first-person perspective* than with a second-person perspective and might, thus, appear to convey the impression that Levinas's understanding of morality is closer to that of Korsgaard than to Darwall's, given that Korsgaard also emphasizes the self-constitutional character of morality. However, for Levinas, the first-person perceiving and acting subject does not occupy a privileged position within ethics since, in the ethical relation, the subject experiences precisely that someone, the other who, already signifying and exerting their claim, is thereby prior to the subject and thus extends a relation to the world in which the subject is only in second position.

Admittedly, for Levinas—as, too, for Kant or Korsgaard—morality is constitutive for being a subject in the sense that only moral beings are fully *human* beings (otherwise, they would miss a constitutive element of their personhood). But, unlike Korsgaard, Levinas is not concerned with the subject taken as the active origin of world perception but, rather, with the subject conceptualized primarily as a form of pure passivity—a form of sensuality that does not depend on cognitive or intellectual performance and is comparable, for example, to the experience of aging over time (cf. Levinas 1981, 51). Passive in this way, the subject is called upon by the other and exposed to them: something that Levinas describes as "vulnerability," "trauma" (cf. Levinas 1981), or even "persecution."[8] In this sense, "exposition" (Levinas 1981, e.g., 15ff., 48ff., 74, 78) refers to the same radical exposure of the subject that also infuses Levinas's recurrent use of the phrase "the-one-for-the-other," with which he emphasizes the underlying structure of both subjectivity and responsibility.

All notion of the subject *as individual* is called fundamentally into question: the *one-for-the-other* is not *indivisible* but is, rather, a complex structure in *itself* that implies the other as constituent of the subject's own subjectivity. Thereby, Levinas wavers between "for" (pour) and "by" (par) in this relation and sees both variants blending into each other: "The for-the-other [. . .] turns into by-the-other" (Levinas 1981, 50). Where "for . . ." is concerned, the *ethical* aspect of the connectivity is more strongly expressed (human existence only has a meaning *for the other*), while "by . . ." underlines the *ontological* dimension: only *by* the other does the subject constitute themselves in their existence.[9] Accordingly, Levinas describes subjectivity also as "substitution" (cf. Levinas 1981, 13f. and especially chapter IV, *The Substitution*, 99–130), whereby human subjectivity consists precisely in having taken the place of the other, even prior to all conscious, active subjectivity: "Subjectivity is structured as the other in the same, but in a way different of that of consciousness. [. . .] The other in the same determinative of subjectivity is the restlessness of the same disturbed by the other" (Levinas 1981, 25). Thus, the subject is no longer characterized by the self-conscious *cogito*, but by the uncertainty, the insecurity, or the anxiety—*l'inquiétude*—arising from the encounter with the other as a being that transcends the subject's consciousness. The subject is subjected (*sujeté*) to the other because, although it cannot totally apprehend the other, it is nonetheless always determined by them.

Rather than expanding further on Levinas's specific conception of responsibility and reinterpretation of other philosophical concepts, let me very briefly take up Levinas's disjointed and partly apodictic argument for a subjectivity based on responsibility for the other in a more conventional language, and suggest the following interpretation: in their subjectivity, even before their formation as a subject and without conscious awareness of this, every human being is affected by the other. As subjects who position themselves in the world, they have already internalized the other, who therefore not only impels their actions but constitutes their very beings as subjects. For Levinas, this passive receipt of the other is the nonconscious ground of all intentionality and consciousness, as he outlined in one of his latter texts titled *Ethics as First Philosophy* (Levinas 1992). Even prior to consciousness, the subject is addressed by the other to whom it has to respond and through whom all its existence is legitimated. Since the subject cannot not respond to the "other," it is responsible, for it cannot do otherwise than *be with*, *for*, and even *by* the other.

Hence, Levinas has reversed the traditional founding relation. I think he is correct and that this reversal is precisely, in his analyses, what furnishes the starting point of all ethical considerations. Responsibility for the other does not have a rational foundation but is, for Levinas, the very reason why we ask for reasons and can give them to others. We cannot but acknowledge the demand to respond to the other, and we actually always do so even if we cannot conceptually grasp in what, exactly, such demand consists and even if we do not correspond to it. For Levinas, this unconditional (and thus irreducible) responsibility is itself something like the ground of all grounding; and it is only in light of this structure, which relates a person to the other, that questions pertaining to reasons and concrete relations of responsibility can meaningfully be posed.

Yet let us come back to the question of the perspective we have as moral beings. For Levinas, this perspective is clearly that of the subject, even though subjectivity here differs from its more typical articulations within the philosophical tradition, and even though the nonperception of the other by the subject is nonintentional. In accepting this perspective as that of the moral being, I believe we can say that Levinas is correct to describe the relation to the other, initially—and in contrast to Darwall—not as a reciprocal, but as an asymmetrical, relation.[10] For the subject does not perceive themselves as responsible for the other in the same way they perceive the responsibility of the other for themselves or someone else, which could only be possible by means of intentionality (at least partially) transcending the immediacy of the ethical experience.

However, the responsibility of the subject for the other is asymmetrical, not because the responsibility carried by the subject is greater than that which the other carries for them, but because the subject, from this ethical perspective, does not perceive the other's responsibility for them. For this perspective is, according to Levinas, characterized by the "radical impossibility of seeing oneself from the outside and of speaking in the same sense of oneself and of the others" (Levinas 1969, 53). Yet the metaphysical asymmetry postulated by Levinas cannot be attributed to "different properties" or to "different psychological dispositions," but has its grounds in the "I-Other conjuncture, to the inevitable *orientation* of being 'starting from oneself' toward 'the Other'" (Levinas 1969, 215).

2.

The subject, however, never inhabits this perspective exclusively, but finds themselves also within an intentional world relation. The change from the nonintentional ethical perception to the intentional world relation becomes reality because, in the world, we do not perceive ourselves as claimed by only one single other but always by many others. This brings us to the question of how to respond in the most adequate and just way to which claims—a question that belongs for Levinas to the realm of politics. I return to this in a moment.

Throughout his work, what clearly matters most for Levinas is how best to articulate the ethical relation as a dyadic relation. Yet he emphasizes that the relation to the other human being already implies a relation to the other of the other and, thus, to third persons: "The third party is other than the neighbor but also another neighbor, and also a neighbor of the other, and not simply their fellow.[11] What am I to do? What have they already done to one another? Who passes before the other in my responsibility? What, then, are the other and the third party, with respect to one another? *Birth of the question*. The first question in the interhuman is the *question of justice*" (Levinas 1996, 168). The encounter with the other is always influenced, arranged, and disturbed by the presence of other others who also lay claim on the subject. It is in this sense that our responsibility, in the first instance understood as immeasurable, infinite, and asymmetrical, finds a limit in the other of the other. This limit is also the condition of possibility of our capacity to act: "My responsibility for all can and has to manifest itself also by limiting itself [. . .]. The fact that the other, my neighbour, is also a third party with respect to another, who is also a neighbour, is the birth of thought, consciousness, justice and philosophy" (Levinas 1981, 128). Although Levinas consistently emphasizes that our responsibility is infinite, he also argues that the subject, in being aware of the additional responsibility for the other of the other, is already confronted with the question of who has the greater right to a response and to support; because, to respond at all, the subject has to compare the other to the *other* other, to examine with care and to consider to whom they need to respond first, in what way, and to what extent.

To undertake any such comparison, the subject must have intentionality and consciousness at their disposal, since only a conscious human being can compare and decide between the demands of the one other and the other others. Thus, it is a mistake to view the nonintentional experience of being called on by the other in our responsibility as being in any way detached from our intentional world relation.

The capacity of intentionality also permits us to cognize another human being—even in their absence—as a being that the subject can encounter in a nonintentional way. This cognition is also important insofar as it cannot be expected that the subject encounter every other human being personally or therefore experience their fundamental alterity that commits them with regard to the other. Intentional and cognitive capacities, together with the nonintentional experience of their responsibility for the other, characterize the subject while at the same time enabling it to consider any other human being—including any other future human being—as someone for whom they are responsible. For even as we need to respond to the singular other, so need we also respond to anyone who is one step further removed from us, without in any way altering the basic fact that moral responsibility is about other, and fully concrete, human beings, for "all the others that obsess me in the other," as Levinas emphasizes, "do not affect me as examples of the same genus united with my neighbor by resemblance or common nature" (Levinas 1981, 159). Rather, they concern us—each in their unique alterity—as concrete others, *even if not present to us in a second-personal way at the moment of concern*. And this is equally true for the generation(s) to come.[12]

It is at this level that it becomes possible to also include the experience of responsibility in measurable, just—and in this sense reciprocal—relations between many human beings that, nevertheless, remain marked by asymmetry. Only at such a level of consciousness can the subject switch, at least partially, between different perspectives.

Thus, for Levinas, the relation to the third—which is the term used by Levinas to capture the fact that we are never only confronted to the claim of one other but always already to the claims of a plurality of others—is the moment where the alternation and the connection between the different world relations are going to become necessary and possible. In taking account of the third, the cognitive aspect of our relation to the other comes to the fore, allowing the subject to universalize the responsibility experienced, originally, for the singular other as an obligation towards all—including future—human beings. Moreover, at the cognitive level, the subject is also able to consider the responsibility of other others to or for themselves in which the fundamentally asymmetrical experience is perceived as part of a reciprocal relation. Finally, only at the level of cognition can the responsible subject *act intentionally and thus assume its initially nonintentionally acknowledged responsibility*. Therefore, even though Levinas emphasizes the perspective of a subject that is always already addressed by the other, it seems as though we must always also think *of* others and ourselves *as* third persons in considering and balancing out how to respond.[13]

To compare, to balance, and to decide presupposes thought, consciousness, and a certain distance that not only let us respond to others but also allow us, and even urge us, to make a well-considered choice between different possible responses: for Levinas, as I mentioned earlier, this is the realm of *politics*. As we are always more than just two, our social reality is always political. Human beings must arbitrate between the numerous claims of others and the natural need of all human beings to also fulfill their own interests and needs that are possibly in conflict with those of the others and try, as far as possible, to do justice to them all. In this very broad sense—as the conscious and balancing actions within a field of many and often competing claims, interests, and needs—politics should be guided by an idea of justice: a justice however that always, and without losing sight of the singular others and their particular claims, strives for the good of the many, taken not as the masses but as individuals.

For Levinas, the ideal of such politics is *fraternity* (cf. Levinas 1969, 214ff., 278ff.; see also Flatscher 2015, 207f., and extensively Bedorf 2005). By this term, Levinas does not mean a form of attachment based on a biological relationship. Instead, without offering a positive definition, Levinas describes a mode of attachment between different individuals who are not hierarchically sub- or super-ordinate to each other but who—like brothers or sisters (!)—relate to each other on an equal footing and experience themselves as being responsible for one another. Just as brothers and sisters do not choose to have siblings, we do not choose to relate to those others with whom we live. Thus, fraternity does not refer to an abstract collective, but a kind of community: to something one would call today—a little more abstract and bearing in mind the gender mainstreaming—a "community of solidarity." Ideally, all human beings—and that includes all future human beings—are brothers or sisters; they are all individuals and yet, standing on the same level, they are also bound to one another by reciprocal relations of responsibility. And this community, as Fritsch also asserts, is a community that neither is, nor ever can be, limited to the present. Thus, brothers and sisters are contemporaries, but at the same time they are also the pre-born and post-born, who live on before or after us and, in this way, are connected with other others: generations do not detach themselves from each other, but are interwoven with each other.[14]

3.

Levinas deliberately leaves open the question of how to respond to all others affected by us. The tension between our infinite responsibility for the single other and the justice we owe to the many others cannot be fully resolved. Nevertheless, as Levinas indicates, we can deal with this tension in various ways, and a number of theories responding to Levinas propose a range of solutions (with different levels of suitability) to take this into account. Yet, while Levinas himself emphasizes very fundamentally and generally that we always live in an ethical and political reality, he declines to say more about how we might deal with this reality. So, although I agree with his central thesis that the entirety of our sociopolitical reality falls under the ethical claim of others, I find it necessary to think beyond Levinas's account. For it seems clear that in his broad understanding of the political, Levinas does not address many essential questions that arise within this sphere, such as the question of how to relate action at the level of the individual to action at the level of the political institution; and theories taking up and responding to Levinas seem equally unable to answer this question satisfactorily.[15] Pascal Delhom (2000, ch. 3.2), for example, gives a thorough analysis of the tension between, on the one hand, the necessity of state institutions for the dispensation of justice in response to the claims of others, so far as this is possible, and, on the other hand, the violence they inflict on the single other in his or her particularity. Yet he does not provide any answer to the question of how institutions ought best to be structured and how they might operate to address and resolve this.

Thus, it seems useful to bring some of the basic insights of discourse ethics into play. Discourse-ethical approaches such those of Karl-Otto Apel and Jürgen Habermas seem productive insofar as their discourse principle—derived from Kant's categorical imperative—advances a procedure for moral decision-making that takes specific agential situations and needs into account (see Apel 1988; Habermas 1990, 1991). This procedure is clearly not an end in itself but is intended as a dialogue, maintained intersubjectively so as to give voice to all possibly affected persons; so as to enable all due consideration for the interests and claims of—ideally—*all* others; and so as to facilitate just arbitration among them. Hence, the dialogue itself must be conducted by those affected—an important advancement on Kant's basic intention; and only where those others are not available, as in the case of future generations, does the need arise for representatives or substitutional hypotheses, as Apel has suggested (Apel 1998, 625). Here a prudential argument should be made: since we lack secure knowledge and certainty as to their needs and circumstances, the way in which we take future generations into account must be more general and open, while being ever conscious of its own fallibility and, thus, dynamically responsive to change.[16] As a first move in this direction, we might accept Jonas's ecological imperative that urges us to act in such a way that the "effects of [our] action are not destructive of the future possibility of such life" (Jonas 1984, 11). This implies that under complex conditions, any possible consequences and side effects of action need to be thoroughly and rigorously scrutinized. However, and in contrast to Jonas, I do not think that the responsibility for this task and for the future of humanity can be met ethically and intellectually *only* by an elite class,[17] but by all affected human beings, together in rational discourse.[18] This seems to me to be important and very much in line with Levinas's basic assumptions (see Apel 2000, 45), for balancing and arbitrating between the different and competing claims of many others also (already) requires the exercise of reason. And, if this process is to respond to the claims of as many as possible among those affected by our actions—at present and in the future—we must avoid atomized, individualistic thinking and instead seek to maximize communication with and among either the affected people or others who can imagine or inquire into the needs and endeavors of those possibly affected in the future, so that—ideally—each particular other with their interests and needs will be heard. Needless to say, the hypothetical status of such dialogues must be kept in mind so that they remain ever open to corrections and revisions in response to concrete communication as it arises.

The principle of the most comprehensive communication possible with all those currently or potentially affected can be considered the central regulative idea of discourse ethics. For this to be more than just a pious wish, however, institutional arrangements are needed with which this communication can be achieved and sustained even through crises. With this very intention, Habermas brings his concept of the democratic constitutional state into play: for, in his view, moral discourse alone is insufficient to guarantee the stability of the social order or the management of internal conflict in modern and culturally heterogeneous societies. Rather, he finds that these ends, underpinning the project of social integration, are better achieved through political institutions and laws, which furnish the possibility for the actors themselves to *"come to some understanding* about the *normative regulation of the strategic interactions"* (Habermas 1996, 26f.). Thus, based on the discourse principle, the rule of law, in Habermas's consideration and understanding, is to be an important guarantor for the viability of democracy, which in turn is the source of the legitimacy of the law. Furthermore, the constitutional state with its rule of law and the idea of democracy do not merely coincide historically with each other, but stand in a "conceptual or internal relation" with one another (Habermas 1996, 449). The law provides a structure beyond the limitations of communication and the restrictions of strategic action; and by introducing and enforcing codified law, politics can support and stabilize the social order of a society where morality lacks any internal means for its own enforcement. For law can compensate for three deficits of modern societies predicated on individual human agency, relieving agents in the areas of cognition, motivation, and, finally, organization.

Unlike morality, positive law defines precisely what is allowed and what is forbidden, and furthermore, by external sanctions, it can mobilize where morality would conflict with and be subordinated to the agent's personal interests; finally, it can assign obligations for acting where moral obligations do not initially result in concrete demands on concrete individuals.

To ensure that the law does not fulfill these positive tasks only de facto, the law needs to be regarded as *legitimate* for all addressees. Habermas finds "the democratic procedure of the production of law evidently" to be the "only post-metaphysical source of legitimacy" (Habermas 1996, 448). It is based on a "principle of democracy" as a specification of the discourse principle analogous to the principle of universality that is central to his discourse theory of morality: "the only regulations and ways of acting that can claim legitimacy are those to which all who are possibly affected could assent as participants in rational discourses" (Habermas 1996, 458). Habermas thus proposes a procedural system for the development of legal norms that could be accepted as widely as possible, and in which the citizens would be not only the addressees, but also the "authors of the law" (Habermas 1996, 449) as a direct entailment of their more comprehensive and effective involvement in the legislative processes.

Initially, Habermas developed his political model of deliberative democracy as the basis of the democratic state of law at the level of the nation-state; yet, against the background of increasing globalization, he is also concerned with the consequences of such a model for a "postnational constellation." Here, however, he admits a "discrepancy between, on the one hand, the human-rights content of classical liberties and, on the other hand, their form of positive law which initially limits them to the nation state." This discrepancy has the effect of generating awareness that the "discursively grounded 'system of rights'" points beyond the dominion of the constitutional state in the singular and towards the globalization of rights. As Kant realized, and by virtue of their semantic content, basic rights require an international, legally administered "cosmopolitan society" (Habermas 1996, 456). This cosmopolitan society is not only, or even not yet, a present one but already has a future by its contemporary and future members. One of the advantages of a procedural conception of societal norms lies in the fact that it implies the possibility of their nonviolent transformation whenever new parameters, unforeseeable events, or changing societal priorities require this or appear desirable. Since the current generation often does not know what the generations to follow in the future will require or desire, but can only anticipate their needs hypothetically, a great deal depends on keeping procedures open for any and all possible changes, including their own future revisions.[19] Thus, if one adopts from Levinas a concept of responsibility that extends to future generations, then discourse ethics can give us indications as to how this responsibility can be institutionally anchored within a democratic constitutional state.

Notes

1. I would like to thank Matthias Fritsch and the participants of the Nature Time Responsibility conference at Munich in 2018 for their helpful comments. Megan Foster and Rebecca van der Post have been extremely helpful in making this a (hopefully) readable English text. I would also like to thank them very much!

2. Jonas 1984, 21f. A very convincing proposal was recently put forward by Matthias Fritsch in his book *Taking Turns with the Earth* (2018), in which he criticizes above all the "presentism" of current moral theories.

3. Wallace (2007) also emphasises that "the sergeant stands in a hierarchical relation to her troops, and her authority in relation to them is strikingly asymmetrical"; likewise, Wallace points out, in the Humean example of someone whose gouty toe we have stepped on, "the second-personal reason to refrain from stepping on the victim's toe" is only given "until the protest was issued" (ibid., 26).

4. Sam Fleischacker shares this worry when he emphasizes that Darwall's book "is a very third-personal study of the second person" in which he "discusses his subject as if from the vantage point of a disembodied reason: as if he occupied the view from nowhere, the third-personal stance from which, in morality, he wants to pry us away." In Fleischacker's view, this shows that Darwall "is less interested in second-personal itself than in the presuppositions for such address." These could be "studied third-personally," though "the nature of second-personal address may not be so readily accessible" (Fleischacker 2009, 121). Therefore, Darwall is only able to show the similarity between the I and the you and not the radical difference. Experiences of the second-person standpoint, Fleischacker argues, "cannot be captured in any theory, philosophical or otherwise, given the third-personal nature of theory" (ibid., 122). Nevertheless, he mentions Martin Buber and Emmanuel Levinas, who, by employing "a cryptic, poetic style," hint at "the difficulty of capturing what goes into the standpoint that constitutes "you" from outside that standpoint" (ibid., 121).

5. Although Levinas methodically follows Husserl's phenomenology of the perceiving subject in his descriptions, he assumes that the perceiving subject experiences the call of the other before it has even attained consciousness. Thus, the phenomenal area of the perceiving subject *sensu stricto* is on the one hand just constituted, but also transcended.

6. Cf. Buddeberg 2016, on which the following explanations are partly based.

7. Levinas's objection against the phenomenological tradition is that the other's signification does not depend on the subject perceiving the other as someone,

but that the other signifies in themselves even without being perceived intentionally as someone by the subject.

8. Cf. Levinas, 1992, passim. To illustrate this extreme form of passivity, Levinas uses even more metaphors in *Otherwise than Being*, such as "obsession," "maternity," and "captivity" or "hostage" (*otage*).

9. Concerning the thesis of the subject constituted by the other, cf. also Simon Critchley, 2007. A similar idea underlies Fritsch's ontological "turn-taking," not only between different generations but also with regard to our relationship toward our environment: individuals as well as generations emerge from their "environment" or the "earth" as they go back into it—and not only or only at the beginning and end of their lives but rather in perpetual exchange with it. See Fritsch 2018.

10. This, as Fritsch also argues in his book (2018, see above all chapter 3), can certainly be an "asymmetrical reciprocity."

11. The neighbor of the neighbor must and should be thought of not only spatially but also temporally. This suggests the idea of an intergenerational chain, on which Fritsch also bases his idea of asymmetrical reciprocity: "each generation addresses the next as one that is to carry on the project of justice in an iterative manner" (Fritsch 2018, 140).

12. Certainly futurity does not come into play in Levinas just via the third party, since already in the dyad of the self and the other, the other's alterity is characterized in part by a futural temporality that means the other is always in some sense outliving my death. However, it seems doubtful to me that the "diachronical" temporality of the encounter with the other suffices to include future generations, who are definitely not the ones we concretely encounter, in our actions. Therefore, we are in need of cognitive performances, perhaps, certainly also the insight that the future of future generations may not be so different from the future of concrete others.

13. For the interweaving of different perspectives, cf. Robert Bernasconi, who describes the intersection of the ethical (the encounter with the other) and the political (the relation to the other of the other) as one "in which they coexist in tension with each other" where both have "the capacity to question the other" (Bernasconi, 1999, 77).

14. But beyond that, and Fritsch makes this much clearer than others do, there is also a connectedness with the earth and world that was and is before us, and will continue to be after us.

15. Fritsch definitely says something more, namely that it has to be about a democratic politics, but not exactly how this is to be shaped.

16. The German Federal Constitutional Court, for example, in its justification for its judgment on climate change, did not refer to the protection of life or health of future generations but to the protection of freedom of future generations (BVerfG, Beschluss des Ersten Senats vom 24. März 2021;- 1 BvR 2656/18 -, Rn. 1–270). Hans Jonas already used a similar formulation: "[. . .] but ultimately because of the *spontaneity* or freedom of the life in question—the greatest of all unknowns,

which yet must be included in the total responsibility. Indeed, precisely that in the object for whose eventual self-assertion the original agent can no longer be held responsible himself, namely, the own, autonomous causality of the life, under his care, is yet an ultimate object of his commitment."

17. See Jonas's description of the statesman (1984, 14f).

18. Iris Marion Young pleads for a "social connection model of shared responsibility," which comes very close to Apel's conception of a primordial co-responsibility. From her point of view, when assuming responsibility, it is not only important to take into account who has what kind of "power" or "privileges" but also what "interest" someone has in changing the existing situation, as well as their collective ability (Young 2006).

19. See once again the reasons of the German Federal Court of Justice for its judgment with regard to climate protection.

Bibliography

Apel, Karl-Otto. 1988. *Diskurs und Verantwortung*. Frankfurt am Main: Suhrkamp Verlag.

———. 1998. "Universale Prinzipien und partikulare (inkommensurable?) Entscheidungen und Lebensformen: Eine Auseinandersetzung mit Peter Winch über ein Problem der Ethik in der philosophischen Situation nach Kant und nach Wittgenstein." In *Auseinandersetzungen: In Erprobung des transzendentalpragmatischen Ansatzes*, 609–47. Frankfurt am Main: Suhrkamp Verlag.

———. 2000. "First Things First: Der Begriff primordialer Mit-Verantwortung: Zur Begründung einer Makroethik." In *Angewandte Ethik als Politikum*, edited by Matthias Kettner, 21–50. Frankfurt am Main: Suhrkamp.

Bedorf, Thomas. 2005. "Andro-fraternozentrismus: Von der Brüderlichkeit zur Solidarität und zurück." In *Verfehlte Begegnungen: Levinas und Sartre als philosophische Zeitgenossen*, 223–57. München: Wilhelm Fink.

Bernasconi, Robert. 1999. "The Third Party: Levinas on the Intersection of the Ethical and the Political." In *The British Society for Phenomenology* 30 (1): 76–87.

Buddeberg, Eva. 2016. "Ethik und Politik im Anschluss an Levinas—zwischen dem einen und den vielen Anderen?" In *Zeitschrift für Praktische Philosophie* 3 (1): 93–124.

Critchley, Simon. 2007. *Infinitely Demanding: Ethics of Commitment, Politics of Resistance*. London: Verso.

Darwall, Stephen. 2006. *The Second-Person Standpoint: Morality, Respect and Accountability*. Cambridge: Harvard University Press.

Delhom, Pascal. 2000. *Der Dritte: Lévinas' Philosophie zwischen Verantwortung und Gerechtigkeit*. München: Wilhelm Fink.

Flatscher, Matthias. 2015. "Das Verhältnis zwischen dem Ethischen und dem Politischen: Überlegungen zu Levinas' Figur des Dritten." In *Levinas: Schwierige Freiheit—50 Jahre Difficile liberté*, edited by Miriam Fischer-Geboers and Alfred Bodenheimer, 182–214. Freiburg: Alber Verlag.

Fleischacker, Sam. "Stephen Darwall, *The Second-Person Standpoint: Morality, Respect and Accountability* (Cambridge: Harvard University Press, 2006), pp. xii + 348)." *Utilitas* 21: 117–23.

Fritsch, Matthias. 2018. *Taking Turns with the Earth*. Stanford: Stanford University Press.

Habermas, Jürgen. 1990. *Moral Consciousness and Communicative Action*. Cambridge: MIT Press.

———. 1991. "What Is Universal Pragmatics?" In *Communication and the Evolution of Society*, by Jürgen Habermas, 1–68. Cambridge: Polity Press.

———. 1996. *Between Facts and Norms: Contributions to a Discourse Theory of Law and Democracy*. Cambridge: MIT Press.

Honneth, Axel. 2008. *Reification and Recognition: A New Look at an Old Idea*. Oxford: Oxford University Press.

Jonas, Hans. 1984. *The Imperative of Responsibility: In Search of an Ethics for the Technological Age*. Chicago: University of Chicago Press.

Korsgaard, Christine. 2009. *Self-Constitution: Agency, Identity, and Integrity*. Oxford: Oxford University Press.

Levinas, Emanuel. 1969. *Totality and Infinity*. Pittsburgh: Duquesne University Press.

———. 1981. *Otherwise Than Being or Beyond Essence*. The Hague: Martinus Nijhoff.

———. 1992. "Ethics as First Philosophy." In *The Levinas Reader*, edited by Sean Hand, 76–87. Cambridge: Blackwell.

———. 1996. *Basic Philosophical Writings*. Edited by Adriaan T. Peperzak, Simon Critchley, and Robert Bernasconi. Bloomington: Indiana University Press.

Wallace, Jay R. 2007. "Reasons, Relations and Commands: Reflections on Darwall." *Ethics* 118 (1): 24–36.

Young, Iris Marion. 2006. "Responsibility and Global Justice. A Social Connection Model." *Social Philosophy and Policy* 23 (1) (winter): 102–30.

6

Jonasian Grounding of Future-Oriented Responsibility and the Idea of the Human

Hiroshi Abe

Undeniably, current environmental issues such as climate change, deforestation, loss of biodiversity, waste production, and so on challenge us to protect nature and humans in the future from catastrophic anthropogenic disasters. However, this challenge also raises certain puzzles, particularly in terms of the question of care for non-overlapping generations in the distant future. Is it possible for us to take responsibility towards distant future generations, *even though they do not yet exist*? And *if* this is possible, then *how*?

The objective of this chapter is to tackle these basic questions by pursuing an interpretive analysis of Hans Jonas's future ethics. As the reader might already know, Jonas's magnum opus *The Imperative of Responsibility* has established itself as a canonic investigation into the theoretical grounding of responsibility towards future generations, whose moral imperative urges: "In your present choices, include the future wholeness of the Human being among the objects of your will" (Jonas 1984, 11; alteration added).

Nevertheless, there is an enigmatic passage in this work over which many commentators have, no doubt, puzzled: a passage where Jonas clearly contends that "we are not at all responsible towards future people but towards the idea of the Human (Wir [sind] gar nicht den künftigen Menschen verantwortlich, sondern der Idee des Menschen)" (Jonas 1989, 91; my translation). Is there an inconsistency here? Why does Jonas think that we incur responsibility towards the "idea of the Human" rather than towards unborn posterity?

According to my reading, as this chapter sets out to show, it is possible to provide a consistent interpretation of Jonas's grounding of the future-oriented responsibility despite its apparent disharmony. In the process, it will become clear that Jonas's notion of the idea of the Human is crucial to the primary questions this chapter seeks to address.

Three Jonasian Conditions for Responsibility

What is implied by Jonas's notion of the current generation's responsibility towards the idea of the Human? To address this question, I think it is helpful to lay out some preparatory considerations, beginning with some clarification of the main characteristics of Jonas's account of responsibility.

Jonas regards two different kinds of responsibility as being "eminent paradigms" (Jonas 1984, 98). One is the parent's responsibility for their children, which is "instituted by nature" and "independent of prior assent or choice" (Jonas 1984, 94). The other is the responsibility of political leaders for the people, which, unlike parental responsibility, is not natural but artificial inasmuch as "the choice [to become a leader] comes first [. . .] and only then procures for itself the power necessary for implementing it" (Jonas 1984, 96). Despite this difference, Jonas argues, these two types of responsibility share common traits that "make them blend into the one, most integral and paradigmatic representation of the primordial phenomenon of responsibility" (Jonas 1984, 98). In order, then, to grasp Jonas's idea of responsibility, we need to understand what he means by the "representation of the primordial phenomenon of responsibility." And this requires us to elucidate the traits that mark parental and political responsibility as paradigmatic exemplification.

The first feature of parental and political responsibility that Jonas points out is that they are both human-to-human relationships that, he finds, expose the "archetype of all responsibility," showing us that "responsibility is first and foremost of humans for humans" (Jonas 1984, 98; alteration added).

The other notable traits that the responsibility of both parents and political leaders have in common are "totality," "continuity," and "future." By "totality" he means that responsibility is for "the total being" of other people who cannot realize this very being for themselves, and covers all aspects ranging "from physical existence to the highest interests, from security to abundance of life, from good conduct to happiness" (Jonas 1984, 101, 102).

Furthermore, such responsibility for the integrity of their being as a whole cannot be constrained within the narrow limit of a specific situation or time period. For instance, parental duties demand that one should raise one's child with constant and long-term care. Thus, in the case of the total responsibility, "its exercise dare not stop" but "must proceed "historically," embracing its object in its historicity" (Jonas 1984, 105, 106). In this way, a further new characteristic follows from the "totality" of responsibility, namely "continuity."

In the context of these two features (i.e., totality and continuity), I believe, we can extract three key conditions for responsibility from *The Imperative of Responsibility*, hereafter referred to as the "three Jonasian conditions": (1) Objectivity, (2) Transiency, and (3) Power-Knowledge Proportion. Let me explain each of these in turn.

1. Objectivity. As we have seen, parental responsibility towards children as an example of total responsibility is "not specified but global (i.e., extending to everything in them that needs caring for)" (Jonas 1984, 94). For Jonas, the complete one-sidedness of this relationship suggests that responsibility has an objective character as long as the object of responsibility makes a claim for existence against the subject, which is expected to hear and accept this appeal. As he puts it, "first comes the 'ought-to-be' of the object, second the ought-to-do of the subject who, in virtue of his power, is called to its care" (Jonas 1984, 93).

2. Transiency. As the trait of "continuity" suggests, those for whom we take responsibility are characterized by their historicity or temporality. Jonas takes this to imply that the object of responsibility is "entirely contingent in its facticity, perceived precisely in its perishability, indigence, and insecurity" (1984, 87), and that "the locus of responsibility is the being that is immersed in becoming, surrendered to mortality, threatened by corruptibility" (Jonas 1984, 135). Thus, unlike Spinoza's *Ethics*, Jonas's ethical theory of responsibility sees things "*sub specie temporis*" (Jonas 1984, 135), emphasizing that the transiency and vulnerability of the object of responsibility warrant particular consideration.

3. Power-Knowledge Proportion: The characteristic of totality tells us that the total being of those for whom I am responsible

> is dependent on me. As Jonas tells us: "The 'what for' [of my responsibility] lies outside me, but in the effective range of my power, in need of it or threatened by it. [. . .] The matter becomes mine because the power is mine and has a causative relation to just this matter" (Jonas 1984, 92). "The first and most general condition of responsibility is causal power [. . .]; the second, that such acting is under the agent's control; and the third, that she can foresee its consequences to some extent." (Jonas 1984, 90; alteration added)

In short, as the object of our responsibility, the other (i.e., someone other than ourselves) lies within the scope or range of our power. Thus, the greater our power over them, the greater the responsibility we ought to take for their safety or well-being and the greater the knowledge we require as to the anticipatory causality of our power. In this sense, responsibility can be characterized as "a function of power and knowledge" (Jonas 1984, 123).

These conditions do not seem, however, to be true of responsibility towards those future generations that are yet to be born. Why? The first two conditions, objectivity and transiency, presuppose the existence of the object of responsibility: if it did not exist, it would not be in a position to claim existence by virtue of its vulnerability. But future people are not existent, nor do they yet have a right to exist. The third condition, power-knowledge proportion—which derives, as discussed, from totality—demands that the anticipative knowledge should be "commensurate with the causal scale of our action" (Jonas 1984, 7f.). On the other hand, this demand is refused by "future," that is, the trait of parental and political responsibility that I have yet to address. Why? Jonas depicts "future" as follows:

> It is the future of the whole existence [of the object of parental or political responsibility], beyond the direct efficacy of the responsible agent and thus beyond her concrete calculation, which is the invisible co-object of such a responsibility in each of its single, defined occasions. These occasions [. . .] are each time about the proximate particular, and this lies more or less within the range of informed prescience. The totality [. . .] is beyond such prescience [. . .] ultimately because of the spontaneity or freedom of the life in question—the greatest of all unknowns, which yet must be included in the total responsibility. (Jonas 1984, 107; alteration added)

As "children outgrow parental care" and "communities outlive statespersons" (Jonas 1984, 106; alteration added), the object of responsibility ought to become autonomous. Thus, the trait of "future" makes us responsible for "the object's self-owned futurity" (Jonas 1984, 107) or its spontaneous freedom in the future, which is absolutely unforeseeable. Hence, in this case, the causal effects of the power of our responsible actions towards the object must lie beyond our anticipatory knowledge. To put it another way, unlike "totality," "future" teaches us that "power-knowledge proportion" does not extend to the unpredictable future of the object of responsibility that is existent in the present.

This inapplicability of "power-knowledge proportion" is also true in the case of distant-future nonexistent generations, and all the more so because of the increasing causal complexity arising from the greater temporal distance as well as an additional major factor that cannot be ignored: technology. In this context, Jonas contends: "The predictive knowledge falls behind the technical knowledge that nourishes our power to act" (Jonas 1984, 8). Warning that modern technology has radically enhanced the impact of human activities on the environment, he argues that these augmented human powers will be all the more perilous because "developments set in motion by technological acts [. . .] tend to make themselves independent, that is, to gather their own compulsive dynamics, an automotive momentum, by which they [. . .] overtake the wishes and plans of the initiators" (Jonas 1984, 32). In other words, he finds that our technological power will be subject to a higher power that is the "self-feeding compulsion of [our technological] power to its progressive exercise" (Jonas 1984, 141) so that even the keenest anticipative knowledge cannot completely foresee its most significant consequences in the far distant future.

Thus it appears that the three Jonasian conditions are simply not applicable to the present generation's responsibility towards future people. In fact, however, unless I am mistaken, this is not so. In the following sections, I build and develop the case for my interpretation by arguing the following two points: (A) our responsibility towards the *Idea of the Human* satisfies the three Jonasian conditions; (B) this very responsibility makes our responsibility towards future people possible.

Responsibility towards the Idea of the Human

In this section, I begin by clarifying what Jonas means by "the Idea of the Human." As mentioned earlier, Jonas seems to think that the three conditions are inapplicable to the question of future-oriented responsibility. In words that raise a challenge to the third condition—power-knowledge proportion—he insists that "[our] ignorance of the ultimate implications [of technological power] becomes itself a reason for responsible restraint" (Jonas 1984, 22). In other words, where the future of humanity is at stake, restraint in the face of high-reward technological advancement is, in itself, a vital expression of responsibility. In this way, Jonas draws the precautionary principle into his discussion: the principle that requires us to avoid prospective worst cases ahead of the fact. But it is also worth our while to reflect on what such worst-case scenarios might have to teach us. The point here is that when the future holds possibilities that may in some way be threatening, the potential objects of fear do not present themselves independently but, in an un-thematic way, as an accompaniment to something else: something *for the sake of which* we are in fear. Jonas refers to the essence of this appresentation of the object of fear as the "heuristics of fear," arguing, "it is an anticipated *distortion* of humans that helps us to detect that in the normative conception of the Human which is to be preserved from it. And we need the *threat* to the image of the Human [. . .] to assure ourselves of her true image. [. . .] *We know the thing at stake only when we know that it is at stake*" (Jonas 1984, 26f.; alteration added). In the same way that we do not realize what health is until we become ill, things that are essential but normally invisible to us can, nonetheless, be encountered as privation. As the passage cited above shows, Jonas thinks this is true of our "image of the Human," by which he understands "what is humanly desirable and what should determine the choice [of our technological actions affecting the future]" (Jonas 1974, 80).

To understand better the notion of the "image of the Human," it is helpful to have a rough outline of Jonas's view of "image-making" as the *differentia specifica* unique to humans. As he sees it, this faculty of reproducing reality provides us with freedom in the following way:

> The remaker of things is potentially also the maker of new things [. . .]. The freedom that chooses to render a likeness may as well choose to depart from it. The first intentionally drawn line unlocks that dimension of freedom in which faithfulness to the original, or to any model, is only one decision: transcending actual reality as a whole, it offers its range of infinite variation as a realm of the possible, to be made true by human at her choice. The same faculty is reach for the true and power for the new. (Jonas 2001, 172; alteration added)

The point is that thanks to the ability to create an image (i.e., an *eidos* or a symbol), we humans have "eidetic freedom (*eiditische Freiheit*)" (Jonas 1997, 284; my translation), namely the freedom to carry out "the symbolic making-over-again of the world" (Jonas 2001, 173). In other words, we are in a position to project and objectify purposely the external world as "the possible" that is available to us in our imagination. However, as Jonas puts it, this eidetic freedom enables us, simultaneously, to objectify ourselves through self-reflection:

> The fateful freedom of objectification, which confronts the self with the potential sum total of the "other," the "world," as an indefinite realm for possible understanding and action, can and eventually must turn back [. . .] upon the subject itself and make it in turn the object of a relation which again takes the detour via the *eidos*. The "form" here involved [. . .] concerns the self's relation to all outwardness. The new dimension of reflection unfolds, where the subject of all objectification appears as such to itself and becomes objectified for a new [. . .] kind of relation [between itself and the world]. (Jonas 2001, 185)

Jonas's suggestion is that through reflection, one is forced to be concerned not with one's self taken as the inner self isolated from the outer world but, rather, with one's "relation to all outwardness" in the world or one's being-in-the-world as a whole. To put it another way, such reflection thrusts upon each of us the following questions: "What is human, what is my place and part in the scheme of things?" (Jonas 2001, 185; alteration added). For Jonas, it is the image of the Human that is the source of such answers as are possible to these questions, and without which we would be rudderless in our journey through life in this world. In Jonas's words, "one models, experiences, and judges her own inner state and outward conduct after the image of what is human" which "never leaves her" (Jonas 2001, 185, 186; alteration added). In addition, as he continues, for most of us "that image is worked out and entertained in the verbal intercommunication of society" (Jonas 2001, 186). So in this sense, one's image of the Human is not so much personal as public, and is generally "ready-made" (Jonas 2001, 186) as a mirror of the time in which one lives.

However, to the extent that the present-day view of humanity is governed by Darwin's theory of evolution, we can hardly expect the public or social image of the Human to arise from within our own present time, since the theory concerns itself with the question of transient traits adapted to specific circumstances and offers no role model for the formation of our own selves. Hence, if the "indefinite realm" of understanding (see quotation on previous page, Jonas 2001, 185) is circumscribed by the horizon of today, then we can have, at most, "an 'image-less' image of the Human" (Jonas 1974, 170; alteration added), which implies a non-normative principle of conduct towards future people that could be summed up as *anything goes*.

In other words, we cannot derive a guiding image of humans exclusively from the present. Thus, Jonas says: "We must learn from the past what humans 'are,' namely what humans *can* be in a positive and negative sense. [. . .] As long as there is something to 'learn' from history from a practical viewpoint or for the purpose of planning and acting, [. . .] we must set about a projection of the future with this sole knowledge that we have about humans" (Jonas 1989, 384; my translation). Here, however, a question arises. Which specific model of human beings should be chosen to guide our conduct from the vast range of possibilities that human history teaches? We might imagine, given his critique of today's "image-less" or non-normative image of humans, that this question would be of particular concern for Jonas. Remarkably, however, we find that in *The Imperative of Responsibility* it seems to be, at most, of only secondary importance, for he tells us: "In the total danger of the world-historical Now we find ourselves thrown back from the ever-open *question*, *what* the human ought to be (the answer to which is changeable), to the first *commandment* tacitly always underlying it [. . .]: *that* she should be—indeed, *as* a human being. This 'as' brings the essence, as much as we know or divine of it, into the imperative of 'that'" (Jonas 1984, 139; alteration added). This quotation indicates that, for Jonas, the priority is *not* to advocate any concrete image of 'what the human ought to be' that is fixed by particular historical generations but, instead, to demand '*that* she should be': to respect and secure humanity's *existence*, which substantializes its *essence* as we, the current people, know (or presume) it to be. This is the human essence to which we succeed as "the heritage from a past evolution" (Jonas 1984, 32), biological and cultural, and that makes us who we are *now*. Why, then, does Jonas prioritize human *existence*? This question merits some further discussion on Jonas's part: "What now matters most is [. . .] to keep open the horizon of *possibilities* which in the case of humans is given with the existence of the species as such and [. . .] will always offer a new chance to the human essence" (Jonas 1984, 139f.; alteration added). This passage confirms that, for Jonas, our human existence itself furnishes "the horizon of possibilities" for the self-manifestation of the human essence as particular human images and, extending it indefinitely into an open future, thereby enables all generations to project at any time whatever image of the Human they prefer. Hence, the reason for the priority of the human existence to human images is apparent: without the former, the latter would be impossible.

Here, it is important to note that this respect for human existence eventually serves to save the human essence and its potential self-manifestations. To put it briefly, we—today's people—exist, so to speak, for the sake of the human essence that we concretely represent in and through our own existence. What does this unilateral relationship between us and the human essence imply? According to my reading, it is "the idea of the Human" to which Jonas appeals in explaining this issue. In the German version of *The Imperative of Responsibility*, this term is rephrased as "the idea which demands the existence of its own content (*die auf der Existenz ihres Inhaltes bestehende Idee*)" (Jonas 1989, 92; my translation), in the form of "the essence of human beings (das *humanum*) that has a [. . .] claim on a responsible person" (Jonas 1989, 184; my translation). Judging from his own paraphrases, what Jonas means by "the idea of the Human" can be interpreted, I believe, as the human essence insofar as it (a) makes an ontological claim for its self-realization (or its presence); and (b) requires us to exist so that we should be in charge of maintaining "the horizon of possibilities" for it—that is, the horizon on the basis of which we can inherit it (the human essence) from the past, embody it, and bequeath it to the future. In this sense, as Jonas puts it, we have "the abstract 'ought' which from the ontological claim of the idea of the Human [. . .] secretly goes out to all humans and searches among them for its executors or guardians" (Jonas 1984, 99; alteration added).

Should this interpretation of the idea of the Human be correct, then what does our responsibility towards it imply? When we take responsibility towards something, we can distinguish between two components of our responsibility: "to be responsible *for*" and "to be responsible *to*." I understand what we are responsible *for* to be the object of our responsibility, that is, that which is in our charge. On the other hand, what we are responsible *to* is the object of our accountability, in other words, that which gives something in our charge and is in a position both to condemn us and to demand an account for what we have done to it.

Given this distinction, I believe, it follows from the above discussion that our responsibility towards the idea of the Human implies that we are responsible *to* the idea of the Human and responsible *for* the horizon of possibilities.

If so, then it is clear that such responsibility towards the idea of the Human satisfies the three Jonasian conditions of Objectivity, Transiency, and Power-Knowledge Proportion. First, it is the object of our accountability (namely the idea of the Human) that makes a claim for our existence and thereby puts us in charge of "the presence of its embodiment in the world" (Jonas 1984, 43). In this regard, the responsibility towards the idea of the Human fulfills the first condition. Second, the object of our responsibility, the horizon of possibilities, is fragile in the sense that its expansion completely depends on our human existence, which can be always endangered by our own power of technology. This shows that being responsible towards the idea of the Human (which is, precisely, being responsible for the horizon of possibilities and to the idea of the Human) meets the second condition. And last, it also satisfies the third condition, for unlike the people of the far-future, the horizon of possibilities is not at all distant from us temporally, so that there is no overwhelming gap between the causal scale of our power and the scope of its anticipatory knowledge.

Having discussed the first point, (A), the issue will be the second point, (B). How does our responsibility towards the idea of the Human make it possible that we take responsibility towards future generations? Let me deal with this question in the final section.

Jonas's Grounding of Responsibility towards Future People

As I have been arguing, the responsibility towards the idea of the Human implies that we, the current generation, are responsible *to* the idea of the Human (or the human essence) and responsible *for* the maintenance of the "horizon of possibilities," which will also enable the next generation to project any image of the Human that is preferable for them. But even if this is so, are we really obliged to pass on this horizon of possibilities to those who come after us? Jonas's answer to this question is positive. But why must such duty towards people of the forthcoming generation be imposed on us? Remarkably, he insists that the reason is not "their right to happiness" but "their duty" (Jonas 1984, 42). What does Jonas mean? To answer this question, I think, the following passages from *The Imperative of Responsibility* and Jonas's later essay *Toward an Ontological Grounding of an Ethics for the Future* are very helpful:

> The general principle [. . .] is that any total responsibility [. . .] is always responsible also for preserving, beyond its own termi-

nation, the possibility of responsible action in the future—that is, for its own precondition." (Jonas 1984, 118)

> The capacity for responsibility as such [. . .] becomes its own object in that having it obligates us to perpetuate its presence in the world. This presence is inexorably linked to the existence of creatures having that capacity. Therefore, the capacity for responsibility per se obligates its respective bearers to make existence possible for future bearers. (Jonas 1996, 106)

According to my reading, the first passage can be interpreted as arguing that we have a duty towards the "possibility" of responsibility in the future, for example, the nearest future of the coming generation; while, in the second passage, Jonas is arguing that the obligation to shoulder this burden of duty falls not only to its current bearers—the living—but also, in turn, to "its respective bearers" in each generation to follow. Should this be the case, then in my view the point of Jonas's arguments, above, is this: for the sake of the fragile being of the horizon of possibilities there should be humans who have a duty to secure it in the present (say, the Nth generation) and who should raise and be responsible for those who will carry the same duty in the next generation (= the N+1st generation); and this next generation should, in turn, be responsible for their own successors who will do this in the generation after next (= the N+2nd generation), *ad infinitum*.

In this way, we can see that our responsibility towards the idea of the Human enables us to take not only *direct* responsibility towards the next generation closest to us but also *indirect* responsibility towards distant-future people at the same time. At the same time, this is also our answer to the main questions raised at the beginning of this chapter. We can even take responsibility towards not-yet existing generations in the distant future, because we will be able to hand, so to speak, a torch of responsibility from generation to generation as long as we are responsible to the idea of the Human or the human essence inherited from past generations.

In short, human responsibility is in itself "responsibility for responsibility." Let me close this chapter by quoting from *The Imperative of Responsibility* to show that Jonas himself emphasizes this very point: "Put epigrammatically: The possibility of there being responsibility in the world, which is bound to the existence of humans, is of all objects of responsibility the first" (Jonas 1984, 99; alteration added).

Bibliography

Jonas, Hans. 1974. *Philosophical Essays: From Ancient Creed to Technological Man.* Englewood Cliffs: Prentice-Hall.

———. 1984. *The Imperative of Responsibility: In Search of an Ethics for the Technological Age.* Translated by Hans Jonas with the collaboration of David Herr. Chicago: University of Chicago Press.

———. 1989. *Das Prinzip Verantwortung: Versuch einer Ethik für die technologische Zivilisation.* Frankfurt am Main: Suhrkamp.

———. 1996. *Mortality and Morality: A Search for the Good after Auschwitz.* Edited and with an introduction by Lawrence Vogel. Evanston: Northwestern University Press.

———. 1997. *Das Prinzip Leben: Ansätze zu einer philosophschen Biologie.* Frankfurt am Main: Suhrkamp.

———. 2001. *The Phenomenon of Life: Toward a Philosophical Biology.* Evanston: Northwestern University Press.

7

"The Race of the Poor"

Intergenerational Lessons from Anarchist Eugenics

Anne O'Byrne

> Anarchists love everyone . . . Usually, however, we become erotically engaged with thinking through the political ramifications of any contemplated liaison, and miss our chance.
>
> —Ruth Robson

> Things created by interest and love will be objects of beauty and joy.
>
> —Alexander Berkman

In 1923, a Spanish anarchist journal appeared bearing the title *Generación Consciente* and, until it closed in 1929, published articles promoting a variety of strategies for human improvement. Contributors to the journal and its related publications, *Estudios Revista Ecléctica*, which disappeared in 1937, and Barcelona-based *Eugenia*, argued for sex education, the right of women to control of their bodies, birth control, and unconstrained sexuality while at the same time advocating healthy nutrition, fresh air, rewarding work, nudism, and free clinics to combat venereal disease. Social problems could be solved and misery eliminated by the full exercise of individual freedom. Yet, if the liberty that would save us was to be the liberty of the *individual*, why did these anarchist theorists describe their ambitions as *eugenic*? How could some advocate the sterilization of undesirables? How could *Eugenia* describe itself in 1921, unabashedly, as "the organ of the future eugenic society"?

In practice, the sheer scope of twentieth-century eugenic ambitions required a large, authoritative apparatus of knowledge, education, medicine, surgery, social manipulation, publicizing, policing, and enforcement. In contrast to the eugenic communities of the nineteenth century, these later political movements saw no sense in modest eugenic schemes. They envisioned programs carried out on the scale of entire populations, since any trace of contagion, unwholesomeness, or degeneracy that remained would be a threat to health. The agency most ready to embark on such a project, most able to command such an apparatus, most willing to use force, and most interested in managing biopolitical production, has always been the state, that is, the prime target of anarchist intervention.[1] Thus, the expression *anarchist eugenics* leaves us puzzled.[2] The familiar eugenic programs of the era were run by governments—in the United States, Britain, and elsewhere—and the most thoroughgoing was implemented by the totalitarian state of the Third Reich. How could eugenics be implemented without force and without a state?

Anarchism also revolts against eugenics in principle. How could an ideology that holds the individual's freedom as the most fundamental value reconcile itself to a eugenic ideal of the healthy race—human, Aryan, or national? Maria Lacerda de Moura, writing in *Estudios* in 1931, insists on a woman's right as "an individual vindication of herself, the right to be the owner of her own body, of her will, of her wishes and her mental expansion, to live life in the fullness of its potential" (Jiménez-Lucena and Molero-Mesa 2012, 232). Contrast this to the hyperbolic self-abnegation of the young women of the earlier eugenic community in Oneida, in the United States: "We do not belong to *ourselves* in any respect . . . we have no rights or personal feelings in regard to child-bearing . . . we will, if necessary, become martyrs to science" (quoted in Richards 2004, 53). Anarchism rejects the surrender of individual freedom to representatives or representations; the ideal of perfected humanity is just such a representation. While the anarchist works to be free here and now, the eugenicist acts now for the sake of a future perfection. How could an anarchist eugenics adjudicate these clashing temporalities?

Lastly, individual anarchist freedom must be freedom for all individuals, equally. As Nicholas Walter puts it: "Freedom without equality means that the poor and weak are less free than the rich and strong, and equality without freedom means that we are all slaves together" (Ehrlich 1979b, 43). What, then, would allow anarchism to make the essential eugenic distinction between the desirable and the undesirable? What criteria would count as anarchist criteria?

I argue here that, while eugenics could never be an anarchist *program*, it emerged as an effect of the sexual struggle that is fundamental to anarchism and brought the movement face-to-face with the quandary of its self-perpetuation. For the existing Spanish state, as for any conservative institution, there was no such quandary. State institutions, with the support of a traditional Catholic Church, pursued a biopolitics that ensured the physical and social reproduction of a large and expendable workforce of peasants and industrial laborers. Biopolitics manages and governs the life process, populations, and all of us as living, reproducing beings; by efficiently controlling and exploiting sex and directing libido, it manages the continual generation of life and secures institutional continuity. Once anarchism states its libertarian principle as a matter of sexual liberation, it engages biopolitics at its core.

It is a complex and dangerous engagement. Historically, some varieties of anarchism would embrace procreation, understood as a transcendent labor in the service of human perfectibility;[3] others could commit themselves to present pleasure to the point where any claim on the part of the future is incomprehensible.[4] I propose something else: that the engagement of anarchism, understood as a doctrine of individual and social freedom, in the sexual struggle confronts biopolitics with *politics*. That is to say, it resists the management of life by challenging us constantly to develop a principled response to the question of how we are to live together well. Biopolitics succeeds by making sure we experience sexuality as private and personal, working all the while to have sex serve institutional ends; anarchism brings the personal into the political sphere by interrogating sexual mores as part of the question of living well together. The sexual struggle is a struggle for pleasure, but that also means that it concerns the individual understood in the *context* of her erotic and generational relations. I want to be free to find my pleasure here and now but perhaps I also enjoy the anticipation of it, its deferral, the recollection of it, the prolonging of it, pleasure shared, the pleasure of experience and also of creation and procreation. This is where we confront the tension embedded not just in anarchism but also in every politics that strives to both promote freedom and sustain *itself* as the best possible structure for the realization of that freedom. It is the struggle of present and future. The anarchist rejects the authority of tradition, so what can her relation be to what comes after? With her commitment to resisting power, how can she grasp her own inevitable power over the generations that come? Will the anarchist parent always find herself instructing her child: "Obey no authority!"?

Pleasure

Eugenic thought developed in Spain in the first decades of the twentieth century in much the same way that it developed elsewhere, becoming a part of all but the most reactionary or conservative political ideologies of the period. Reformers, republicans, socialists, and anarchists all believed that society must be transformed and that the problem demanded the most efficient measures; when these convictions coincided with the growing reverence for the power of science to produce transformation, social thinking became biological thinking (Peláez 1995, 40). If biology and evolutionary theory held the key to social problems, then social problems must be understood as having their origin in the degeneration of the race. Political priorities differed, but certain characteristics were shared. Reformers interested above all in *strengthening* and modernizing the Spanish state emphasized marriage, the role of medical professionals, and the need for efficiency in the project of regeneration; anarchist writers committed to *dismantling* the state emphasized exactly the same things. Anarchist positions were necessarily diverse and constantly evolving. In the period between the First Spanish Eugenic Days—a congress held in Madrid in 1910—and the collapse of Spanish anarchism at the end of the civil war in 1939, the movement continually tried to address the immediate social problems of poverty, disease, and inequality, at certain points stressing theories of inheritance, at others eugenic strategies (e.g., requiring medical approval for marriages) and at yet others the classical anarchist commitment to anti-authoritarianism (Cleminson 2000, 260). Although they could never be univocal about what *nature*, *culture*, and *nurture* referred to and what their relative importance might be as causes and cures of misery—after all, what critical theory could be?—the Spanish anarchists' commitment to free love followed from the commitment to personal liberty.

As soon as we know how to control our fertility, sex is transformed. The anarchist contributors became deeply interested in sex and pleasure, and sex as pleasure. (Month after month, the covers of *Generación Consciente* featured nude women in natural settings and in states of considerable happiness.) By exhorting intervention in nature to separate sex and reproduction, they produced a new nature and aligned themselves with a new ideology of nature in the form of natur*ism*. Casting off clothing was the performance of casting off the traditions that had exploited human sexuality by keeping people ignorant of their own sexual possibilities. In the name of nature, people would rise against the church and the state, since those were the institutions that had imposed themselves between men and women and between each of us and his or her own natural being, deforming our bodies and constraining our relations. Sex and love would be freed, and Emma Goldman's vision of a healthy grown woman, full of life and passion, could become a reality; no longer obliged by fate and convention "to subdue her most intense craving, undermine her health and break her spirit . . . stunt her vision and abstain from the depth and glory of sex experience until a 'good' man comes to take her unto himself as a wife," the free woman could at last experience the pleasure of her own sexual sovereignty (Goldman 1969, 23).

The emphasis is almost invariably—even unrelentingly—heterosexual. The old social institutions continued to exert their influence, and the movement in those years included some who regarded homosexuality as pathological and degenerate, others who treated it as a matter of free choice, and others who praised it as a healthy egoism. This last, though an uncommon position, suggests a train of thought that would emerge again in Genet, and later in Bersani, Edelman, and the queer anarchists and (post-)anarchist queers of the early twenty-first century.[5] Where early twentieth-century anarchism had to work hard against reactionary forces to broach the subject of sexual pleasure liberated from reproduction, queer theory of a century later would have no hesitation in rejecting hetero-norms, reproductive futurism, and the temporality that ticks and tocks through birth, marriage, reproduction, and death (Halberstam 2005, 2). Queer subcultures have emerged and demanded different temporal logics, all the way to a dogmatic future-less temporality that affirms pleasure *now*, understanding it as the dismantling of sexual sovereignty and the operation of the death drive. This is Lee Edelman's argument in *No Future*, and it is relevant here because it brings anarchism face-to-face with its last temptation and its last authority figure, that is, the authority of the future exercised through the figure of "The Child."

According to Edelman, we are unable to imagine a politics without a fantasy of the future, and we are unable to conceive of the future without the figure of "The Child." Who can resist "The Child"? Who can be against "The Child"? In the face of idealistic attempts at social reform, he criticizes the commitment to "The Child" as the figure that holds open the hope that, in the future, we will finally right the wrongs of the world. Radical social movements may exhort us to smash the system, but most, the Spanish anarchist eugenicists included, wanted to see it smashed as a precondition for bringing about something new and better: in their case, the advent of the free and natural man and woman. At that point, any move to affirm this hard-won freedom, or to fend off the reactionary forces that would encroach on this nature, would risk—nay, would *aim at*—consolidating the anarchic structure in all its newness and transmitting it to the next generation. Historically speaking, Edelman writes, "the Child has come to embody for us the *telos* of the social order and come to be seen as the one for whom that order is held in perpetual trust" (Edelman 2004, 11).

If the anarchist project is individual liberation, then the source of resistance will be the commitment to sexual freedom above all—above the future and above "The Child." At its extreme, the heteronormative worldview sees sex reaching its completion in children. Deploying all the normative forces of naturalism, sex is regarded as a moment in the arc of reproduction, and all the many instances of un-reproductive sex are precisely that: *un*reproductive and either incidental or accounted for in more or less elaborate accounts of drive and libido. For Edelman, heterosexual, reproductive, married sex will not produce the disturbance of identity he advocates, because that experience, whatever its ecstasies and *ex-stases*, always risks—even courts—appropriation by the future child. What he has in mind is, rather, queer sex. If "The Child" is the figure of life, the future, and our social being, then queer (or queerness or the queer) is conjured as the figure of the death drive, that is, "the negativity opposed to every form of social viability" (Edelman 2004, 9). This has become known as the antisocial or antirelational thesis.

The argument is most striking in its account of how the category of "queer" becomes powerful in its disruption not just of straight identities but also of *identification* as such. Those who work to make lesbian or gay identity something substantial play the identification game and establish an opposition of identities that reinforces the rules of that game. But if all identities are in fact disjointed; if all our attempts to match up to a substantial or authentic identity fall short; in Lacanian terms, if noncoincidence of this sort means that every identity must reckon with a constitutive gap; then, while reproductive futurism struggles to suture identity by closing the gap, queerness struggles to hold it open. Edelman writes: "queerness undoes the identities through which we experience ourselves as subjects, insisting on the Real of a jouissance that social reality and the futurism on which it relies have already foreclosed" (Edelman 2004, 25). So when heteronormative culture displaces its anxieties onto the figure of the queer, and when queers then take on this figural identity, when they em*body* this figure, they are opposing identity *and* the logic of opposition.

The antisocial thesis leaves behind generation, good or bad, for better or worse. An anarchism that was queer in Edelman's sense would have no place for eugenics, but it would also have no place for politics. By taking the anarchist commitment to present individual liberty and pushing it beyond sovereignty and beyond identifiable individuals, by finding the splits and cracks in us and keeping them open, by embracing the negative, it would make absurd the other anarchist commitment to equality and would render moot the question of resistance to *inequality*. Edelman rejects the question of living well together, of living well, even of *living* when he rejects the criterion of social viability. Yet eschewing politics does not mean escaping biopolitical management. On the contrary. As Todd May writes (in response to a different challenge to the subject of anarchism): "Traditional anarchism is founded on the conception of the individual as possessing a reserve that is irreducible to social arrangements of power; to remove [that conception] . . . effectively precludes the possibility of resistance" (May 2010, 30). Who could resist? Who could be compelled to resist? Who, us?[6]

The antirelational thesis has meaning in a context understood according to a relational thesis, specifically, according to the familiar sense that sexual contact is a matter of connection and intimacy. Antirelational sex has meaning in a world of relational sex. Moreover, the rejection of the figure of the child is undertaken by former children, in a world where people persist in having more children. Jack Halberstam describes the antirelational thesis as "a radically realistic recognition of both the selfishness of sex and its destructive power" (Halberstam 2005, 140); we can share that recognition and at the same time recognize, realistically, its productive power. Sex produces experience, pleasure, relationships, and babies. People keep having children, some of them even consciously. Homonormative gay couples, rejecting the role of saboteurs of the biopolitical machinery, keep having children quite consciously. Our resistance, whatever form it takes, will happen against the backdrop of generational life and the slow, stepwise movement of death and birth and death, bequest and inheritance and bequest.

The Race of the Poor

Political anarchism, in the tension between freedom and equality, asks: "How are we to live well together, freely?" Anarchist eugenicists isolated an essential part of the problem by asking: "What it is to be *born* well and *born* free?"[7] Anxiety about what it meant to be well-born has a distinctive history in Spain, beginning in the sixteenth century. After Muslims and Jews were forced to convert or be expelled after 1492, anxiety centered on the activities of the converts: were they just behaving *like* Christians and continuing to be Jews and Muslims behind closed doors? Even if not, weren't they still really Jews and Muslims in some important and unshakeable way? In this way, anxiety shifted to the matter of blood. Surely there had to be a difference between those born Christian of long generations of Christians and those born Jewish or Muslim or born of converts. Surely there was a device that could guarantee that the Christian descendant of a Jew or Muslim could be excluded from the ranks of the well-born. The blood of inheritance emerged as that device.[8] Thus, at the moment when global imperialism was taking shape, and the groundwork was being laid for modern theories of race, the blood relationship was taken on as the natural—that is, naturalized and racialized—determinant of good birth. To be born well was to be the scion of good (Christian, Spanish) stock.

Writing in *Generación Consciente* in 1929, Dr. Isaac Puente explains what it is to be born poor, appealing in the same way to both social and naturalized categories. The misery of the lower class was caused by the church, the state, and capitalism, which kept people ignorant, impoverished, and chained to the process of breeding new congregants, citizens, and workers. He views it as a class created by historical social structures, yet names it "the *race* of the poor" (my emphasis). This is no mistake, but the indication of a double structure. Children are born whether we think about it or not, and whether our lives are formed by these specific social structures or different ones. What Puente diagnoses is the rhythm by which church, state, and capitalism at that time gave shape to the heedless or unconscious process of reproduction, naming it *natural*; the natural acts of reproduction in turn sustained the system that gave them their form. Thus the church could forbid contraception and exhort married couples to accept all the children God sent, while couples continued to have sex, beget, conceive, and give birth as though it were only natural or merely the will of God. Why devote thought to what was beyond human control? If the church, the state, and capital could naturalize—and simultaneously sacralize—unconscious reproduction *for* peasants and workers, and thereby naturalize the reproduction *of* new generations of peasants and workers, they had effectively created a group that would perpetuate itself through birth. Add a rigid social structure established along lines of blood, and a frenetic pace of self-perpetuation leading to large families, hand-to-mouth existence, labor for all from a young age, and little education, and the result is that social mobility is made impossible and the fate of the poor is as thoroughly naturalized as the fate of any immobilized, naturalized race.

"The race of the poor" is the name for socially produced poverty that has been naturalized and racialized.

The task of anarchist eugenics is to interrupt this rhythm. From the reactionary point of view, conscious generation punctuates the natural cycles that sustain life; from the anarchist point of view, it punctuates the ideological cycles that sustain ignorance and oppression.[9] Reactionary ideology gives authority to nature and establishes the cycle of naturalization, and when that cycle is interrupted by education, technology, and choice, the game is up for the ideological standoff between consciousness and nature. If everyone knew how sexual reproduction happened, if everyone were allowed to develop the self-possession that is a condition for making choices, and if everyone had access to the technologies of birth control and abortion, then all generation would be conscious *and* natural.[10] We could abandon the language of reproduction and speak instead of procreation and insist on the *creativity* of having babies.

After all, generating the new generation is work. Anarchism strives for our liberation as humans and as sexual beings, but particularly and simultaneously as workers. In 1937, referring to Catalonia's eugenic projects, Dr. Félix Martí Ibánez writes: "above any material interest there exists the supreme desire to create a new, vigorous free generation of workers" (Cleminson 1994, 738). Capitalism desires the reproduction of its workforce, but the question of whether the work is alienating or fulfilling, destructive or creative is incidental to the central purpose of profit maximization. Work is not an incidental or temporary element of the human condition but the way in which we objectify ourselves in the world and, for anarchism, its own central purpose—freedom—is never a matter of freedom *from* work but freedom *to* work together cooperatively and creatively.

Creation

What is the shape of anarchist creativity? Certain forms of work—Hannah Arendt reserves the word *labor* for them—generate what the body needs to survive, and the product is consumed more or less immediately. Other forms—Arendt calls them *work*—produce something that lasts, a thing that both sustains and furnishes the world and stands to endure beyond the life of its creator. Creative work generates something new, and it involves investing our capacity for innovation in something beyond ourselves, leaving the world other than as we found it. That is to say, to create is to invest in the world, a world that has already changed by virtue of our being in it, that will change by virtue of the specific work we do, and the survival of which is therefore of interest to us. Even if we strive to live according to a principle of self-effacement, we cannot efface our being here and our having been here. Yet anarchism cannot prescribe the form of a future social world; in the name of freedom, it cannot steal that right from those to come. Being free, those generations must be left to create modes of existence for themselves.[11]

Yet the future touches us. Implied in anarchist eugenics is the thought that there will be such generations, that we will generate them, and that how we generate them will affect the choices they make. That is to say, our interest here and now is in living a fulfilled sexual life; if that involves a desire to beget or bear children, we have an interest in doing so *well*. To procreate well is to ensure that our children are born well, and to that extent our interests are entirely enfolded in theirs. Yet, from the point of view of individual freedom, our interests are also at odds with theirs. Our power to procreate is inevitably also a power *over* the new beings we create. Just as the conditions of industrial work under capitalism and agricultural labor under the landlords had to be brought to the level of consciousness, so too the social conditions of marriage, sex, and reproduction had come to consciousness and thus passed into the realm of freedom. The result of raised consciousness in the Andalusian countryside was the peasant takeover of farms; the result of raised consciousness among industrial workers in Catalonia was the rise of anarcho-syndicalism; the result of raised consciousness about sex would be the separation of sex and reproduction, free love, chosen parenthood, and fewer, better babies. In each case, the future encroaches—after all, whom were the harvests meant to feed? Didn't the syndicates include young and old workers?—but what is distinctive in the case of procreation is that it is the very condition for the possibility of any political future.

Politics against Biopolitics

Anarchism struggles to throw off the burden of tradition, rejecting not so much the past as the mode in which the past bears down on the present, and the dead generations make their demands on the living. Yet, unlike other brands of revolutionary politics, it must also refuse ideals and utopias that would likewise bear down, this time from the future. At the root of this struggle is the anarchist response to the concept and practice of representation: when we submit ourselves to representation, we surrender our power. This applies to political representation but also, significantly, to representations that are offered as images of our future. Kropotkin writes: "By proclaiming our morality of equality, or anarchism, we refuse to assume a right which moralists have always taken upon themselves to claim, that of mutilating the individual in the name of some ideal" (Kropotkin 2005, 105). Elites arrogate to themselves the right to speak on behalf of the free people, and if we hand over our power of speech, we sacrifice our freedom and give them the tools to oppress us. Likewise, projected images of the good life become instruments of exploitation when they are used to induce us to sacrifice today for the sake of the future. To subordinate myself to an ideal—a utopia, an image of perfected humanity, a promise of eugenic hygiene—is to give away my human freedom.

Yet there were those who took up the eugenic project of breeding the revolution with militant urgency. A neo-Malthusian element aimed to reduce the *size* of peasant and working families, but another, more explicitly eugenic group pointed to the additional need to improve the *quality* of the children by breeding out undesirable characteristics (Rousselle 2014, 36). This was at the root of Puente's promotion of education and his encouragement to identify our own vices and seek out a mate whose virtues would counteract them in the formation of the child. A 1928 editorial in *Generación Consciente* insists that "Respectful of the human personality, enemies of all imposition external to the individual, we aspire, rather than trusting this eugenic labour to governments, to achieve it by means of man's control over himself." Yet, in the same article, the editors push further: "We believe that this is not practicable for those in whom their inheritance, illness or vice has destroyed their human personality, almost to the point of erasing them in their entirety" ("Redacción" 1928, 293, quoted in Cleminson 2008, 237). Some of those born into the race of the poor had lost or had failed to ever attain human personality. Lacking consciousness, they could be treated as non-persons: confined, placed under medical supervision, and sterilized. Apparently, individuals could be mutilated for an ideal after all.

In 1933, Germany introduced laws permitting forced sterilization of people with inherited mental and physical conditions—schizophrenia, blindness, so-called mental deficiency—and in 1934 an article appeared in *Estudios* denouncing such practices as "penal and vindictive" (Rousselle 2014, 38). The anarchist movement rejected forced sterilization in 1936, turning its attention instead to sex education at Clinics for the Psychosexual

Orientation of Youth and the Institute for Sexual Science, and to the promotion of motherhood. Of course, the struggle between the commitment to freedom and equality, on the one hand, and the appeal for revolutionary violence, on the other, had long been part of the history of anarchism. Spanish anarchism was soon bound for violent destruction in the civil war. Yet this specific retreat from force to exhortation, from talk of sterilization to sex education classes, represents another strand of anarchist thinking. If we see it as the reassertion of Kropotkin's principle, we begin to see how this anarchist politics confronts biopolitics.

Rejecting ideals does not mean rejecting principles. Rather, it means espousing principles in the knowledge that they will always be matters for contestation among us. Instead of making a choice between fundamental rules and nothing, we find ourselves inheriting, struggling over, inventing, fixing, letting go, cobbling together a collection of principles as we go along. This is familiar as a description of anarchist ethics. Todd May writes: "Rather than relying on their own moral intuitions and their capacity to reflect upon them in irreducible concrete situations, individuals are asked to submit to an ideal which claims to realize their highest nature but in fact disjoins them from their capacities for critical reflection and thoughtful action" (May 2010, 28–29). This is still more compelling as an account of politics. Ethics deals essentially with the relation between one and another, whereas politics deals with plurality; the central theme for ethics is the ethical subject, whereas the central theme for politics is the world, that is, the site of all our irreducible concrete situations (Arendt 1994, 153). The ethical question may take the form "What should I do?" or "How should I live?," but the political question is the one already noted: "How are we to live well, together?" It is not necessary to appeal to the upheavals of war and conquest or the ebb and flow of migrations to acknowledge that who *we* refers to will change; the fact of generational existence means that the old are always passing away and the young are always coming to be, and the world we inhabit together is the forum where we overlap and try to answer the question.

The object of biopolitics is the generational life flow of populations; the object of politics is the *question* of our worldly living. Anarchist answers to that question are unrelentingly temporary, and while they are guided by commitments to freedom and equality, they are driven by a deeper commitment to perfectibility, though a perfectibility without a vision of perfection. It is an immanent perfectibility, a capacity to discover by means of critical reflection what it might be to live together better, and to engage on that basis in thoughtful action. It is not a matter of building a world according to the model of a no-place, but of tending to ourselves and to the world where we find ourselves.

"Child! Obey no authority."

To tend to the world is to attend to it consciously, to respond to it and take responsibility for it. This is not the moral responsibility I ought to take for my own misdeeds—did *I* create the world?—but a shared responsibility for the world as it is.[12] It is shared among ourselves, the old and the young, the dead from whom we inherited it and those still to come. Handing down is an exercise of power. For traditional inheritance, it is a matter of preservation, privileging the power of the old to shape the young and confer on them the obligation to keep up their good work; for anarchists, it is also a matter of continuity but, in addition, a concern with protecting the contingency and otherness of the inheritors and conferring on them the responsibility to achieve the capacity for freedom and revolutions of their own.[13] For anarchism, power is not always a constraining and oppressive force but the power to procreate and create, empowering us to forge a freedom to judge according to the principles we make, love according to our desires, and re-create the world. Again.[14]

Notes

1. This is not to claim that only states have pursued eugenic schemes. Numerous utopian or supremacist communities attempted them too, e.g., Bernhard Förster and Elisabeth Förster-Nietzsche's Nueva Germania established in Paraguay in 1887, or the Oneida community established by John Humphrey Noyes in New York in 1848.

2. And yet there were numerous anarchist publications in Spain in the 1920s and 1930s, for example: *Amor, conveniencia y eugenesia* (1929) by Gregorio Marañón; *Moral, eugenesia y derecho* (1930) by Joaquín Noguera; *Un siglo de civilización bajo la influencia eugenésica* and *Pedagogía y eugenesia, cultivo de la especie humana* (1932) by Enrique Madrazo; *Eugenesia y matrimonio* (1932) by Francisco de Haro; and *Eugenesia de la hispanidad y regeneración de la raza* (1937) by Vallejo Nágera (see Cleminson 2000, 84–88 and Alvarez Peláez, 203). These were in addition to the three journals already mentioned.

3. This was the editorial position of *Eugenismo*.

4. See Edelman 2004.

5. see Bersani 2009; Edelman 2004; and Yekani, Kilian, and Michaelis 2016.

6. There is a more complex argument to be made here regarding the political role of negativity. As Halberstam writes, "Negativity might well constitute an anti-politics but it should not register as apolitical" (Halberstam 2008, 148. See also Grassi 2016; O'Rourke 2011; and Muñoz 2009).

7. Jimenez-Lucena and Molero-Mesa write: "The sexual struggle was nothing other than the social struggle to be born well and live well" (Jiménez-Lucena and Molero-Mesa 2012, 225).

8. See Anidjar 2014.

9. Both Puente and Higinio Noja Ruíz rejected determinism, arguing that nature deserved respect only insofar as it was respectable. See Jiménez-Lucena and Molero-Mesa 2012, 228.

10. Crucially, anarchist thought broke explicitly with the distinction between nature and society, public and private. See Jiménez-Lucena and Molero-Mesa 2012, 233.

11. See McLaughlin 2007.

12. See Arendt 1968.

13. Judith Butler writes: "Perhaps anarchism is linked to productive power—the production of new social structures, based on a critical analysis of existing structures" (Heckert and Cleminson 2011, 99).

14. See Ehrlich 1979b and Ehrlich 1979a.

Bibliography

Anidjar, Gil. 2014. *Blood: A Critique of Christianity*. New York: Columbia University Press.

Arendt, Hannah. 1968. "The Crisis in Education." In *Between Past and Future*, 173–96. New York: Penguin.

———. 1994. "Collective Responsibility." In *Essays in Understanding*. New York: Schocken Books.

Bersani, Leo. 2009. *Is the Rectum a Grave?: And Other Essays*. Chicago: University of Chicago Press.

Cleminson, R. 2008. "Eugenics without the State: Anarchism in Catalonia, 1900–1937." *Stud Hist Philos Biol Biomed Sci* 39 (2): 232–39.

Cleminson, Richard. 1994. "Eugenics by Name of by Nature? The Spanish Anarchist Sex Reform of the 1930s." *History of European Ideas* 18 (5): 729–40.

———. 2000. *Anarchism, Science, and Sex: Eugenics in Eastern Spain, 1900–1937*. New York: P. Lang.

Edelman, Lee. 2004. *No Future: Queer Theory and the Death Drive*. Durham: Duke University Press.

Ehrlich, Howard J. 1979a. *Reinventing Anarchy, Again*. Chico, CA: AK Press.
———. 1979b. *Reinventing Anarchy: What Are Anarchists Thinking These Days?* New York: Routledge & K. Paul.
Goldman, Emma. 1969. *Anarchism and Other Essays*. New York: Dover.
Grassi, Samuele. 2016. "The Anarchy of Living with Negativity." *Continuum* 30 (5): 587–99.
Halberstam, Judith. 2005. *In a Queer Time and Place: Transgender Bodies, Subcultural Lives*. New York: New York University Press.
Heckert, Jamie, and Richard Cleminson, eds. 2011. "On Anarchism: An Interview with Judith Butler." In *Anarchism & Sexuality: Ethics, Relationships and Power*. Abingdon, UK: Routledge.
Jiménez-Lucena, Isabel, and Jorge Molero-Mesa. 2012a. "Good Birth and Good Living: The (de)Medicalizing Key to Sexual Reform in the Anarchist Media of Inter-War Spain." *International Journal of Iberian Studies* 24 (3): 219–41.
Kropotkin, Peter. 2005. "Anarchist Morality." In *Kropotkin's Revolutionary Pamphlets*. Whitefish, MT: Kessinger Publishing.
May, Todd. 2010. "Is Post-Structuralist Theory Anarchist?" In *New Perspectives on Anarchism*, edited by Nathan J. Jun and Shane Wahl, 25–38. Lanham, MD: Rowman & Littlefield.
McLaughlin, Paul. 2007. *Anarchism and Authority: A Philosophical Introduction to Classical Anarchism*. Aldershot, UK: Ashgate.
Muñoz, José Esteban. 2009. *Cruising Utopia: The Then and There of Queer Futurity*. New York: New York University Press.
O'Rourke, Michael. 2011. "The Afterlives of Queer Theory." *Continent* 1 (2): 102–16.
Peláez, Raquel Alvarez. 1995. "Eugenesia y darwinismo social en el pensamiento anarquista." In *El anarquismo español y sus tradiciones culturales*, edited by Bert Hofmann, Pere Joan i Tous, and Manfred Tietz, 29–40. Madrid: Vervuert.
Richards, Martin. 2004. "Perfecting People: Selective Breeding at the Oneida Community (1869–1879) and the Eugenics Movement." *New Genetics and Society* 23 (1): 47–71.
Rousselle, Elizabeth Smith. 2014. "Militarism and Maternalism: Anarchist Eugenics in Halma Angélico's Ak y La Humanidad." *Confluencia* 29 (2): 35–48.
Yekani, Elahe Haschemi, Eveline Kilian, and Beatrice Michaelis. 2016. *Queer Futures: Reconsidering Ethics, Activism, and the Political*. New York: Routledge.

Section 3
Amor Mundi in Presentist Modernity

8

Critical Theory, Natal Alienation, Future People

Matthias Fritsch

Natal Alienation

A critical theory of modernity would do well to recognize what Marx called primitive or original accumulation (*ursprüngliche Akkumulation*) as an indispensable aspect of capitalism's principal presupposition and ongoing mode of operation: the separation of human populations from the land and the insertion of the market in commodity and labor between land and life (Marx 1992, Part 8). To be sure, Marx's 1867 diagnosis in *Capital* suffers from teleological assumptions of historical progress to which we cannot subscribe today. The Indigenous scholar Glen Sean Coulthard has given a helpful tripartite of these assumptions. First, Marx specifically ties primitive accumulation (PA) to the birth of capitalism, but for Coulthard (following the early critiques of Piotr Kropotkin and Rosa Luxemburg as well as the more recent Federici 2004; Alfred 2005; Smith 2005; Harvey 2005, and others), state-orchestrated dispossession has always accompanied capital accumulation and continues today in neoliberal times. The endemic threat of overaccumulation and underconsumption generates an ongoing need for state power, with military, infrastructural, and legal force, to create an "outside"—such as nature—that can serve as resource for surplus capital looking for investment (Harvey 2005, 139–41). The crisis tendencies of capitalism could thus, in part, be offset by state interventions aimed at further privatization of the commons, including dispossession (especially of land, but also of water, intellectual property, etc.), warfare, state-assisted access to inexpensive inputs such as cheaper labor, and so on.

Second, Marx thought PA took place by overt, often state-orchestrated violence (the slave trade, colonial dispossession, vagabond laws, warfare, etc.), but, as indicated, less visibly coercive means may take its place, such as the asymmetrical exchange of mediated forms of state recognition and accommodation in the context of colonial relations of power (Coulthard 2014, 15). These first two assumptions are further connected to Marx's "normative developmentalism" (Coulthard 2014, 9), that is, the teleological account of history. For Marx, PA was necessary for the eventual goal of history as communism or the classless society. This permits the view that noncapitalist (including precolonial) human societies are, in Marx's own words, "mediocre" (Marx 1992, 906, 928), that is, backward, primitive, and undeveloped, and so betrays a lingering Eurocentrism. This further suggests the view that PA and capitalism are historically inevitable processes that may ultimately be expected to yield benefits even for those violently drawn into the capitalist maelstrom. In fact, history's *telos* in the classless society may even be said to justify and redeem the bloody violence needed to achieve it (Fritsch 2005).

And yet, stripped of these problematic Eurocentric and teleological assumptions, PA remains a critically crucial explanation of the basic processes that, in the "long 16th century" (roughly 1450 to 1640; see Braudel 1949; Wallerstein 1972) and beyond, shaped the modern world and continue to structure its fundamental dynamic. PA offers a coherent account of slavery, colonialism, and the end of serfdom in Europe (Wallerstein 1972, 1974; Perelman 1984; 2000; Moore 2016). Original, or primitive, accumulation names the separation of the "immediate producers" (serfs, peasants, Indigenous peoples, and so on) from the land, by way of such signature processes as the European slave trade, colonial dispossession the world over, and the forcible removal of European peasants from the land. This separation is the precondition for the basic relation between capital and labor, as it freed the land for capital accumulation, reducing it to mere property and profit making, while forcing the populations that lived off the land to work as slaves or for wages. Privatization of the means of production and proletarianization of immediate producers, then, came to form capital as a social relation between owners of productive resources and wage laborers. The former privatized by force what were once collectively held lands and resources (including Indigenous territories), while, over time, enclosure and dispossession engendered a class of workers whose newly found "freedom," as Marx famously argued, consisted chiefly in having to move to wherever they could sell their labor power for access to basic necessities. Hence, the older Marxist focus on exploitation as the central concept of critical theory (Nielsen & Ware 1997).

While the privatization of land is overshadowed in Marx's account by the question of proletarianization, the emphasis has shifted more recently to dispossession and land grabbing as central concepts for critical theory (next to Coulthard 2014, see Butler and Athanasiou 2013; Nichols 2020). Arguably, these accounts, too, stand to gain from Indigenous (Deloria 1992, 2001; Simpson 2011; see also "Land Back," Yellowhead Institute 2019) and phenomenologico-ontological accounts of the role of land in the constitution of agency, identity, and community life (Gauthier 2016; Mei 2017). But here I would like to highlight, and address with the help of the phenomenological tradition, another aspect of PA, and one that I think tends to be neglected: the severing of generational ties, which often, and crucially, accompanied slavery, colonialism, and the end of serfdom. Separation from the land often also meant separation from community. If land is not only resource, but also identity conferring for many communities—as especially Indigenous anticapitalist struggles often maintain against Eurocentric extractivism (Coulthard 2014, 61)—then the avoidance of Eurocentrism in our analysis also involves the recognition that the division into aspects (dispossessing alienation from land and alienation from community) can only be a heuristic device.

In fact, the phenomenon of genealogical isolation or natal alienation cuts across both privatization and proletarianization: destroying communities and cultures often served the goal of access to their land. And we should recognize that, alongside the privatization of land, the proletarianization of people involves more than just inserting the goods and labor market between people and their means of production. Proletarianization requires cultural and psychological processes that structure the individualization and disciplining of bodies of labor. The enslaved and the colonized were usually deliberately separated from their families and communities, typically at a young age, and prohibited from speaking their mother tongue or practicing their culture. It is impossible in this context not to think of the residential school system of settler colonial states such as Australia and Canada, or the native boarding schools in the United States. In Canada, where I live on unceded Indigenous lands, more than 150,000 First Nations, Métis, and Inuit children were forced to attend church-run, government-funded schools between the 1870s and 1997. The recent (2021–2022) discoveries of unmarked graves of unnamed children near such schools, long known to exist among Indigenous peoples but neglected or denied by white settlers, rekindled the discussion of whether we should speak of attempts at cultural genocide or just plain genocide.[1]

According to the Truth and Reconciliation Commission report of 2015, Canada did indeed take the US boarding and "industrial" schools as a model, and both were modeled on the European reformatories for the urban poor that Foucault (focusing on the French rather than the British systems, and especially the Mettray Penal Colony) saw as emblematic of the "disciplinary power" and the "carceral system" that came to mark capitalist societies (Foucault 1995, 293/300ff.).[2] In Europe, too, poor children were often seized from their families and institutionalized in the reformatories, with the aim at the production of "bodies that were both docile and capable," disciplined, and prepared for service in the military, in the school system, in factories, and so on (Foucault 1995, 294/301). The link to Foucault's work shows, I think, that the treatment of Indigenous peoples in settler colonial states, unique and uniquely brutal in many respects, is nonetheless part of the continuation of forms of original accumulation that structured modern capitalism and continues to shape it. Separation both from the land and from family and culture can be seen as preconditions, as well as core elements, of the disciplinary society that seeks to produce subjectivities serviceable to labor and commodity markets. If the Enlightenment championed freedom and individual rights, Foucault dryly remarks, it also invented the disciplines (222/224). The reference to Mettray, a penal colony Foucault sees as being emblematic of the "carceral archipelago" or "carceral continuum" (297/304), also indicates the link between PA (including slavery and colonialism) and widespread practices of incarceration, the latter being one of today's most prevalent forms of social death and natal alienation (Price 2015; Adelsberg, Guenther, and Zeman 2015).

We should ask, then, how or in what way the question of freedom intersects with the question of natal alienation, and how we can better integrate the phenomenon and its critique into a critical theory of modernity. As feminists and ecofeminists in particular have long argued, freedom as a critical concept demands reflection on the conditions of agency, including care relations and natural environments (Plumwood 1993). Critical theory should not just update the Marxist concept of alienation (Rosa 2013; Jaeggi 2014) but also link it to the account of PA and the non-Marxist—and, as we will see, broadly phenomenological—account of "natal alienation."

Orlando Patterson famously introduced natal alienation in the context of the history of slavery. Among the present effects of the ongoing legacy of slavery, especially in the United States, we must count racism; poverty among Blacks in particular; social, cultural, and political disenfranchisement; mass incarceration of young Blacks; and disproportionate police violence. In this context, scholars continue to take an interest in those aspects of slavery specific to natal alienation that help us grasp the scope and intensity of its impact on the affected individuals and cultures. In his 1982 historical study of slavery—from which I have, admittedly in a rather brutal fashion, merely extracted the elements of the concept I focus on here—Patterson describes natal alienation as the second, the "symbolic" or "cultural" constituent element of slavery, the first and physical constituent being brute force, ranging from the ever-present whip to death (Patterson 1982, 5). He elaborates as follows:

> I prefer the term "natal alienation," because it goes directly to the heart of what is critical in the slave's forced alienation, the loss of ties of birth in both ascending and descending generations. It also has the important nuance of a loss of native status, of deracination. It was this alienation of the slave from all formal, legally enforceable ties of "blood," and from any attachment to groups or localities other than those chosen for him by the master, that gave the relation of slavery its peculiar value to the master. The slave was the ultimate human tool, as imprintable and as disposable as the master wished. And this is true, at least in theory, of all slaves, no matter how elevated. (Patterson 1982, 7)

Natal alienation, then, refers to removal of an individual both from "ties of blood" and from "native status," and so to the loss of membership in any legitimate social order. Historically and sociologically, the term offers a useful way in which to understand one feature of (perhaps even a central aspect of) not only slavery, but also, as we heard, of genocide, human trafficking (e.g., of sex slaves; see Patterson 2012), forced migration, colonization and the residential school systems, and so on. Suitably adapted, natal alienation and the closely connected concept of "social death" might even be helpful if we are to talk about some of the harms involved in environmental and climate destabilization, which uproots not only those individuals who thereby become climate refugees, but also entire long-standing, long-settled societies, especially in low-lying coastal areas and islands such as Tuvalu and the Maldives. In this context, we should also recall Hannah Arendt's assessment of refugees after WWII as being denied "the right to have rights" (Arendt

1979 [1951], 296ff.), which can be understood as the unconditional right to belong to a political, status-conferring community. Kelly Oliver (in this volume) links this right to an Arendtian *amor mundi* that overcomes other forms of alienation, what Arendt calls "world alienation" and "earth alienation."

Forced removal from kin and culture tends to result in post-traumatic stress disorder as well as intergenerational trauma: harms that can last over many generations and that hamper human agency and freedom.³ Fanon's analysis of the psychological situation of racially oppressed subjects is, of course, the classic study of the effects of colonization—subjective effects that he describes, among other things, as "inferiority complexes," "psycho-existential complexes," and "alienation," although not as natal alienation (Fanon 1991, 14, 18, 25, 33, 48, et passim). However, in his view, these subjective effects can only be addressed when change is also brought about in the objective, material, and economic circumstances of the oppressive practices, as Coulthard's reading of Fanon stresses (2014, 33, 140).

From the perspective of a critical social theory capable of accounting for and critiquing some of the harms I just mentioned, a crucial question concerns what the phenomenon of natal alienation might tell us about the conditions under which human agency flourishes. Patterson stresses the loss of community over the loss of native habitat and largely fleshes out community in political terms ("legitimate social orders"), in symbolic terms (heritage, tradition, customs, language), and in terms of the obligations involved in family and kinship relations ("blood ties") (1982: 5). However, he notes that these social relations have a generational aspect to them, and it is this element that I wish to investigate further here. To be sure, the generational linkages seem most prevalent in kinship ties, but Patterson does not overlook the political and symbolic anchoring of "the living present in [a] conscious community of memory."⁴ Why are natal alienation and genealogical isolation not conducive to human freedom—a freedom that we otherwise may be more likely to associate with the ability to *leave behind* generational relations into which we are thrown? Why and in what way does intergenerational belonging constitute an indispensable element of agency or freedom, the human power to fashion and pursue ends of one's own? Why is natal alienation a form of alienation in the first place?

My overall argument is that what I would like to call "modern presentism"—an enduring feature of the legacy of primitive accumulation—tends to overlook the constitution of "the living present," the present of freedom, out of the social-ontological-cum-normative intersection and overlap of two sorts of intergenerational relations: past and present generations on the one hand, present and future generations on the other. By "presentism," I mean the favoring of the present at the expense of past and future generations (see Thompson 2005, 2010). By "social-ontological," I mean an account of the enabling conditions of individuals that focuses on such factors as space, historical time, and intersubjective relations. The account is "social-ontological-*cum-normative*" if the constitutive conditions entail obligations to oneself or to others. The claim then is that both backward- and forward-looking intergenerational relations are co-constitutive of human agency, and that is a central element in explaining why forced removal from these reciprocal relations is so devastating. Presentism would then be closely linked to modern individualism and atomism, to the belief that individuals are nonrelationally autonomous (Mackenzie and Stoljar 2000), as if free individuals could give birth to themselves, matricidally, as Derrida might say (2013, 91), without generational others—ancestors, parents, descendants, whether linked by blood ties or not. This individualist-presentist bias may explain in part why theories of justice often assume contemporaries as parties to justice, and intergenerational ethics usually abstracts from generational overlap (see Vergani, in this volume; Menga, in this volume; also Fritsch 2018, chapter 1). As Foucault suggests, increasing individualization in modernity should not, *pace* Durkheim, be seen as the cause of a new regime of power, but rather as its effect (Foucault 1995, 23/28).

Mortality and Natality

I adopt the normative ontology of human agency from the phenomenological tradition, broadly construed; for lack of space, I do not emphasize exegesis, but adopt and recontextualize what seems crucial to elucidating natal alienation. Given its central emphasis on temporality in the constitution of a human world—from Husserl's time-consciousness to Heidegger's historicity, from Arendt's natality to de Beauvoir's reflections on aging, from Levinas's fecundity to Derrida's living-on—the phenomenological tradition might reasonably be expected to offer central insights into intergenerational relations—the very reason for this anthology. Speaking generally, we may say that the phenomenological tradition stresses not only the belonging of individuals to historical lifeworlds but also elaborates the insight that the meaningfulness of the world—its capacity to render lives and actions meaningful—constitutively depends on the past and the future. This nonlinear account of time further implies that the dead and the not yet born are not as distant as one may have assumed: they are *with* us and *of* us in ways that modern presentism and individualism tend to overlook. Hence, intergenerational ethics does not have to *extend* an otherwise preferred or assumed presentist theoretical framework, let alone in ad hoc or piecemeal fashion (see Menga, this volume). Among the many possible routes opened up by phenomenology, let me render this more concrete by tracing a path from Heidegger to Arendt and Levinas.

We may begin with Heidegger's deepening of Husserl's intentionality thesis, the claim that consciousness is not a blank slate but, as consciousness-of-something, is necessarily related to things in the world (cf. Overgaard 2004). The deepening takes the form of characterizing human existence as "being-in-the-world": humans have been "thrown" into traditions and social relations that are not mere accidents, but constitutive elements of Dasein's disclosure of a meaningful world. Heidegger's ontological account of Dasein as disclosive of actionable possibilities by way of an authentic temporalizing in the face of death is also, thereby, "normative" to the extent that it insists that this temporalizing implies the ineluctable responsibility to appropriate inheritance for oneself (*Sichüberliefern*), so as to free up possibilities for understanding and action from the past for the future (Heidegger 1962, 435/383; §74).

For the Heidegger of *Being and Time*, the being of Dasein is characterized by *Sorge*, the care for its being not merely in the sense of survival, but in the sense of questioning inherited understandings of its being and the meaning thereof. While its own being, as well as being in general, is given to Dasein, since the meaning of being and its interpretation are initially taken over from tradition, the gift (*Gabe*) is always at the same time a task (*Auf-gabe*): in contrast to, say, a stone, being for Dasein has to be interpreted and assumed. The "ultimate demand" for Dasein, says Heidegger, is that it "takes upon itself again, expressly and explicitly, its own being-there and be responsible for it" (Heidegger 2004, 254). In this "taking up," not only does the gift or event of being precede the self, but the self in fact comes about only in such a responding or corresponding. Rewriting Kant's "respect for the moral law," Heidegger writes: "Only in responsibility [*Verantwortlichkeit*] does the self first reveal [*enthüllt*] itself, and indeed the self not in a general sense, as the knowledge of an I in general, but the self as in each case mine [*als das jeweils einzelne faktische Ich*]" (Heidegger 1997, 194).

Responsible appropriation of being's gift, however, requires singularly facing up to one's mortality. In *Being and Time*, Heidegger famously argues that a world, understood as the context within which entities and possibilities for action appear meaningful, arises for an agent in confrontation with death: only "being-for-death" permits the authentic temporalizing from out of the future that allows entities and the agent herself to appear in a meaning-conferring context of reference (Heidegger 1962; for discussion, see e.g., Caputo 1988; Gethmann 1993; Dahlstrom 2001). This relation to death is necessary for an agent who has to grasp the present moment not as "is" but as "to be": ripe with futural possibilities to be actualized by the agent herself against the background she has inherited alongside others.

Although he uses the word "generation" sparingly, Heidegger is aware that this account of human agency places Dasein into inextricable generational relations.[5] The two arguably most well-known criticisms of this account extend and deepen its intergenerationality. The first is Arendt's argument that Heidegger's account of the finite temporality of agency illegitimately privileges death over birth; the second critique is Levinas's claim that Heidegger's death privileges solitude over sociality. Arendt argues that natality, the fact of being born, is not just an accident from which an account of moral personhood may abstract but is central to human agency (Arendt 1958). Birth indicates that humans are both of this world, empirically and corporeally belonging to its facticity and history, yet never coincide with it on account of birth's resistance to conscious grasp and causal explanation. Birth exceeds the memory of those born and, more generally, remains irreducible to natural laws. Natality means that a human being is not one with its birth or its natural kind, for as creative, free beings that give rise to something new against the background of inherited circumstances, we are not born once and for all but, rather, remain in the process of being born.

Human natality, then, comprises being thrown as a body into unchosen circumstances, and the demand to appropriate these circumstances to the point of giving birth to something new, the hallmark of human action (Arendt 1958, 8–12, 246–47).[6] If birth is a constitutive feature of agency, then, as feminist elaborations of natality have argued, agency is intrinsically referred to previous others, birth-giving mothers above all (Durst 2004; Diprose 2009; Cavarero 2014). Human existence is, in Lisa Guenther's felicitous phrase, a "being-from-others" (Guenther 2008). The relation to previous generations is not just mediated by inheritance in the form of language, culture, norms, habits, and institutions, but also necessitates corporeal, intimate relations, care for material and symbolic needs, and so on. Agency comes with intricate social and moral relations, among which Patterson's natal alienation stresses, above all, parental obligations (Patterson 1982: 5ff.).

Turning now to mortality, the embodied nature of freedom demands that it also be related to the threat of violence, to passive exposure to forces beyond human freedom, including death and other people. According to

Levinas's critical reading of Heidegger (Levinas 1969, Levinas 2001), mortality is constitutive of moral agency in that vulnerability must be understood on the basis of death as the ultimate and utterly unknowable imminence of a time we cannot anticipate. In contrast, in its invulnerability, an immortal being could not become the object of moral concern. According to Heidegger's argument, it also could not disclose meaningful, actionable possibilities. Like natality, then, mortality is not accidental to agency; subjects must access death in some form. However, Levinas argues against Heidegger that death is not accessible "as such" but only indirectly, by way of, or at least not without, other people.[7] To experience meaning-conferring death as a threat to be avoided, we mix (or have already mixed) the experience of a foreign will with death; hence, the widespread personifications of death (the Grim Reaper, Thanatos, Yama, etc.). Without the social dimension, death could not be understood in its menacing approach from the outside as something beyond my knowledge or control. Further, as Levinas argues in departure from Husserl, understanding in general requires the presence of a judging Other to confirm my reidentifications of objects and thus my access to an objective world beyond what Levinas calls its "mythical format" (1969, 140/149), that is, a world where objects could, for example, disappear at any moment (Crowell 2012; Mensch 2015). Understanding death thus demands exposure to the face of an other. Accessing one's own temporalizing disclosure cannot bypass other people. However, the other is also mortal and vulnerable, so that their judgment on me is not just an affirmation or negation of my own perspective, but a demand that I let them live, possibly beyond my own death. On the face of the other, mortality issues both the threat of murder and the imperative to let the other live. Agents are born as mortals surpassed by a world of future people.

On this view, the interpersonality of access to death entails that my death does not amount to nothingness, at least not the existentialists' nothingness of anxiety (Levinas 1969, 266/298). Constitutively, there is a world beyond death: the world of future generations. For access to their own world of action and meaning, agents must have a relation to others whose futurity in principle outlives the agent's time. Hence, against Heidegger's being-towards-death, Levinas speaks of human existence as "being-against-death" (Levinas 1969: 224/247, 235/261). More strongly still, agency is conceived as "being-for-beyond-my-death" [*l'être-pour-au-delà-de-ma-mort*], a generative being "for a time that would be without me" (Levinas 1987b: 93/45). Freedom and responsibility thus can also be characterized as "fecundity" (Levinas 1969: 267) and, no doubt problematically (Chanter 2001, Gürtler 2001), as "paternity" (without, of course, making agency depend on biological parenthood). If, as we just saw, a meaningful world is disclosed only in confrontation with a death that also commands us to let the other live, to give the gift of life beyond our own, then meaning is constitutively referred to and depends on the relation of the present to a future time belonging to others, including overlapping and nonoverlapping future people. As Samuel Scheffler has argued beyond the phenomenological tradition, many of our current projects depend on future generations (Scheffler 2013, 2020).

Here, too, Arendt's reinterpretation of Heidegger's "mortality" in terms of "natality" may be seen to concur with Levinas. In *The Human Condition*, Arendt writes:

> The miracle that saves the world, the realm of human affairs, from its normal, "natural" ruin is ultimately the fact of natality, in which the faculty of action is ontologically rooted. It is, in other words, the birth of new men and the new beginning, the action they are capable of by virtue of being born. Only the full experience of this capacity can bestow upon human affairs faith and hope, those two essential characteristics of human existence which Greek antiquity ignored altogether. (Arendt 1958, 246)

Arendtian *amor mundi*, then, seems to commit us to love of new people and new beginnings, beyond our own natural ruin. Natal alienation is best grasped in its relation to natality as well as to "world alienation" (see Oliver, this volume).

Critical Theory

The conditions of human agency, on this phenomenological-ontological sketch, involve the temporal connectedness of human lives across birth and death. Birth and death are not merely empirical facts of life, but necessary features of agents who confront the world not as is, but as to be—full of possibilities for change by action and reinterpretation, and thus as meaningful. This is what we can learn from Arendt and Heidegger as well as Levinas, albeit in different ways. But birth relates us to forebears and death to descendants, intergenerational relations that are thus also co-constitutive of the world understood as meaningful and alterable. That is why forced removal from ancestors and progeny is devastating for agency and meaning-making. Agency is constitutively tied to ancestors and descendants.

These ties should not be interpreted in a particularist and deterministic way: no doubt, freedom also consists in un-binding and re-binding such bonds in their specificity. In the definition of natal alienation as forced removal from kin and community, it is not only the removal but also the force that is crucial, including the violence of cutting ties of love and care. The force is directed against the free will whose general conditions we are tracing here as one of the elements of freedom. After all, the intergenerational web is crisscrossed by Levinasian discontinuity or what he calls diachrony (1987a, 105; 1998, 7/20 et passim) as well as by Arendtian natality and its fashionings of new beginnings in a necessarily plural political world. Nonetheless, at this level of general conditions, private and political relationships must be seen to include not only living co-presence, but also a moment that points beyond contemporary life to a time both before and after the present.

In moral and political terms, we may say, the present is constituted by two reciprocally conditioning forms of involuntary asymmetrical reciprocity: the present receives gifts and benefits from previous generations that are, individually and collectively, constitutive; in return, the present owes memory and gratitude, in the case of previous but overlapping generations, also care, attention, and the like.[8] With respect to subsequent generations, the present is, in turn, the donor, but also already a recipient: to wit, the recipient of the possibility of a meaningful world, without which, as Levinas puts it, actions would appear to be "desperate blows of a head struck against the wall" (Levinas 1969: 236/263). However autonomous and discontinuous, children carry a promise—to pick up Arendt's words, a faith or a hope—that not all was in vain. In turn, they demand, at the very least, a habitable world. As Liebsch (in this volume) and Guenther (2006a, b) have argued—both with reference to Levinas—giving birth implies the promise to render acceptable the life thus given. Generativity, biological and nonbiological, is inseparable from the promise of a habitable world, and this promise entails offering the means by which the next generation can come to reaffirm the acts that generated them, even if these acts will always remain insufficiently justified.

On this basis, we may be better able to understand the wrong of natal alienation. Given that the social and normative webs of generations may be expressed in terms of (albeit odd and often denied[9]) forms of reciprocity, we may be tempted to critique such wrongs as consisting principally in cutting off relations of reciprocity. And in fact, much of the normativity involved in intergenerational relations has been formulated as varying forms of reciprocity, a term common among sociologists, social anthropologists, and, above all, economists (who, however, typically neglect nonfinancial transfers).[10] However, what I think the phenomenological-ontological account permits us to see is that what is at stake in natal alienation is more than reciprocity withheld, ordinarily understood as refusing the receipt and donation of obligatory benefits and gifts. While reciprocity is an important normative concept in many contexts involving intergenerational justice, natal alienation goes to the heart of agency itself, to the extent that freedom in the living present depends on the nonliving, the dead and the unborn. Forcibly removing someone from their parents and/or from a wider community of memory is not just—though that is obviously bad enough—to withhold parental care, love, and attention, and this or that memory, heritage, language, and culture. Rather, genealogical isolation also tends towards denying an elemental condition of the person and their agency. Similarly, separation from one's children and other minors in one's community, actual or threatened, removes, or significantly weakens, access to a future world of meaning on which present agency draws. To the extent that PA built the modern capitalist world by systematically cutting or weakening generational ties and fostering a presentist individualism, its difficulties responding to long-term threats, such as environmental destabilization, are perhaps no coincidence. Just as modern capitalism entails the systematic conditions for exploitation, so it also generates the systematic conditions for natal alienation and matricidal presentism or buck-passing short-termism, and thus intergenerational injustice.

I would like to conclude with a few telegraphic pointers regarding the critical theory I promised at the outset as suggested by such a normative social ontology.

First, it might be helpful to give some philosophical, conceptual underpinning to the historical claim that individual freedom in modernity is a response to slavery. In a follow-up to his book on slavery, Patterson argued that freedom must be understood as slavery's antithesis (Patterson 1991). This historical point, if it can be defended, should not lead us to overlook that, philosophically and politically, freedom draws on several sources for its enabling conditions and defining features. Here, I mean only to suggest that intergenerational relations are one such (albeit co-constitutive) element. If freedom can hardly be conceived without responsibility, we should, with Levinas, grasp this responsibility as inseparable from what Anne O'Byrne has called our generational being (2010, 6, 41). The pair slavery-freedom would then be matched by the couple natal alienation-generational being.

Second, the claim that agency draws on a past before one's birth and a future beyond one's death is not meant to suggest that lives spent without having or adopting children of one's own are meaningless. The connection between presently lived meaning and future people, though experienced by many to be direct, is here merely claimed to be indirect, passing by way of culture, tradition, language, society, communities, political institutions, and nature, or what I have elaborated as the earth (Fritsch 2018, chapter 5): these supra-individual, quasi-holistic, and shared elements of life would lose almost all of their meaning if there were no afterlife—human or perhaps nonhuman—to continue and transformatively inherit them (see Scheffler 2013). This indirect connection invites nonprocreative people to participate in legacy creation and what psychologists call generativity: the always partial and conflicted conferral of meaning on one's life by leaving positive traces beyond one's death (McAdams and de St. Aubin 1998; Feiler and Wade-Benzoni 2009). Levinas, too, insists that fecundity is not merely a biological notion, though he also points out that social ontology does not stand above biology in the way Heidegger's fundamental ontology had hoped (Levinas 1969, 247/225, 277/254ff.).

Third, given the different roles men and women play, for biological and cultural reasons, in giving birth, nurturing, and care (not only for the young but often also for the elderly), the critical theory that understands the centrality of intergenerational relations will have to avoid an abstractive egalitarian universalism. A universalism that trusts in normatively contentful accounts of the human sufficiently above gender pluralities to disregard them is in jeopardy of becoming repressively heteronormative. Norms and policies that foster freedom must always be double-checked against their particular and possibly differential implications for women as well as nonbinary and queer folks, especially if a primary concern is the effects of such norms and policies on "the child" and future people (Edelman 2004; Fritsch 2017b).

The third point leads to the fourth, for being wary of accounts of freedom and agency that tend towards abstractive universalism should not lead us towards biological-genealogical determinism. The former tends to miss constitutive intergenerational relations in part because it attenuates embodiment, and thus the role of natality and mortality. In stressing embodiment and filiation, however, critical theory must avoid embracing the view that one's body, race, bloodline, family, and culture spell out one's destiny, a fate that one must affirm (Guenther 2012).[11] While freedom is inseparable from intergenerational relations, these relations are not predetermined in terms of kinship or culture, let alone "race." The tension between being "thrown" into unchosen inheritance and its critically filtering appropriation and relaunching—to the point, perhaps, of voluntary deracination—is constitutive of freedom.

Finally, my major concluding point regarding critical theory circles back to primitive accumulation. I have sought to suggest that to the list of basic critical concepts, including exploitation, domination, inequality, discipline, and the like, the critical theory of modernity should add both dispossession (as divorce from land) and natal alienation or genealogical isolation, and perhaps asymmetrical reciprocity. I must leave it open here how genealogical alienation should be related to Arendtian alienation and the concepts of alienation offered by Jaeggi (2014) and Rosa (2013). I note in passing, however, that Rosa's recent account of alienation and its antonym "resonance" (Rosa 2021) is already linked to a highly pertinent historical-sociological account of intergenerational relations. Briefly, a major source of alienation from world relations is claimed to be social acceleration, which tends to disconnect generations from each other. In premodern societies, we can summarize, social change occurred at a generation-transcending pace in that the three or four generations that tend to overlap at any given time share many practices and planning horizons in an inherited lifeworld. In the classical modern era and into the twentieth century, social change in modern capitalist societies became largely generational, neither predetermining individual and collective identities nor undermined by constant reinvention. In late modernity or "postmodernity" (Harvey 1990), acceleration has led to a "contraction of the present" that renders social change *intra*generational, disconnecting the overlapping generations from each other and their inherited lifeworlds while shrinking the planning horizons of individuals and collective polities such as democratic institutions (Rosa 2013, 109ff.; see also Scheuermann 2004, Fritsch, 2023).

A critical theory of modernity that seeks to connect the sociology of acceleration with the critique of alienation, then, may stand to learn from elaborating and integrating the phenomenological account of natal alienation I sought to sketch here. As indicated, natal alienation (and arguably social acceleration too) should be understood against the broad background of original accumulation (including dispossession and divorce from land) and to modern presentism, that is, the current disregard, in our times of environmental destabilization, for the earth as well as for future generations. In this way, the theory of intergenerationality positions itself critically against forms of presentism that underplay the role of the past in constituting the present, as perhaps most clearly in Enlightenment definitions of freedom as "self-beginning" (à la Kant) and the related stress on a clean slate or tabula rasa, such as the claim that modernity must "construct" its moral and other resources—its own legitimacy—only from out of itself (Blumenberg 1985; Habermas 1987). But presentism also tends to misconstrue the relation between present and future, often assuming a version of historical progress according to which contemporaries contribute to the future without getting anything in return.[12] In Rawls's words, "We can do something for posterity but it can do nothing for us" (Rawls 1971: 291). By contrast to this complaint of what Rawls calls "chronological unfairness"—"those who live later profit from the labor of their predecessors without paying the same price" (Rawls 1971: 291)—our present must recognize that it already draws an advance credit on future generations. It is not only that we must overcome this optimistic view of progress in general and of capital accumulation in particular, a view that PA should always have put in doubt, and that today has become particularly questionable because of environmental devastations such as climate change, resource depletion, and loss of biodiversity. It is also that we must recognize that the advance credit comes with a freedom-constituting responsibility that has already pulled our being beyond the present.

What the phenomenological argument against presentism can help us see, above all, is that the relation to the dead and future people is not a relation yet to be achieved. To say that the natal-mortal relation to non-present times is co-constitutive of the present is to say that the self-relation of contemporaries—to themselves and to each other—is also a relation to the past and the future beyond one's own time. Rather than linear time, it is the present's diremption, its non-presence to itself, that first of all entails the obligatory relation to the dead and the unborn.

Presentism, however, also consists in figuring the future as merely a continuation of the present. To construe the future as one more, one further, future present, should be seen as a narcissistic overburdening of future people. To insist on the advance "credit" drawn in the present on the future is not to homogenize different times, as if the present and the future could indeed be calculated in terms of equivalences, like debt, credit, and money. The future is both a continuation and a radical novelty, both constrained and molded by the present, as well as forever beyond its reach. Descendants may not be oppressed to take over the present's projects, shoring up contemporary subjectivities over and against a death denied or disavowed. As Levinas puts it so well, speaking of the child as figuring the futural relation in general: "*C'est moi étranger à soi*" (1969, 267/299). We can translate this as "It is me a stranger to myself" or "It is me, a stranger to oneself." The "child"—the future person, biological or not—is not me in identification (parent and child are one) or in appropriation (the child is mine), but in "trans-substantiation" (1969, 269/301): the child in fact makes me a stranger to myself, renders my "substance" one of an ongoing trans-cending (Guenther 2006a, 78). As a result, I am not at home in my own home. My home is delivered over to the other, who makes me transcend myself towards a temporal alterity I cannot appropriate for myself. I respond to this alterity as something not made by me, but in fact (and from the perspective of linear time, paradoxically) preceding me, beckoning from a future always already beyond my reach. Levinas calls this a transcending towards the one who transcends, a "fecundity engendering fecundity" that "accomplishes goodness: above and beyond the sacrifice that imposes a gift, the gift of the power of giving" (1969, 269/301).

Having received the power of giving from beyond myself, this transcending in my life is a responsibility, and one that consists not in charging the child with one's responsibilities and projects, but in assuming the responsibilities of the future other in the present. In this way, the Levinasian "infinity" of intergenerational responsibility has implications, for example, for such burning issues as climate destabilization. In the face of a generation's genuine possibility of severely, and perhaps irremediably, compromising the wherewithal of future people to correspond to their obligations to their next generation, mitigation as well as adaptation (and compensation, or—to use the UN terms as of the Paris Accord 2015—"loss and damage") may be mandated not first of all by the rights of future generations or future people as a collective (and distant) entity, but by the responsibility to enable future others to handle their duties to others.

No doubt the dividing line between charging the future with one's projects and enabling it to address its responsibilities is not pregiven but to be negotiated and redrawn ever anew. To stress that the relation to the future is above all a mortal-natal relation to inappropriable alterity, one marked by moral, political, and environmental responsibilities, it would indeed be fascinating to figure the future subject not in the first instance as a human child, but merely as living being: as Derrida once did, as ant or bird.[13] In the present context, however, to insist on future people as radical alterity in the present means first of all that sustainability or sustainable development should not be construed as sustaining a capitalist modernity born in primitive accumulation.

Notes

1. "Cultural genocide" is the term the Truth and Reconciliation Commission settled on in its 2015 report:

> The history of residential schools presented in this report commenced by placing the schools in the broader history of the global European colonization of Indigenous peoples and their lands. Residential schooling was only a part of the colonization of Aboriginal people. The policy of colonization suppressed Aboriginal culture and languages, disrupted Aboriginal government, destroyed Aboriginal economies, and confined Aboriginal people to marginal and often unproductive land. When that policy resulted in hunger, disease, and poverty, the federal government failed to meet its obligations to Aboriginal people. That policy was dedicated to eliminating Aboriginal peoples as distinct political and cultural entities and must be described for what it was: a policy of cultural genocide. (TRC Report 2015, 133)

However, some argued already at the time of its publication in 2015 that the term "cultural genocide" glosses over the real, physical genocide the state of Canada committed on Indigenous populations (see e.g., https://rabble.ca/blogs/bloggers/pamela-palmater/2015/06/what-happened-residential-schools-was-genocide-what-matters-j). See also Herschkopf et al. 2011 and Akhavan 2016.

2. The French penal colony of Mettray—the principal object of Foucault's analysis—is indirectly present in the 2015 TRC report. The report cites Driver (1990) on Mettray as a model for the British reformatories, which in turn became models for the Canadian residential schools: "The model for these residential schools for Aboriginal children, both in Canada and the United States, did not come from the private boarding schools to which members of the economic elites in Britain and Canada sent their children. Instead, the model came from the reformatories and industrial schools that were being constructed in Europe and North America for the children of the urban poor. The British parliament adopted the Reformatory Schools Act in 1854 and the Industrial Schools Act in 1857" (TRC 2015, 57). The appended note at this point refers to Driver, who discusses Foucault's work on Mettray.

3. As a recent study of the Canadian residential school system concluded, "On an individual level, the long-term impact of residential school experiences has left many former students facing significant psychological challenges. These range from heightened feelings of anger, anxiety, low self-esteem, and depression to post-traumatic stress disorder and high rates of suicide, among other things." See https://www.thecanadianencyclopedia.ca/en/article/intergenerational-trauma-and-residential-schools.

4. Here is the full passage:

> Not only was the slave denied all claims on, and obligations to, his parents and living blood relations but, by extension, all such claims and obligations on his more remote ancestors and on his descendants.

He was truly a genealogical isolate. Formally isolated in his social relations with those who lived, he also was culturally isolated from the social heritage of his ancestors. He had a past, to be sure. But a past is not a heritage. Everything has a history, including sticks and stones. Slaves differed from other human beings in that they were not allowed freely to integrate the experience of their ancestors into their lives, to inform their understanding of social reality with the inherited meanings of their natural forebears, or to anchor the living present in any conscious community of memory. That they reached back for the past, as they reached out for the related living, there can be no doubt. Unlike other persons, doing so meant struggling with and penetrating the iron curtain of the master, his community, his laws, his policemen or patrollers, and his heritage. (Patterson 1982: 5)

5. See Heidegger 1962 (429/508, §74), where "generation" is placed in quotation marks and referenced to Dilthey for fuller discussion (see also 1962, 41/27, §6). See also Heidegger 2002, his 1925 essay on Dilthey. Anne O'Byrne has analyzed the reference to generation in *Being and Time* as a suppression of birth: "The mention of . . . 'generation' . . . marks the moment when Heidegger might have embarked on a new attempt to elucidate the whole of Dasein's being by finally broaching that being as specifically generational, which is to say, natal, historical, and essentially with others" (O'Byrne 2010, 35). See also McMullin 2013.

6. I believe a comparable account, without using the word "natality," can be found in Levinas 1969, esp. 238ff. For more on this correspondence between Levinasian responsibility and Arendtian natality, see Astell 2006; Markovits 2009; Mensch 2015, 168ff.; Fritsch 2018.

7. Levinas writes: "Death, source of all myths, is *present* only in the Other, and only in him [sic] does it summon me urgently to my final essence, to my responsibility" (Levinas 1969: 179; Levinas's emphasis; cf. 233). Time does not permit me to go into the details of Levinas's argument in this context, an argument well investigated in the secondary literature (Beardsworth 1995; Rolland 1998; Chanter 2001; Köveker 2004; Cohen 2006; Klun 2007).

8. On asymmetrical reciprocity, see Fritsch 2017a; 2018, chapter 3; 2020.

9. It is a widely accepted claim in literature on intergenerational justice that no reciprocity is possible between generations, in particular not with future people; see Beckman and Page 2008, Page 2007; for an attempt at a counterargument, restricted to overlapping generations, see McCormick 2009. For a counterargument not so restricted, see Fritsch 2018, chapter 3.

10. Patterson seems to draw on some of this literature; for instance, in talking about the intergenerational relations from which slaves are forcibly and deliberately removed, Patterson distinguishes between ascending and descending relations (1982:

5). This language is quite common in social anthropology and sociology, intergenerational economics, and some philosophical literature on justice between generations (see Arrondel and Masson 2006; Kolm 2006; Gosseries 2009).

11. In her account of natal alienation and Levinas, from which I have taken much inspiration, Guenther (2012) shows that Levinas's work, especially the concept of fecundity, is in good measure inspired by rejecting such generational determinism, which he encountered early on in the form of Nazism. Guenther also argues that Levinasian fecundity remains insufficiently nuanced to negotiate the difficult passage between universalism and biological-generational determinism.

12. In this context, we do well to recall that the moral universalism of the European Enlightenment typically went along (and often still does go along) with a conception of progressive social-economic development that permits casting other "races" or "cultures" as backward (McCarthy 2009).

13. In conversation with Jean-Luc Nancy and Philippe Lacoue-Labarthe, Derrida notes that if *Dasein* is always *Mitsein*, then Heidegger cannot conceive of dying in entirely solitary terms. To think this togetherness in dying, neither dying for the people (as in the infamous paragraph 74 of *Being and Time*) nor being a member of a generation quite suffices for Derrida (2014, 21–22). He then links dying together to what he calls a "testamentary desire, the desire that *something* survive" of me "that does not come back to me" (23), what I called generativity above, the desire to leave a legacy. He then distances this desire from the Spinozist claim that "We feel and know by experience that we are immortal" and says: "[. . .] naturally, I don't believe in immortality. But I know that there is an I, a *me*, a living being who is related to itself through auto-affection, who might be a bird, and who will feel alive like me . . . When I am dead, there will be a bird, an ant, who will say "me" for me, and when someone says "me" for me, that's me" (26).

Bibliography

Page numbers after a "/" indicate the original of a translation.

Adelsberg, Geoffrey, Lisa Guenther, and Scott Zeman, eds. *Death and Other Penalties: Philosophy in a Time of Mass Incarceration*. New York: Fordham University Press.
Akhavan, Payam. 2016. "Cultural Genocide: Legal Label or Mourning Metaphor? *McGill Law Journal* 62 (1): 243–70.
Alfred, Taiaiake. 2005. *Wasáse: Indigenous Pathways of Actions and Freedom*. Peterborough, Ont.: Broadview Press.
Arendt, Hannah. 1979 [1951]. "The Decline of the Nation-State and the End of the Rights of Man." In *The Origins of Totalitarianism*. New York: Harcourt Brace Jovanovich.
Arendt, Hannah. 1954. *Between Past and Future*. New York: Viking Press.

———. 1958. *The Human Condition*. Chicago: University of Chicago Press.
Arrondel, Luc, and André Masson. 2006. "Altruism, Exchange or Indirect Reciprocity: What Do the Data on Family Transfers Show?" *Handbook of the Economics of Giving, Altruism and Reciprocity: Applications*. Vol. 2, edited by Serge-Christophe Kolm and Jean Mercier Ythier, 955–1053. Netherlands: Elsevier.
Beckman, Ludvig, and Edward A. Page. 2008. "Perspectives on Justice, Democracy, and Global Climate Change." *Environmental Politics* 17 (4): 527–35.
Blumenberg, Hans. 1985. *The Legitimacy of the Modern Age*. Translated by Robert M. Wallace. Cambridge: MIT Press.
Braudel, Fernand. 2017 [1949]. *La Méditerranée et le monde méditerranéen à l'époque de Philippe II*. Tomes 1–3. Paris: Colin.
Butler, Judith, and Athena Athanasiou. 2013. *Dispossession: The Performative in the Political*. Cambridge: Polity.
Caputo, John D. 1988. *Radical Hermeneutics: Repetition, Deconstruction, and the Hermeneutic Project*. Bloomington: Indiana University Press.
Cavarero, Adriana. 2014. "'A Child Has Been Born unto Us': Arendt on Birth" *philoSOPHIA* 4 (1): 12–30.
Chanter, Tina. 2001. *Time, Death, and the Feminine: Levinas with Heidegger*. Stanford: Stanford University Press.
Coulthard, Sean Glen. 2014. *Red Skin White Mask: Rejecting the Colonial Politics of Recognition*. Minneapolis: University of Minnesota Press.
Crowell, Steven. 2012. "Why Is Ethics First Philosophy? Levinas in Phenomenological Context." *European Journal of Philosophy* 23 (3): 564–88.
Dahlstrom, Daniel. 2001. *Heidegger's Concept of Truth*. Cambridge: Cambridge University Press.
Deloria, Vine Jr. 1992 (1972). *God Is Red: A Native View of Religion*. Golden: Fulcrum Publishing.
———. 2001. "Power and Place Equal Personality." In *Power and Place: Indian Education in America*, by Vine Deloria Jr. and Daniel Wildcat. Golden: Fulcrum Publishing.
Derrida, Jacques. 2013. "The Night Watch." In *Derrida and Joyce: Texts and Contexts*, edited by A. Mitchell and S. Slote. Albany: State University of New York Press.
———. 2014. *For Strasbourg: Conversations of Friendship and Philosophy*. Edited and translated by Pascale-Anne Brault and Michael Naas. New York: Fordham University Press.
Diprose, Rosalyn. 2009. "Women's Bodies Giving Time for Hospitality." *Hypatia* 24 (2): 142–63.
Driver, Felix. 1990. "Discipline Without Frontiers? Representations of the Mettray Reformatory Colony in Britain, 1840–1880." *Journal of Historical Sociology* 3 (3): 272–93.
Durst, Margaret. 2004. "Birth and Natality in Hannah Arendt." *Analecta Husserliana* 79: 777–97.

Edelman, Lee. 2004. *No Future: Queer Theory and the Death Drive*. Durham, NC: Duke University Press.

Fanon, Frantz. 1991 [1967/1952]. *Black Skin, White Masks*. Translated by Charles Lam Markman. London: Pluto Press.

Feiler, Daniel, and Kimberly A. Wade-Benzoni. 2009. "Death and Intergenerational Behavior: A Tale of Power and Immortality." In *The Impact of 9/11 on Psychology and Education*, edited by Matthew Morgan, 187–200. London: Palgrave Macmillan.

Foucault, Michel. 1977. *Discipline and Punish: The Birth of the Prison*. Translated by Alan Sheridan. New York: Vintage Books. Originally published as *Surveiller et Punir: Naissance de la Prison*. Paris: Gallimard, 1975.

Frederici, Silvia. 2004. *Caliban and the Witch: Women, the Body and Primitive Accumulation*. New York: Autonomedia.

Fritsch, Matthias. 2005. *The Promise of Memory: History and Politics in Marx, Benjamin, and Derrida*. Albany, NY: State University of New York Press.

———. 2017a. " 'La justice doit porter au-delà de la vie présente': Derrida on Ethics Between Generations." *Symposium* 21 (1): 231–53.

———. 2017b. "Between Generational Presentism and Reproductive Futurism: How to be Concerned About the Future of Children Without Becoming Repressively Heteronormative." In *Responsabilità verso le generazioni future: Una sfida al diritto, all'etica e alla politica*, edited by Fabio Ciaramelli and Ferdinando G. Menga. Naples: Editoriale Scientifica.

———. 2018. *Taking Turns with the Earth: Phenomenology, Deconstruction, and Intergenerational Justice*. Stanford: Stanford University Press.

———. 2020. "Asymmetrical Reciprocity in Intergenerational Justice." In *Future Design: Incorporating Preferences of Future Generations for Sustainability*, edited by Tatsuyoshi Saijo, 17–36. Berlin: Springer, 2020.

———. 2023. "Democratic Representation, Environmental Justice, and Future People." In *Representations and Rights of the Environment*, edited by Peter Stoett and Sandy Lamalle. Cambridge: Cambridge University Press.

Gosseries, Axel. 2009. "Three Models of Intergenerational Reciprocity." In *Intergenerational Justice*, edited by Axel Gosseries and Lukas H. Meyer. Oxford: Oxford University Press.

Guenther, Lisa. 2006a. *The Gift of the Other: Levinas and the Politics of Reproduction*. Albany: State University of New York Press.

———. 2006b. " 'Like a Maternal Body': Emmanuel Levinas and the Motherhood of Moses." *Hypatia* 21 (1): 119–36.

———. 2008. "Being-from-others: Reading Heidegger after Cavarero." *Hypatia* 23 (1): 99–118.

Guenther, Lisa. 2012. "Fecundity and Natal Alienation: Rethinking Kinship with Emmanuel Levinas and Orlando Patterson." *Levinas Studies* 7 (1): 1–19.

Gürtler, Sabine. 2001. *Elementare Ethik: Alterität, Generativität und Geschlechterverhältnis bei Emmanuel Lévinas*. München: Wilhelm Fink Verlag.
Habermas, Jürgen. 1987. *The Philosophical Discourse of Modernity*. Translated by Frederick G. Lawrence. Cambridge: MIT Press.
Harvey, David. 1990. *The Condition of Postmodernity*. Oxford: Blackwell.
———. 2005. "Accumulation by Dispossession." *The New Imperialism*. Oxford: Oxford University Press.
Heidegger, Martin. 1962. *Being and Time*. Translated by John Macquarrie and Edward Robinson. New York: Harper and Row. Originally published as *Sein und Zeit*. Tübingen: Max Niemeyer Verlag, 1984 [1927].
———. 1997. *Die Grundprobleme der Phänomenologie* (Sommersemester 1927). 3rd. ed. Edited by Friedrich-Wilhelm von Herrmann. Frankfurt: Klostermann.
———. 2002. "Wilhelm Dilthey's Research and the Struggle for a Historical Worldview" (1925). In *Supplements: From the Earliest Essays to Being and Time and Beyond*, edited by John van Buren. Albany: State University of New York Press.
———. 2004. *Die Grundbegriffe der Metaphysik. Welt - Endlichkeit—Einsamkeit* (Wintersemester 1929/30). 3rd ed. Edited by Friedrich-Wilhelm von Herrmann. Frankfurt: Klostermann.
Herschkopf, Jayme, Julie Hunter, and Laurel E Fletcher. 2011. "Genocide Reinterpreted: An Analysis of the Genocide Convention's Potential Application to Canada's Indian Residential School System." Draft report prepared for the Truth and Reconciliation Commission of Canada, Winnipeg, April 2011, unpublished.
Jaeggi, Rahel. 2014. *Alienation*. Translated by Frederick Neuhouser and Alan E. Smith. New York: Columbia University Press.
Kolm, Serge-Christophe. 2006. "Reciprocity: Its Scope, Rationales and Consequences." In *Handbook of the Economics of Giving, Altruism and Reciprocity*. Vol. 1, edited by S. Kolm and J. Mercier Ythier. Amsterdam: Elsevier.
Levinas, Emmanuel. 1969. *Totality and Infinity*. Translated by A. Lingis. Pittsburgh: Duquesne University Press. Originally published as *Totalité et infini. Essai sur l'extériorité*. La Haye: M. Nijhoff, 1961.
———. 1976. *Difficile liberté*. Paris: Albin Michel.
———. 1987a. *Time and the Other and Additional Essays*. Translated by Richard A. Cohen. Pittsburgh: Duquesne University Press. Originally published as *Le Temps et l'Autre*. Montpellier: Fata Morgana, 1980.
———. 1987b. "Meaning and Sense." In *Collected Philosophical Papers*, translated by Alphonso Lingis. The Hague: Martinus Nijoff. Originally published as *Humanisme de l'autre homme*. Paris: Le Livre de poche, 2012.
———. 1989. *The Levinas Reader*. Edited by Sean Hand. Oxford: Blackwell.
———. 1998. *Otherwise than Being, or Beyond Essence*. Translated by A. Lingis. Pittsburgh: Duquesne University Press. Originally published as *Autrement qu'être ou au-delà de l'essence*. La Haye: M. Nijhoff, 1974.

———. 2000. *God, Death, and Time*. Translated by Bettina Bergo. Stanford: Stanford University Press.

Mackenzie, Catriona, and Natalie Stoljar, eds. 2000. *Relational Autonomy: Feminist Perspectives on Autonomy, Agency, and the Social Self*. Oxford: Oxford University Press.

Marx, Karl. 1992. *Capital Volume 1*. Translated by Ben Fowkes. London: Penguin.

McAdams, Dan P., and Ed de St. Aubin. 1998. *Generativity and Adult Development: How and Why We Care for the Next Generation*. Washington, DC: American Psychological Association.

McCarthy, Thomas. 2009. *Race, Empire, and the Idea of Human Development*. Cambridge: Cambridge University Press.

McCormick, Hugh. 2009. "Intergenerational Justice and the Non-reciprocity Problem." *Political Studies* 57: 451–58.

McMullin, Anne. 2013. *Time and the Shared World: Heidegger on Social Relations*. Evanston, IL: Northwestern University Press.

Mei, Todd S. 2017. *Land and the Given Economy: An Essay in the Hermeneutics and Phenomenology of Dwelling*. Evanston, IL: Northwestern University Press.

Mensch, James. 2015. *Levinas's Existential Analytic: A Commentary on* Totality and Infinity. Evanston, IL: Northwestern University Press.

Nichols, Robert. 2020. *Theft Is Property! Dispossession and Critical Theory*. Durham: Duke University Press.

Nielsen, Kai, and Robert Ware. 1997. *Exploitation: Key Concepts in Critical Theory*. Atlantic Highlands, NJ: Humanities Press International.

O'Byrne, Anne. 2010. *Natality and Finitude*. Bloomington: Indiana University Press.

Oliver, Kelly. 2015. *Earth and World: Philosophy after the Apollo Mission*. New York: Columbia University Press.

———. "Earth: Love It or Leave It." In *Eco-Deconstruction: Derrida and Environmental Philosophy*, edited by Matthias Fritsch, Philippe Lynes, and David Wood. New York: Fordham University Press.

Overgaard, Soren. 2004. *Being in the World in Husserl and Heidegger*. Dordrecht: Kluwer Academic Publishers.

Page, Edward A. 2007. "Fairness on the Day after Tomorrow: Justice, Reciprocity, and Global Climate Change." *Political Studies* 55 (1): 225–42.

Patterson, Orlando. 1982. *Slavery and Social Death*. Cambridge: Harvard University Press.

———. 1991. *Freedom in the Making of Western Culture*. New York: Basic Books.

———. 2012. "Trafficking, Gender, and Slavery: Past and Present." In *The Legal Understanding of Slavery: From the Historical to the Contemporary*, edited by Jean Allain. Oxford: Oxford University Press.

Perelman, Michael. 1984. *Classical Political Economy: Primitive Accumulation and the Social Division of Labor*. Totowa, NJ: Rowman & Allanheld.

———. 2000. *The Invention of Capitalism: Classical Political Economy and the Secret History of Primitive Accumulation*. Durham: Duke University Press.
Plumwood, Val. 1993. *Feminism and the Mastery of Nature*. London: Routledge.
Price, Joshua M. 2015. *Prison and Social Death*. Ithaca: Rutgers University Press.
Rawls, John. 1971. *A Theory of Justice*. Cambridge: Harvard University Press.
Rosa, Hartmut. 2013. *Alienation and Acceleration: Towards a Critical Theory of Late-Modern Temporality*. Ann Arbor: University of Michigan Press.
———. *Resonance: A Sociology of Our Relationship to the World*. Translated by James Wagner. Cambridge: Polity.
Scheffler, Samuel. 2013. *Death and the Afterlife*. New York: Oxford University Press.
———. 2020. *Why Worry About Future Generations?* Oxford: Oxford University Press.
Scheuerman, William. 2004. *Liberal Democracy and the Social Acceleration of Time*. Baltimore: Johns Hopkins University Press.
Simpson, Leanne. 2011. *Dancing on Our Turtle's Back: Stories of Nishnaabeg Re-Creation, Resurgence and a New Emergence*. Winnipeg: Arbeiter Ring Press.
Smith, Andrea. 2005. *Conquest: Sexual Violence and American Indian Genocide*. Boston: South End Press.
Tatransky, Tomáš. 2008. "A Reciprocal Asymmetry? Levinas's Ethics Reconsidered." *Ethical Perspectives* 15 (3): 293–307.
Thompson, Dennis. F. 2005. "Democracy in Time: Popular Sovereignty and Temporal Representation." *Constellations* 12 (2): 245–61.
———. 2010. "Representing Future Generations: Political Presentism and Democratic Trusteeship." *Critical Review of International Social and Political Philosophy* 13 (1): 17–37.
Truth and Reconciliation Commission of Canada. 2015. *Honouring the Truth, Reconciling for the Future: Summary of the Final Report of the Truth and Reconciliation Commission of Canada*. Cited as TRC Report 2015. http://www.trc.ca/assets/pdf/Honouring_the_Truth_Reconciling_for_the_Future_July_23_2015.pdf.
Wallerstein, Immanuel. 1972. "Three Paths of National Development in Sixteenth-Century Europe." *Studies in Comparative International Development* 7: 95–101.
———. 1974. *The Modern World-System I: Capitalist Agriculture and the Origins of the European World-Economy in the Sixteenth Century*. New York: Academic Press.
Yellowhead Institute. 2019. "Land Back. A Yellowhead Institute Red Paper" Report 2019. https://redpaper.yellowheadinstitute.org/.
Young, Iris Marion. 1996. "Asymmetrical Reciprocity. On Moral Respect, Wonder, and Enlarged Thought." *Constellations* 3 (3): 340–63.

9

In Our Element

Rebecca van der Post

Prelude: A Post-Progress World

In a small shop in a quieter corner of Rome, I ask if the shirt comes in a bigger size. "Oh miss," the shop assistant protests sweetly, "it IS a bigger size."

Many years later, turning my thoughts for this chapter towards a future that is somehow losing its shine, and finding myself marooned for the umpteenth time in the age-old conundrum of how or where to catch a guiding glimpse of a better world, I hear a smiling Italian voice saying to me, "Oh miss, it IS a better world." And it strikes me that there is an unhappy ring of truth to these words, for, whatever the discomforts of our ill-fitting present, the future seems on track to be very much worse. Which is, perhaps, why I find myself haunted by these few brief lines from Oscar Wilde: "A map of the world that does not include Utopia is not even worth glancing at, for it leaves out the one country at which Humanity is always landing. And when Humanity lands there it looks out, and, seeing a better country, sets sail. Progress is the realisation of Utopias" (2001, 141). As a teleocratic[1] civilization, our present is powered by the future that it adumbrates. So perhaps it is unsurprising that for Western modernity, as a capitalist technocracy in thrall to its industrialized visions of perpetual material transformation, even Utopia is a disposable item. But from our moorings in the present, the future looks less like a land of beckoning promise and more like a repository for those problems that we cannot resolve, or choose not to resolve, in the here and now. The very word "progress" seems to reverberate with the gnawing intuition that somehow or other we missed the mark: that in our restless impulse to transform our world, and without quite noticing when or where or how, we sailed on past peak progress and are now beating our way against the laws of diminishing return. In the words of Kingsnorth and Hine: "Even within the prosperous liberal societies of the West progress has, in many ways, failed to deliver the goods. Today's generation are demonstrably less content, and consequently less optimistic, than those that went before . . . They fear crime, social breakdown, overdevelopment, environmental collapse. They do not believe that the future will be better than the past" (2014, 7–8). Far from giving us pause, however, the intensifying presentiment of disaster ahead seems only to increase our thirst for ever more radical change in ever more dimensions of existence, and finds us setting sail in ever faster boats to ever further shores. As George Steiner wrote, with words that have surely only grown in relevance in the fifty years since their first delivery: "We no longer experience history as ascendant. There are too many cardinal points at which our lives are more threatened, more prone to arbitrary servitude and extermination, than were those of civilized men and women in the West at any time since the sixteenth century . . . Yet, at the same time, our material forward motion is immense and obvious" (1971, 68–69).

And so we muscle onwards, for such is our westernized way. But in this strange, post-progress society that is our home, we are caught within the vertiginous and contradictory evolutions of a civilization whose motivating and legitimating belief in its own continuing improvement is withdrawing from the way of life and the framework of meaning and possibility that it has bequeathed. Ours is a post-progress world, not because global transformation at human hand is unthinkable or unworkable, but because the possibility of any such transformation yielding a better world is increasingly felt to be draining away from this one. In this way, it is not only the future as we imagine it but also the present as we experience it that is undergoing profound transformation. Adorno once remarked that "the horror is that for the first time we live in a world in which we can no longer imagine a better one" (Adorno and Horkheimer 1956, 40), but the horror, now, is that we live in a world in which it is becoming increasingly difficult to imagine anything but a *worse* one. Casting an eye towards the crisis in childhood mental health, or recent eruptions of anti-natalism (as but two obvious examples), we appear to be poised at a critical juncture where the general forecast is rendering the present uninhabitable to the extent that our own enduring contribution to posterity may well be a way of being human, an experience of selfhood, that is becoming unbearable in itself and for which nonbeing is becoming the coherent, desirable, and *decent* option: a state of affairs that brings its own disquieting inflexions to the question of intergenerational justice. So it seems to me that there are pressing concerns as to the impact not only of the present upon the future but of the future upon the present; and it strikes me that under the doctrine of progress, the perpetual filtration of the present through the future has become incapacitating to both.

The question, then, is how to rehabilitate the present for those within it when progress is losing its grip; the future confronting our children, their children, and their children's children is looking grim; and the "better country" ahead seems less like an article of faith and more like a reprimand.

I am waist deep in treacherous waters here, because of course—as is noted in the introduction to this volume, and as Menga points out—there is a growing and hugely important body of work tracing humanity's troubled trajectory in terms of the "presentism" of Western modernity and the "preeminence of the contemporary" (Menga, this volume), so that the call to take the present as the primary target of our regenerative efforts seems to demand justification. But, as I see it, the problems lapping against the shores of the future are not to do with the preeminence of *the* contemporary, but the preeminence of *our* contemporary. In Jean-Luc Nancy's words: "No culture has lived as our modern culture has in the endless accumulation of archives and expectations. No culture has made present the past and the future to the point of removing the present from its own passage" (Nancy 2014, 40). Another way of putting this is that the problem with our Western presentism is that it erases the present. And so, although this chapter is preoccupied with the impact of our outcome-oriented, goal-dependent worldview and teleocratic subjectivity upon present conditions and well-being, my suggestion is not at all that we must therefore ignore the plight of future generations, but that their well-being, like ours, depends upon the restoration of the present to its own dimensions, meanings, and possibilities—to its "own passage"—*for its own sake*; and the argument I advance is that this requires the rekindling, on our part, of sustained sensorial intimacy with our material environment.

The chapter falls in two main sections, albeit with subdivisions along the way. In the first of these, which takes its point of departure from Alphonso Lingis's phenomenological account of the emergence of sentient selfhood (an account that both draws, and deviates, from Levinas and Merleau-Ponty, whose major works were translated into English by Lingis), I trace a structural shift in the qualitative experience of selfhood to show that in the transition from antiquity to modernity, meaning undergoes a two-part displacement, syphoned away from the ancient enchanted cosmos to be deposited in the future by the agential determinations of the rational subject. Finding that this embeds the underlying structures of depression within our basic framework of self-experience and, most problematically, within our imagination, I argue in the second main section that we must turn to the sensorial dimensions of our reality if new possibilities are to emerge from within the present and new horizons are to open towards the future.

Awash with the World

In his depiction of sensorial self-awareness, Lingis speaks of a primordial sentience holding us in perpetual communion with a cosmos that permeates our being from the outset and bookends and cradles our own brief moment of consciousness and specificity.

"To be born," he tells us, "is not to be cast into the imminence of nothingness but to find oneself in a sustaining medium" (Lingis 2018b, 46). Space undulates around us not as empty distances stretched between a profusion of things, but as a seamless envelopment of light, sound, density, aridity, haze, humidity, breeze, warmth, and boundless depth. We are swaddled "in atmosphere, in sonority, in redolence or in stench, in warmth or in cold" (2018b, 45) and carried by the "infinite reservoir of support" (2018b, 44) that is the ground beneath and before us, so that we find ourselves "immersed from the first in the superabundance of the elements" (2018b, 46). And the elements are immersed in us. Light "invades the eyes," sounds "invade one's ears," and the ground "rises up into one's posture" (2018b, 49). The contours that demarcate us are not boundaries but thresholds, and the elements that flow back and forth across them saturate us (2018b, 47).

"Life," Lingis exclaims, "lives on sensation; the elements are a nourishing medium" (2018b, 47), but, more than this, the elements are a pleasurable medium, a generous, overflowing medium. We are awash with the world, porous to its sensorial infusions; and as sentience awakens, he continues, "the movement that senses the elements is not the movement of need or want, the movement of an emptiness that seeks, in the distance, a content; sensuality finds itself in a gratuitous abundance." As Tom Sparrow comments, in his wonderfully insightful overview of Lingis's work: "The elements that *give* life to each one of us by offering themselves as the very stuff of our existence are sensuous material—luminosity, tactility, and sonority bathe our sensitive bodies. As the real source of our nourishment, they *lend* us sensibility and illuminate our world (Sparrow 2007, 113; emphasis added).

Roused by their elemental infusions, our senses are drawn through the "plenum of the elements" (Lingis 2018b, 52) and "cast forth their eddies of involution" (2018b, 49), so that it is in our exclamatory surprise and *pleasure* (2018b, 49) at the world they open to us that we catch our first glimpse of ourselves; and our nascent self-awareness, the "first eddy of ipseity" (2018b, 48), begins to unfurl: "The primary sense of self is not a movement that reflects itself and maintains itself by continuing and consolidating or synopsizing a multiplicity of elementary sense data. Essentially exclamatory, it is a moment of involution that intensifies and releases its energies into the elements in which the sensual body is immersed" (Lingis 2018b, 48). Emerging from raw immediacy, we transcend ourselves not *towards* a world but ever further *into* a world that has already stirred us from within, so that ipseity,[2] our *sense* of self, is born as immersion and its primary modality is integration. And from here to reflective, intentional self-awareness there is no schism, no daylight, but only a continuum along which the primordial, sensorial sense of self distills and concentrates. "The movement that diagrams a self, the as-for-me is not an intuition but an intensification" (2018b, 48), so that the originary basis of the modern Western subjectivity[3] and the ordering, categorizing, objectifying subject is not the agential self in confrontation with an external reality, but a broad-spectrum sensorial predilection for our world. Always for Lingis, as Sparrow tells us, "the subject stripped down is a bare enjoyment of the depths, of the countless levels of unfounded sensations" (Sparrow 2007, 109); and it is this "bare enjoyment" that elicits our sensorial forays into the expanses beyond our own contours, opening our horizon of meaning and possibility within a world that gradually becomes legible to us—that *makes sense* to us. And so, for Lingis, "sensuality becomes the fertile ground of being-in-the-world" (2018b, 112). Ipseity comes *to* us from an elemental cosmos and the multiplicity of things within it, which, preceding human intention, unsolicited in their affective exertions upon us, have *autonomy*: "the fact of their being there is imposed on us" (Lingis 2018d, 14). As Sparrow elaborates: "the countless objects and levels of the world are not dependent on us for their sensual energy, they offer themselves as so many avenues of pleasure that go about their business even when humanity is nowhere in sight" (2007, 113).

Little surprise, then, to find that for Lingis, "life has been understood negatively, when it is needs and lacks suffered in a material system that were taken to agitate it and move it towards outside resources." Expanding on this, he writes that:

> Needs and wants are not the essence of life; they are partial and superficial, accidents that befall the plenitude of an organism which is alive for itself in its sensuality. The ego that arises as an awareness of needs and wants, the self that forms as the cramp knotted over this negativity, is intermittent and shallow. Sentient life is not a succession of initiatives driven by need and want and aiming at objectives. Life is not the recurrence of need and satisfaction, eating and getting hungry and drinking and getting thirsty again, in an enterprise that is gradually losing its reserve, in an anxiety repeatedly postponing death. (Lingis 2018b, 46)

Instead, for Lingis, "prior to the practical perception that draws out a practicable layout and pursues objectives, there is the appetite for the elements." Irreducible to the pangs of biological need, this is the appetite for delight: for "savoring what one assimilates and that in which one is assimilated" (Lingis 2018b, 47). Where, for Lingis, "to be alive is to enjoy," in our sentience "we enjoy our enjoyment" (2018b, 47). And so we become a self in a world *not* because need and desperation demand it of us, but because becoming a self in a world is enjoyable *in itself*. The basis of our selfhood is a primordial *amor mundi* (Arendt 2005, 2003; see also Fritsch, this volume; Oliver, this volume) manifest as subliminal joy in what is already there.

There is an important temporal dimension to Lingis's account that needs to be emphasized. Becoming a self is an emergence without end[4] because "what is already there" is there not in stasis but in flux: as Lingis puts it, "the elements are there by incessant incoming" (2018b, 44; see also 2018d, 17; 1986, 65). And since this incessant incoming "dissolves all traces of its own past tones" and "obturates with its radiance the horizons of its future" (2018b, 44–45), it is also an incessant "now." Captivated by a "now" that fills their entirety, the senses are insensible to the vectors of linear time; our sense of self is ever emerging into a perpetual and undivided present. The instantaneous pinprick of joy that spurs our first glimmer of ipseity is no singular, momentary occurrence but the ongoing, fluvial basis of a selfhood that has its deepest roots within the surging, sensorial transformations of the moment.

But, of course, we are not only sensorial beings, but also social beings; and the world that gradually draws into focus as selfhood takes form has been domesticated over many millennia. The self and its world come to cognition as the acculturated reductions of raw ipseity and the originary, spectral sweep of elemental possibility from which it emerges. In what Sparrow calls "natal trauma," ipseity, en route from first inchoate glimmerings to articulated self-awareness, is stuffed to the brim with "a communal form, a form—a structure, a language—that initiates the body into the stratified world and removes for good the possibility of raw sensation" (Sparrow 2007, 116). Our day-to-day self-experience has introjected, as Lingis puts it, "feelings contracted from others, passed on to others, perceptions equivalent to and interchangeable with those of any other, thoughts which conceive but the general format of the layout about one, sentences formulated such that they can be passed on to anyone" (Lingis 2018d, 18).

Turning to the Western world and ourselves within it, we might then wonder about the long historical distillation of ipseity into the very specific form that is our telic, goal-driven subjectivity. We might wonder what has happened to our appetite for uncomplicated joy in the moment, or what has been done to it. It is as if we have acquired the habit of seeking within the future something that we no longer recognize as already ours within the present. It is as if Western civilization first withholds and then rebrands as righteous reward or grudging compensation what is in fact the very wellspring of our being.

Ipseity and Subjectivity

Within the broader context of the historical and geographical sweep of human experience, a sense of susceptibility to unsought cosmic exertions and elemental infusions of one kind or another, and the understanding that these have formative and sometimes commanding bearing on selfhood, are very far from new.

To this day, there are societies from Amazonia to Africa to Asia to Australasia to the Arctic Circle that have successfully evaded incursions of the Western worldview on their own and have avoided being subsumed within the disenchanted externalized reality that is the perceptual bedrock of our modern westernized subjectivity. In Descola's remarkable account (2014, 2015) of animist society, for example, which is distinguished by what he describes as "the continuity of souls and the discontinuity of bodies" (Descola 2015, 79), particularity and alterity are shown to be matters of physical form *of* which ipseity, unconstrained by material boundary, has diverse immersive experience, but *from* which it has independence. In a way of life where, as

Zerzan has remarked (2012, 196), survival entails "a borderlessness between inner and outer worlds," an uninterrupted or continuous ipseity weaves back and forth between people, things, animals, and spirits, enfolding them seamlessly into "social 'collectives'" (Descola 2015, 85) of extraordinary and fluid diversity (Descola 2014, 3–31), with the result, as Descola tells us, that "most of the entities that people the world are interconnected in a vast continuum inspired by unitary principles and governed by an identical regime of sociability" (Descola 2014, 22). Selfhood, then, is not the discrete or enduring domain of the person, but of the tidal exchanges between the beings and entities of the cosmos in their radically heterogeneous convergences, which can act upon and within the person (or entity), or draw them—sometimes in metamorphosis, sometimes by transposition—into the body or form of another. And so ipseity, in animist society, is not so much constituted and reconstituted by its sensorial and material environment, but is affirmed and deepened in immersive intimacy with physical alterity and the many transformations of perspective that this brings.

There is also an important temporal, as well as spatial, dimension to the continuity of selfhood due to reincarnation,[5] which occurs in hunting and especially in eating: "vitality, energy and fecundity constantly circulate between organisms thanks to the capture, the exchange and the consuming of flesh . . . beings who ingest one another cannot be distinguished by the substances they are made of" (Descola 2015, 80). In this way, the comity of death and life is ever present within the most basic functions of existence, which release ipseity from the mortal temporality of the body. For the uninterrupted, continuous ipseity, birth and death are not beginnings and ends but contours that give shape to the vast continuum of the cosmos and saturate the actions and entities within it with ultimate meaning and significance.

So too in the Western world, before the last lingering tendrils of our own ancient and enchanted order began to retire from the general currency, the permeability of the human mind and body and a general susceptibility to the variegated incursions of a vast panoply of cosmic forces were matters of self-evidence, imprinted upon the basic understanding and experience of life.

Nowadays it is more or less commonplace for the West to applaud the obsolescence of its ancient enchanted worldview and "porous" ipseity (Taylor 2007, 40) as the triumph of reason, science, and objectivity over credulity and assorted, irrational terrors of one kind or another. The modern mind tends, generally, to be experienced as a bounded, interior space (Taylor 2007, 31) within a self that takes itself to be "master of the meanings of things for it" (Taylor 2007, 38), with the result that to go about life as a modern individual is to act *as if* we have filled in the pores and bricked up the threshold between self and world. No longer hapless pawns tossed about at the merciless hands of invisible forces, we are, as Taylor puts it, "buffered" (Taylor 2007, 40) agents, self-possessed individuals at the helm of our own minds and actions and imbued with a sense of invulnerability to nonhuman interference in our practical, emotional, and psychological affairs: an invulnerability that cloaks the entire framework of our day-to-day reality but is now so thoroughly and deeply ingrained as to be more or less invisible to us (Taylor 2007, 31). In this way, as a modern individual operating within what Roszak so memorably describes as "the subliminal boundaries of the contemporary modern mindscape" (1973, xvii), I carry with me an underlying sense that, as Taylor puts it, "my ultimate purposes are those which arise within me, the crucial meanings of things are those defined in my responses to them" (Taylor 2007, 38).

But the ancient enchanted order was ripe with meaning,[6] charged with significance that, as Taylor comments, "exists already outside of us . . . is there quite independently of us; it would be there even if we didn't exist." Paul Shepard gives a remarkable account of the emergence to mature selfhood in a world where "the clues to the meaning of life were embedded in natural things, where everyday life was inextricable from spiritual significance and encounter" (Shepard 1998, 6); and he describes how, in sensorial intimacy with their surroundings, our ancestors were drawn ever further into the intricacies, possibilities, and meanings of their world:

> The unfiltered, unpolluted air, the flicker of wild birds, real sunshine and rain, mud to be tasted and tree bark to grasp, the sounds of wind and water, the calls of animal and insect voices—all these are not vague and pleasant amenities for the infant but the stuff out of which its second grounding, even while in its mother's arms, has begun. The outdoors is also in some sense another inside . . . The child learns that all life tells something and that all sound—from the frog calling to the sea surf—issues from a being kindred and significant to himself, telling some tale, giving some clue, mimicking some rhythm that he should know. (Shepard 1998, 7 and 11)

In the passage from birth to mature selfhood, which unfolded in sensorial and spiritual intimacy with the subtleties of their environment, our ancestors, as Shephard comments, "[did] not graduate from that world but into its significance" (Shephard 1998, 9).[7] Ipseity took shape within the person as the specific nexus of familial, social, and spiritual bonds, which overlapped with the many ties to place and surroundings (Taylor 2007, 157; Shepard 1998, 1–17); but its outlines were "porous" (Taylor 2007, 40), and among the multiplicity of meaningful entities, beings, and forces that made up our reality were those with the power to take command of our own interiority. The forces of the cosmos held us in their sway (Taylor 2007, 35), affecting not only events and outcomes, but also our ability to falter or flourish in body and mind, so that, once again, the distinction between interiority and exteriority had fluidity and ambiguity in the sense that, as Taylor puts it, "the line between personal agency and impersonal force was not at all clearly drawn" (Taylor 2007, 39).

But the enchanted order, already well in retreat by the late Middle Ages, finally gave away entirely beneath the steamroller momentum of Protestant reform and the various upheavals of proto-capitalist enterprise. In particular, the enchanted porous self and its complex cosmic infusions took a series of heavy blows in their confrontation with the reformist concern for *personal* salvation: a concern that increasingly consumed the popular imagination and was to play a pivotal role in the gradual distillation of the cosmic, social ipseity into the particularized entity of the self as an *individual,* whose salvific future depended upon the strict mediation of all relations—social, material, and spiritual—through the reformist conceptualization of God's providential plan and its enactment in well-ordered *productive enterprise* (Taylor 2007, 90–145, 221–69). The unflinching determination to impose productive order upon the stuff of nature, including *human* nature, was gradually and thoroughly inculcated as the very foundation of the fully moral being, in a society whose ultimate fears and hopes served to perforate the ancient social bonds between humans and nature, and to embed a rigid perceptual and conceptual division between the self and everything else. And the ancient powers of things in the world to impart their own meaning to us came to be supplanted by the disciplined, instrumentalizing application of human reason, with divine purpose as its interpretative lens and human well-being and prosperity as its goal.

As Enlightenment humanism gathered momentum, the pursuit of human prosperity and material progress depended less and less upon reformist anxiety for its motivations and day-to-day operations until, as Taylor comments, "the very scrutability of the whole system left little place for mystery" (2007, 230), with the irony that God himself was gradually painted out of the picture that religion, as belief, had once inspired but, as passion or enthusiasm, had begun to hinder (2007, 263). By the apex of the Enlightenment, meaning had come to be *experienced* as homegrown fruit within the buffered mind of an altogether finite and "discontinuous" subject confronting an external, inanimate universe and the mortal strictures of its own body. Writing in 1755, Diderot summarizes the Western view of the world at the brink of its industrial transformation: "One consideration above all must not be lost sight of, and that is that if man or the thinking, observing being is banished from the surface of the earth, this moving and sublime spectacle of nature is nothing but a sad and silent scene. The universe is dumb; silence and night overtake it. Everything changes into a vast solitude where unobserved phenomena occur in a manner dark and mute" (Diderot, 1755/2002, 641). As we can partly infer from the Diderot's depiction of a dumb, uncommunicative, and meaningless universe, the processes of buffering were not only inward, or "mental," for the buffered mind is contained within a vessel that was to become strikingly desensitized to its environment en route to modernity, as if the body, too, came to be buffered through our long historical departure from the ancient world.[8] In Zerzan's words, "it is possible to see the hallmark of human evolution in terms of a release from proximity, as if estrangement from sensual interface with the natural world, rather than intimacy with it, were a desired goal" (2012, 112). For in the rational production of meaning, as Serres has argued, "one must close one's eyes and cover one's ears to the song and the beauty of the sirens. *In a single blow*, we eliminate hearing and noise, vision and failed drawing" (Serres 1982, 70, emphasis added). We pixelate and filter the spectral sensorial plenitude of the present in which our primal ipseity is immersed, and we dismiss entire regions of its teeming potentialities and possibilities as marginalia or interference: as "noise" (Serres 1982, 70; Lingis 1994, 79). We shut our ears to "the glossolalia of non-human things—the humming, buzzing, murmuring, crackling, and roaring of the world" (Lingis 1994, 78); we filter out the angle of the shoulders, the orbit of the gaze, the "pitch, timbre, rhythm, volume and density" of the voice (Lingis 1994, 78).

This is not to dismiss the importance of being *able* to filter the "incessant incoming" of our sensorial environment. But it is to say that, according to the terms and conditions of the buffered subjectivity, the price exacted by the pursuit of the rational production of meaning is broad-spectrum sensorial repression and dissociation. Lingis illustrates the point with the example of reading:

> The reader systematically neglects not only the erroneous lines but also the particularities with which the letters have to be materialized. He disregards the fact that they are written in blue or black ink, or set in a Courier 10 or Courier 12 typeface. Reading is a peculiar kind of seeing that vaporizes the substrate, the hue and grain of the paper or of the computer screen and sees the writing as will-o'-the-wisp patterns in space disconnected from the layout of things. (Lingis, 1994, 76–77)

Now Shepard has argued that the "quality of attention" of hunter-gatherers is "universal," casting as wide a net as it can maintain, because "the hunter knows that he does not know what is going to happen . . . thus he needs to prepare an attention which does not consist in riveting itself on the presumed but consists precisely in not *presuming* anything" (Ortega y Gasset in Shepard 1998, 22). However, Serres's *single blow* that liberates meaning from noise and interference is neither innocent nor impartial, for it has already determined *what* is meaningful *before* its exposure to the very meaning for which it, the blow itself, is the precondition. This matters because, as Shepard continues, "what people notice, what they expect to encounter, the mix of senses used, even the quality of their inattention and disregard all reveal something about the kind of world it is for them" (Shepard 1998, 21). The single blow of our buffered rationality presupposes narrow interest and, as Lingis argues, "consign[s] to noise the teeming flood of signals emitted by what is particular, perspectival, and distinctive in each thing" (1994, 80). What this tells us about our world, then, is that it is a world from which particularity *itself*, including our own particularity, is prefiltered and marginalized: exiled without trial. In other words, the single blow eliminates vast regions not only of the world around us but also, and especially, of *us*. And what is left behind is merely the common residue. In this way, Lingis continues, "the maximal elimination of noise would produce successful communication among interlocutors themselves maximally interchangeable" (1994, 78). So, in the rational determinations of meaning and significance, the reduction to noise of all but pixelated fragments of our reality and the fungibility of the communicable remainder implicate sentience and meaning in their own undoing, their own erasure, across vast regions of their own spectral possibility. And as for Diderot's thinking, observing beings: gradually dissociated from our primal, sensorial ipseity, "made tonal by society" (Zerzan 2012, 63) and its buffering domestications, we leave the enchanted cosmos in mass migration to "the city of communication maximally purged of noise" (Serres 1982, 68), where, as Thoreau once wrote, "our winged thoughts are turned to poultry" (1995, 49); and love letters and library fines announce themselves in identical font.

IMPLOSION

Throughout the journey from reformist angst to modern buffering, meaning was accelerating through a *temporal* as well as a spatial transposition. Over time, the extraordinary collusion between economic production and Protestant reform, a collusion that saw the remarkable transformation of avarice from—"the foulest of them all" (Hirschmann 2013, 41)—to socially useful self-interest, applied an unremitting pressure on relations between the individual and their sense of the future. There is something disquieting about the fervor to map the quest for spiritual rectitude onto the market-driven pursuit of self-interest; but in their telic structures, the salvific priorities of reform (which profoundly disrupted the ancient acceptance of death as "part of the round of life" [Taylor 2007, 67])[9] and the goal-driven orientation of economic production bear a striking similarity, in that they each subordinate the present to the future and they each prioritize what is yet to be over what *is*. In their temporal and ontological affirmations of one another, economic and salvific concerns worked together over time to undermine the possibility that intrinsic value or meaning is to be found within the present, as opposed to *future*, reality. At the same time, they each place ultimate accountability, be it salvific or fiscal, squarely upon the individual. Thus, whether the goal is to avoid eternal damnation or, later on—under the intensification of enclosure, urbanization, industrialization, and market ideology—to avoid starvation, the newly individualized person is under pressure to be self-determining: to take not only the world around them but also their own self as an object to be worked upon and remade according to their understanding of what the future requires them to be. In this way, meaning, in its gradual transposition to the buffered mind of the agential individual—(who casts their intentions into the future and steers reality towards their realization)—is simultaneously transposed to the future from where it mediates the present, including the self within it.

But when the present is mediated in the future and determined by the subject, the buffered agent, then among the myriad potentialities of the present only those that are in some way relevant to the intentions of the subject survive their spatial and temporal extrusions. In other words, it is what we *already* know and understand and what we have *already* experienced that wrap around to confront the present as its destination. In an odd way, then, the underlying dynamic of telos is a stasis: an ossification of the underlying meaning and significance of things to us, in which the intended future can only affirm the given reality, which is thereby affirmed *in its subjugation to the future*. Reality, then, is condemned ever to be present as an impoverished version of itself. But more than that, in being mediated in a mind that is itself self-mediating, the experience of reality is drained of all substance: the ensemble of reality, mind, and meaning becomes an empty telic structure, whose modality is self-subjugation and whose modus operandi is self-destruction; for, as Paul Shepard points out, "the trouble with the eagerness to make a world is that, being already made, what is there must first be destroyed" (1998, 120).

Mirage

I have been suggesting that the Western economy of meaning runs on perpetual debt: that when that which matters *more* is ever around the next bend in the road, meaning is perpetually "borrowed" from a future that becomes a placeholder for meaning, for value and significance that can never be filled. But in the temporal displacement of value from the realm of action there is a loosening of the moorings, which enables action to drift away from the values to which the present, the realm of action, nonetheless claims to subscribe. Marcuse alludes to this when he writes that:

> It is only the exclusion of cruelty, fanaticism, and unsublimated violence which allows the definition of culture as the process of humanization. However, these forces (and their institution) may well be an integral part of culture, so that the attainment or approximation of the cultural goals takes place *through* the practice of cruelty and violence. [. . .] the re-examination of a given culture involves the relation of values to facts; how are the means of a society related to its self-professed ends? (Marcuse 2007, 15)

The problem, then, as Marcuse proposes, is not only that the way in which we strive to actualize our legitimating values involves their endless postponement, but also that it *sabotages* them.

Within our own market-driven teleocracy, beholden to what Clastres calls the "infinite space of forging ahead" (2010, 112), meaning—tending towards pure abstraction and severed from the originary sensorial conduit that anchors it in our material reality—becomes an empty form, a mirage that not only recedes but also fades with each step we take towards it. We might see this as the very nature of progress, but in which case then, at the level of praxis, the same telic dynamic that enables means and ends to become catastrophically discordant with one another enables their being so *in perpetuity*. In practice, then, means become the negation, and even the destruction, of ends; and progress is not *a* value but, *at most*, the negation of value. "Follow the tireless motion of cogs and wheels back to its source," urge Kingsnorth and Hine, "and you will find the engine driving our civilization: the myth of progress" (2014, 7). But in its very commitment to the "myth of progress," Western modernity is thereby undermining itself from within.

DEPRESSIVE

Oh! but our reality has not *yet* purged itself of *all* noise. Oh! but we don't *actually* live in the "technocratic, hygenic utopia functioning in a void of human possibilities" that Steiner (1971, 69), for example, envisions. True enough, perhaps. But I have been laying out a direction, a trajectory, that has the momentum of millennia as it hurtles onwards. And a trajectory from which our sentience is in intensifying retreat and in which a spectral continuum of meaning and significance is gradually converging upon the unilinear value of progress is also a trajectory in which a plenitude of possibilities is gradually tending towards the singular: possibility *as such* is gradually being erased.

In which case, then, where Heidegger famously proposed that the underlying attunement of the ancient Greeks to their world was wonder (Heidegger 1994, 143–55) and that of modernity was boredom (1995, 74–167), it is not entirely hyperbolic to say that the underlying mood of our post-progress society is depression. For the thing about depression, as Ratcliffe has shown in his remarkable investigations (2015), is that it involves the radical withdrawal of possibility (65–66) and the radical loss of world (Ratcliffe 2015, 14–16). Its catalogue of symptoms (despair, guilt, hopelessness, and so on) arises within a framework of self-experience that has undergone a profound transformation *in its entirety*, closing off the space in which belonging, action, and connection occur. Meaning and significance are exiled to a dimension that is radically elsewhere and utterly inaccessible. And it is highly relevant to my own concerns in these pages that, as Ratcliffe finds: "the world of depression is imbued with *certainty* because it is bereft of other possibilities" (2015, 69; my emphasis). I find myself wondering, then, what happens to us all when we feel possibility gradually collapsing into certainty in our confrontation with a future whose troubles are becoming ever more apparent.

My suggestion, here, is not that we are all suffering from depression, which is clearly not the case (although depression is obviously a huge and growing concern throughout Western society), but that, as Heidegger tells us, our basic attunement to our world determines the possible ways in which we are able to "[let] the world matter to [us]" (2008, 213) or, as Dreyfus puts it, the ways in which "things show up for us" (1991, 172). As beings-in-a-world, our sense of self is inextricable from our sense of reality; and a moribund world from which meaning is in retreat is simultaneously an emptying of the self, a withdrawal of our own immanence and possibility. There may, as I have already suggested, be no daylight between ourselves as subjects and our primary, sensorial ipseity with its straightforward, immersive joy in the present; but as a domain of spectral *possibility*, our sentient self seems to be in danger of slipping ever further from our reach in what is therefore a catastrophic vicious circle. And as our trajectory tears at the seams of our selfhood, it is not only we who suffer the consequences, but also the earth that sustains us: "The fiction . . . is that [his] painful incompleteness is the true mature experience and that the meaningless of the natural world is its meaning. In itself, this philosophy is merely inadequate, no worse than other intellectual dead ends. But, acted upon, it wounds us, and we wound the planet" (Shepard 1998, 70).

Interlude

In the midst of this there is a biting irony, in that scientific reasoning is beginning to accommodate and even promote a worldview that it fought very long and hard to reject; for among the recent discoveries of Western science is that in body *and in mind* we are, indeed, extraordinarily porous, so that, as Zuboff wrote, in a somewhat different context but in words that seem entirely apt: "the lived experience of psychological self-determination is a cruel illusion" (2015, 8).

Biologically speaking, the human body is less an autonomous entity and rather more a series of Mobius twists in a highly porous membrane: a dynamic ecosystem in constant exchange with the world beyond its contours, and in which the myriad microscopic life-forms that make up the human microbiota—the bacteria, viruses, fungi, protozoa, and so on, whose own future generations have multiplied many times over as I have been thinking about these pages—and collapse the distinction between the human and the nonhuman. But, intriguingly, the microbiota also appears to wield a powerful influence on brain development, behavior, and things such as the choice of what to eat, how much, and when (Carding 2015, 24:02–24:20, 34:12–34:40, 37:00–38:30), on creativity and curiosity (Carding 34.40–35.58), and on emotions and moods (Carding 36:00–36:48; Bagga et al., 2019; Limbana et al., 2020). Depression in particular shows strong causal associations with microbial depletion and imbalance,[10] and among the current recommended treatments are probiotics (Wallace and Miley 2017). So, although our basic mood or attunement shapes the way things in the world "show up" for us, for the microbes with which we co-habit, mood can actually *be* the way they show up.

But the causal interactions run in both directions, for the health of the microbiome appears to be highly vulnerable to even subtle alteration in our water, food, air, types of activities, and even accommodation (Carding 2015, 16:40–17:30). Many aspects of our modern way of life can have catastrophic impacts: things such as stress (Carding 27.30–28.03), medications—especially antibiotics (Carding 20:55–23:33)—surgery (Carding 28:07–28:15), our methods of childbirth, the use of infant formulas in place of breastfeeding (Carding 14:30–16:35), ultra-processed foods (Carding 31:16–32:14), as well as the use of pesticides and herbicides, including (and, worryingly) glyphosate (van Bruggen et al. 2021), are particularly damaging. The systems of rational control we impose upon our environment have a trickle-down effect, so that, although the loss of insect species and biomass, soil depletion, and so on are among the more clear-cut results, our technologized ways of addressing our material needs also expose us to a very specific set of vulnerabilities as a direct result of their ability to inflict lasting damage upon the world-in-our-being that conditions our mental health and contributes to the dynamics, content, and experience of our selfhood.

By way of a contrasting example, the Buginese people of Sulawesi *feed* the insects that would otherwise destroy their crops (Rahmatia and Christomy 2020, 5–6), a possibility that is largely obscured in the West by a mindscape that reduces the significance and meaning of a scintillating multitude of species to "germs," "infestations," and "pests." The particularity of extraordinarily diverse and complex needs, behaviors, interactions, and environmental *and sensorial* contributions to our world is little but noise and interference to a telic rationality that sees boreal forest as "overburden" and wildlife and its habitats, as Monbiot dryly comments, as "asset classes in an ecosystems market" (2014).

So Far

I began this discussion with the suggestion that if the pressing *concern* is for the generations who come after us, then we must tend to the well-being of our current self-experience and the health and vitality of our contemporary subjectivity, and that this points to a pressing *need* for the present to be returned *to itself*. I have shown that in Lingis we find, at the origin of self-awareness, a primal, sensorial joy and the porous infusions of the spectral, elemental continuum of our surroundings, so that we are born to anticipate boundless subtleties and possibilities without end (Shepard 1998, 39). I have also been arguing that sensorial dissociation and the telic incline of Western modernity are two sides of a coin that drains substance, meaning, value and possibility from our reality and from the self, so that, under the doctrine of progress, the modern subject and its world are self-emptying forms that are indicative of a depressive framework becoming an embedded structure of the modern self. And I have been suggesting that we are caught in a vicious cycle or perhaps more of a vicious figure of eight: upon the one hand, as we saw in Shepard's commentary, a world drained of meaning damages us and we damage it; on the other hand, as we saw with the impact of our "rational" systems of production upon the microbiome, among the damages we inflict are those that damage us further in return in a series of feedback loops that seem to know no effective circuit breaker.

Undoubtedly, the general thrust of what I am saying here expresses no new sentiment. But in what Zerzan calls our "privatized distress" (2012, 30) there are many signs that our predicament is only intensifying in ways that seem to creep into day-to-day life and embed themselves there as if normal rather than merely commonplace. En masse, we are losing our equilibrium and the qualities of interiority upon which rests, as our most minimal happiness, the ability "to become aware of oneself without fright" (Benjamin 1979, 71).[11]

> Stress, loneliness, depression, boredom—the madness of everyday life. Ever greater levels of sadness, implying a recognition, on the visceral level at least, that things could be different. How much joy is there left in the technological society, this field of

alienation and anxiety? Mental health epidemiologists suspect that
no more than 20 percent of us are free of psychopathological
symptoms. Thus we act out a "pathology of normalcy" marked by
the chronic psychic impoverishment of a qualitatively unhealthy
society. (Zerzan 2012, 26)

In other words, part of the mechanism of our modern mindscape is the burial, even at the price of its own sanity, of the disruptive notion that human existence could do and be better.

But now what? What tools of transformation are simultaneously within our reach but beyond the psychopathologies of daily life? Shepard argues that the human capacity to retrieve both ourselves and our world from moribund descent is innate: "latent in the organism, in the interaction of the genome and early experience" (1998, 128). But clearly, any appeal to our buffered reasoning and telic agency holds us within the very circuitry that needs to be interrupted. This is not to suggest that reason and agency must play no role in our lives but, rather, under the present circumstances, and from within an increasingly manufactured environment that reason designs and agency produces, that the gene pool of possibilities, meanings, and experiences that sustains them is inbred and ailing, so that our telic rationality is devouring its own toxifying tail. The question then—also very far from new—is to what dimension of our being or our reality we might turn to seek out alternative influences: where, in other words, we might catch some experiential glimpse of how "things could be different."

Fantasy, Reverie, and the Apocalyptic Imagination

If, as I have been suggesting, the roots of the problem lie in the increasing distance and tension between subjectivity and primal ipseity on the one hand, and self and world on the other, then proximity and integration would appear to furnish a solution, or at least a place in which to look for one. And this, of course, is precisely what our own culture strongly militates against. The Ancient Greeks already intuited, almost three thousand years ago, that the pleasures of sensorial immediacy were anathema to the workings of a civilization built upon slavery and division of labor. Among their mythic *terrors* was the life of the Lotus eaters and the simple, sensorial pleasures in the moment that erased all memory and all purpose, all past and all future; and from which Odysseus had to extricate his men by force, binding them to the benches of his ship and forging onwards *while they wept.* We can perhaps see, at the heart of the ancient terror, a great fear of a present released from the diktat of telos, and of peaceable and uncomplicated immersion in the moment. But if, today, as Shepard argues, some part of us yearns for something that we feel to have vanished from our lives, some other way of being present in our world, our cultural heritage is remarkably swift to tell us "that this yearning is only *fantasy* and nostalgia for something that 'never' existed" (1998, 104, emphasis added).

And yet fantasy, as Marcuse famously wrote, is the "refusal to forget what *can be*" (Marcuse 1974, 149; original emphasis). For Marcuse, fantasy is the unfolding of a layer in our selfhood that, despite its deep historical submersion, refuses to be consigned to the past. And it is in the lived *experience* of fantasy itself that we find the underlying truth of all fantasy, namely, that we can *be* in a way that is external to the telic framework of a society driven by needless and "distributed" scarcity (1974, 36) and the perpetual postponement of its own values—most especially that of the universal well-being and prosperity of humans *and* nature. And so for Marcuse, the vital truth of fantasy is that of its own existence: "As a fundamental, independent mental process, fantasy has a truth value of its own, which corresponds to an experience of its own—namely, the surmounting of the antagonistic human reality. Imagination envisions the reconciliation of the individual with the whole, of desire with realization, of happiness with reason. While this harmony has been removed into utopia by the established reality principle, fantasy insists that it must and can become real, that behind the illusion lies *knowledge*" (Marcuse 1966, 143). Bachelard expresses something similar when he asks, "doesn't reverie, by its very essence, liberate us from the reality function?" (1969, 13), taking an additional step by adding that "it is perfectly evident that reverie bears witness to a normal, useful *irreality function* which keeps the human psyche on the fringe of all the brutality of a hostile and foreign non-self" (13).

On our way to modernity, he continues, "man 'no longer able to dream, thought.' And the world dreamer begins to think the world through the thoughts of others" (La Jeunesse 1897, 51, in Bachelard 1969, 176–77). But where the "hostile and foreign non-self" are those parts of us that have conformed to the prescriptions of Western modernity—becoming, as Lingis puts it, "maximally interchangeable"—reverie remains a source not only of truth but also of *sustenance* for the non-fungible dimensions of our selfhood.

For Bachelard, reverie, in its most deeply transformative mode, emerges from within the "the soul of the dreamer" (1969, 14). Here, in what he calls "cosmic reverie," we lapse into a pure and unmediated present—an eternity where "time no longer has any yesterday and no longer any tomorrow," and which draws us into layers of our selfhood untouched by the "taught ideas" (188) of others; for "while thinkers who reconstruct a world retrace a long path of reflections, *the cosmic image is immediate*" (175). Unconstrained and unmediated, cosmic reveries "situate us in a world and not in a society" (14) and gently immerse us in an undivided, elemental cosmos whose gateway is poetic imagery of own: "Through the cosmicity of an image then, we receive an experience of the world; cosmic reverie causes us to inhabit a world. It gives the dreamer the impression of a *home (chez soi)* in the imagined universe . . . In dreaming on the universe, one is always *departing*; one lives in the *elsewhere* which is always *comfortable*" (Bachelard 1969, 177).

As a perpetual setting forth, cosmic reverie is the perpetual present-tense emergence of its dreamer into an elemental *welcome* and a "pure exchange which never ends between our own being and the expanses of the world . . ." (Goethe, quoted by Bachelard 1969, 181). As Bachelard continues, "the communication between the dreamer and his world is very close in reverie; it has no 'distance,' not that distance which marks the *perceived world*, the world fragmented by perception" (174). And so, in cosmic reverie, we return to an unedited selfhood and the spectral plenitude of an unfiltered world that we begin to *hear* as we "pass from a human vocabulary to a vocabulary of things" (Bachelard 1969, 189). For a brief moment, we are in a state of union, which, in itself, is a locus of profound well-being, spectral possibility, and transformation. In words that have extraordinary resonance with Lingis's elemental sentience, Bachelard tells us that:

> In a cosmic image as well as in an image of our dwelling, we are in the well-being of a repose. The cosmic image gives us a concrete, specified repose; this repose corresponds to a need, to an appetite. The formula that the world is my appetite must be substituted for the philosopher's general formula that the world is my representation. To bite into the world with no other "care" than the happiness of biting, isn't that entering the world?

It is as if in cosmic reverie, in perpetual stepping forth into the elements, we can rediscover the primordial joy of the "incessant incoming" that our modern buffered sentience withholds from us.

If, as Oscar Wilde tells us and as we saw at the very outset, Utopia is to be found only in the future, in fantasy, as we learn from Marcuse, we are adamant that Utopia "must and can become real"; and from Bachelard we learn one way in which it might be experienced *in the present* when it does so. Perhaps, then, the utopian *impulse* to change our own world, endlessly, for the sake of a better world ahead can usefully be differentiated from the utopian *desire*—fulfilled only in occasional, fleeting moments of fantasy and reverie—to participate unabashedly in a world that we do not feel we *have* to change. The utopian impulse conflates with the very teleocratic subjectivity and structural futurity that serve, so problematically, to pole-vault meaning beyond our own divided and conflicted reality; whereas fantasy and reverie are prefigurative, fulfilling the utopian *desire* to be integrated with our world and immersed without conflict within our own present moment.

But Bachelard makes it very clear that where cosmic reverie is vital to our well-being, well-being is also its *condition*. "You must" he says "tell the man who wants to dream well to begin by being happy." In fact, he continues, "the dreamer then participates in the world by nourishing himself from one of the substances of the world, a dense or rare, warm or gentle substance clear or full of penumbra according to the *temperament of his imagination*" (Bachelard 1969, 178; original emphasis). We seem to be back at square one. And, as Toadvine argues in his own discussion of Bachelard, contemporary images of the world speak more to the gradual disintegration of our environment than to a welcoming, hospitable cosmos: "the cosmic imagination of our times tends in another direction, not toward harmony and well-being, but precisely toward anxiety and, in a word, apocalypse" (Toadvine 2014, 212).

To reflect upon our world today is, increasingly, to confront a slow-dawning awareness of our impact upon it: of "the steady risings of the oceans, the inconspicuous vanishing of honeybees and tadpoles, the patient and silent unworkings of things at scales so small and so grand that we only wait in expectation of the eventual realization that at some point already passed we entered into the entirely unrecognizable" (Toadvine 2014, 212). The space once given over to the idylls of fantasy and cosmic reverie is filled by the "apocalyptic imagination" (212) that points us away from the perpetual beginnings we find in Lingis and Bachelard and towards the eventual disintegration of our universe as it reverts to its basic elements. The world of the apocalyptic imagination speaks of an elemental or "immemorial" time, an eternity that admits of no human participation and from which all possibility has withdrawn: "a world that is no longer ours, no longer an environment for us, a world that is precisely the end of our world" (213). Yet, as Toadvine argues, this elemental cosmos also *precedes* our own as that from which we emerge and back into which we and all things dissolve, and hovers within our present as a phantom whisper so that in our self-awareness our very being carries the constant reminder of its own nonbeing. And so, for Toadvine, the apocalyptic imagination is not only a confrontation with our own violence towards our world but also "an intensification of nature's own fundamental duplicity" (220): of life that, in becoming present to itself, must, at the same time, be stricken by its own finitude. It is as if, beneath and ahead of us, is not the infinite support of the earth that Lingis describes, but the void.

It may well be that the apocalyptic imagination is not imagination at all, but a Trojan horse wheeling itself into the domain of fantasy and reverie that it then destroys from within; that it is the *death* of imagination, the ultimate closure of fantasy and reverie in a mindscape that, entirely given over to our own buffered reality principle, can see only what telic rationality has determined to be the inevitable fate of our world. Recalling Marcuse, the crucial point about fantasy, reiterated by Bachelard, is that as an experiential form it is radically external to the operations of our own contemporary reality. But the apocalyptic imagination brings us to an empty eternity, devoid of all possibility, into which our own universe disintegrates: it confronts us with a totalizing loss of meaning and hope, structural despair, and the grim certitude that is all that is left behind when possibility closes its final door. In so doing, it precisely *reproduces* and *reinforces* our reality function, first, by prefiguring exactly what science has long advanced as the eventual fate of the human universe; and second, by drawing us further into the underlying attunement, and the overall framework and trajectory of modernity, namely *depression*. As I see it, the apocalyptic imagination expresses precisely what modernity is telling us—it reproduces the *meaning* of our modernity, which is that of the undoing of all meaning and possibility. It speaks to the impact of our own way of being upon *us* as well as our world, and to the pervasive and intensifying sense that the meanings and possibilities available to us are impoverished and dwindling. It shows us that the ultimate triumph of modernity is also its fate. And the question of how we might restore the present to itself remains unresolved.

Beginnings

As I move into these last few paragraphs, my purpose is not to argue for solutions but for beginnings. If the pathway that our modern mindscape illuminates leads us without detour to the end of all things, then perhaps our task is not only to retrieve from the elemental cosmos the wonder and astonishment and extraordinary mystery of our being part of it, but also to allow ourselves to be drawn along the way into its tributaries, into the winding ways that open along their own planes and towards their own mysterious vanishing points: to receive the apocalyptic imagination without being consumed by it; and perhaps, to find within the "duplicity of nature" the essential interplay of life and death that held our ancestors in comity with their cosmos. And for this, once again, I turn to Lingis and the senses, for it seems that the only available landscape that remains untouched by the buffered reality we are trying to step beyond is that of sensation.

Toadvine argues that the self that *senses* "can never be fully recuperated by the reflective operations of the personal self" since, as he continues: "As the generative ground of experience, sensibility so understood cannot be a conscious experience; it cannot occur within personal time, the time of reflection, precisely because it makes such time possible. It, therefore, represents, for reflection, an impossible and irrecuperable past, a past that can never be made present" (Toadvine 2014, 216). Lingis may very well agree with this, for, as we saw earlier, he finds that raw sensation is withheld from us by our various acculturations and filtered by our Western subjectivity. But as I see it, this may not matter: we may be able to get close enough for all practical purposes (as the engineer famously remarked to the physicist), and Lingis's account of the spectral continuum of selfhood shows us how.

The subject, for Lingis, is innately dynamic or fluvial, fluctuating "episodically" (Sparrow 2018, xiii) in a constituting and reconstituting correspondence with its surroundings (Sparrow 2018, xi and xii) that is neither entirely passive nor fully intentional but speaks to a generative interplay between affect and response. To remain within the homogenized enclaves of Western civilization, whose manufactured surfaces have replaced the variegations and subtleties of an untamed world with regularity, monotony, and repetition (Shepard 1998, 104), is to condemn our subjectivity to calcification. But to travel, to move within cultures beyond the shores of the Western world, is to court self–transformation: "you can't imagine what ten days of this does to you. It's worth crossing seas for" (Lingis 2018e, 186).

And yet precisely because our domesticated sensorial exposures within Western civilization are so blunted, "travel" itself need not cover great distances and can involve as little as walking barefoot in the forest, as those of us who have tried it will surely know. The searing heat of a dark stone in August, the unexpected warmth and smoothness of fallen leaves, the chilly reservoirs beneath the moss, the unnavigable slipperiness of rocks at a river's edge, ants' nests, pine cones, lichen, roots, mud, and brambles choose our pathway for us and bring us to the reaches of their own sensorial domain that are as unavailable to a pair of boots as they are to a map. To walk barefoot in the woods is to discover that we already have a functional, if vastly underemployed, "vocabulary of things" that grows remarkably quickly when we use it, and that stays with us, fuels our understanding, our imagination, our sense of the possible. Cosmic reverie for the body, perhaps. But at the most basic level it also has a straightforward ability to change, forever, the repertoire of things we do and explore when we have the privilege of being able to improvise our day. And, as Lingis reminds us, "in the enjoyment of the radiance of the spring day and the warmth of the ground, we forget our cares, our cravings and our objectives; we let go of our losses and our compensations and we let go of what holds us" (2018b, 52). Our daily preoccupations are punctuated by uncomplicated pleasure in the moment that, if we grant ourselves—or are granted—time and space for reflection upon it, works against the "prescribed inner world" (Zerzan 2012, 31) of modern selfhood, eroding its priorities and loosening its telic hold.

But there is more. For within the spectral continuum of an undivided sensorial world of infinite dimensions, things glide along its planes as they rise above what Lingis calls the "levels" (2018c), draw into their particularity within our acculturated field of perception, and then sink back down again into the noise or the background hum of our lives. Luminescence, sonority, redolence, pitch—the levels undulate in their density and intensity, moving in and out of focus, emerging from within the sensory elements as "directives that summon" (2018c, 67), perpetually drawing us into the fields they extend and then releasing us from them as they draw us into others: "we listen to the droning of a bee and the murmur of the meadow ceases to throb gently on all sides and within us to become a plane along which the buzzing stops and starts again" (2018c, 56). Our sentient responses—our hearing, our seeing, our tasting and smelling—are movements that, as spontaneous as they are unwilled, are "conducted" by the levels (2018c, 61): always saturated but ever in flux. And so Lingis finds that "sensuality is vulnerable and mortal from the start" (2018b, 49). But this vulnerability is quite unlike the confrontation with mortal finitude that lurks within the apocalyptic imagination: it is "not the vertiginous sense of the contingency of all being, an intuition into the nothingness in which all being would be perilously adrift, and which could be foreseen as a real possibility just beyond the thin screen of being" (2018b, 49). Rather, it is born of the episodic qualities of sensory experience that inhere in the confrontation of the sentient self with the "torrential oncoming" of the ever-shifting, ever-abundant, sensorial elements: a "contingency," Lingis tells us, that "is in the very fullness and abundance of the present" (2018b, 49).

But just as our awareness of *things* fluctuates, so too does our awareness of our own *being*. Self-awareness also comes and goes along a continuum: is always drawn towards itself or released from itself by the levels that open the self to itself as a field of perception, or release it to the summons of the world beyond. From raw sensorial immediacy to sentient self-awareness is, as we saw before, a continuum of spectral intensity: "The movement that diagrams a self, the as-for-me is not an intuition but an intensification" (2018b, 48). Self-awareness emerges not in confrontation with nothingness or its own finitude, but as part of the ebb and flow of its own sentient life, so that subjectivity is an intermittent, interrupted state within the broad spectrum of ipseity, drawn in sensorial summons through its own levels, rising above and falling beneath the radar of its own gaze. The self withdraws from itself, sinks down into the "murmur of the world" to resonate with spectral "vibrancy of things" (Lingis 1994, 96), and, as other levels begin to open other fields to us, we begin to hear the voices of things in their communion with their world:

> There is sound in things like there is warmth and cold in things, and things resonate like they irradiate their warmth or their cold. The quail and the albatross, the crows and the hummingbirds, the coyotes and the seals, the schooling fish and the great whales, the crocodiles infrasonically and the praying mantises ultrasonically continue and reverberate the creaking of the branches, the fluttering of the leaves, the bubbling of the creeks, the hissing of the marsh gasses, the whirring of the winds, the shifting of the rocks, the grinding of the earth's plates. (Lingis 1994, 96–97)

Slipping past the pixelating machinations of our telic mindscape and entering a world restored for a brief moment to its own horizon, we retrieve the very sustenance of imagination, of transformation, of meaning, and joy. And when we reemerge to ourselves, *we remember it*.

To lapse into sensorial intimacy with our world is to approach an undivided, porous ipseity that is known to itself only in its immersion within the vast spectrum of existence. It is to retrieve some dimension of the self that fades as it reaches the surface of modernity, yet leaves its imprint upon us as we float back up to begin again as our agential, modern selves. For as we glide through the densities and viscosities and volumes and intensities of awareness, each emergence to specificity is a beginning that extends its own field of possibility and discovery, and each emergence liberates the horizon of imagination. For our own sakes, then, we must grant ourselves and each other something that our ancestors inhabited as a plenitude and that now, within Western modernity, is marshaled into punitive spirals of escalating debt and shrinking repayment, namely *time* (e.g., Sahlins 1972; Clastres 1989; Suzman 2017). We must give time, and time and time and yet more time to the immersive pleasures of simply being in our world: of bathing in rivers and lakes and oceans, of rolling on damp grass and lying on hot sand; of wading through marshland; of bracing ourselves on a hilltop as the wind bores through us; of being drawn through the woods by the pied-piper call of the hermit thrush or the spoor of an unknown creature; of wondering at the snow fleas that fill up our footprints when the winter air first begins to hint of warmer days to come, or at the seeds of a continent blowing onwards to their spring. And perhaps, then, we may begin to pull back from the brink of extinction the multitudes of tiny creatures of the soil and the air and the water whose future generations are the condition of our own—the "pests" and "infestations" that our systems of meaning consign to their fate—and to feel their fate as our own.

And as we come and go, lapsing in and out of self-awareness; as we move through our days and nights, dissolving into our sleep that speaks to us of the "night beyond the night" (Lingis 2018b, 52) and reemerging to begin our days anew, then our dissolution into the elemental undulates through the breadth and depth of our selfhood, not as apocalyptic horror, not as despair and hopelessness and the end of all things, but as infinite possibility.

Postlude: Neowise, Summer 2020

It is dark now. The late midsummer sky has fallen into shadow behind the trees where the fireflies are beginning their nightly courtship with the stars. The day was hot and the mud that wraps around our feet feels cool as we wade into the lake so gently that the ripples we cast on the shoreline float away into the song of the tree frogs and the barest whisper of a breeze that stirs the aspens. We swim out beyond the point in darkened waters that are as warm as the last of the late afternoon air that lingers above us. And as we look up, the ocher smudge that hangs in the sky over the tallest of the pine trees glows in the corner of our gaze. We float on our backs.

The sky reaches down through the still, black surface of the waters, and the depths beneath and above us are thick with the stars and throbbing with the fireflies so that we can no longer tell sky from earth from water from the surface of our skin as the comet trails its hazy plume of dust and sodium across the millennia. And the future that will one day be our own burns softly into our memory.

Notes

1. I take this term from Schürmann's deconstruction of Heidegger's productionist metaphysics and his depiction of an archeo-teleological dynamic of being that is presupposed by Western metaphysics and that not only frames thought and action in terms of outcomes and end points but functions as a monopolizing and dominating structure of our subjectivity and our uptake of our world, so that, as Schürmann argues, the Western world functions as a teleocracy (10, 257, 259).

2. Throughout this chapter I use the term "ipseity" to denote self-experience, self-awareness, and selfhood in general. This is in contrast to "subjectivity," which, insofar as I understand and use the term in this chapter, is but one particular form of ipseity, to wit, the ipseity of the self as subject—as a discrete and bounded entity confronting an external or object world. So subjectivity expresses a bifurcated reality divided into subject and object, perceiver and perceived, and is the dominant, but not the only possible, mode of ipseity within Western modernity.

3. See previous note.

4. I have in mind a lack of finality or conclusion, but the double meaning of end that Nancy (2015, 37) highlights may also be applicable here: an emergence with neither goal nor cessation.

5. Descola's description of hunting stresses the importance of ritual to the continuity of life through reincarnation, while giving a vivid account of intentional action in pursuit of even the most fundamental of needs as a cooperative and voluntary affair between the relevant parts of the social continuum: "The most common of such relationships and the one that best emphasizes the parity between humans and animals is the bond of friendship that the hunter establishes over time with one particular member of the species. This forest friend is regarded as a companion who will serve as an intermediary among his fellow creatures, who, without balking, will then expose themselves within the range of a shot. No doubt it does involve a minor act of treachery on the intermediary's part, but this is of no consequence to his fellows, as the hunter's victim will soon be reincarnated in an animal of the same species, provided its remains have received the prescribed ritual treatment. Whatever the strategies employed to incite an animal to expose itself to a hunter, when the prey delivers itself up to the one who will consume it, it is always out

of a feeling of generosity. The animal is moved by the compassion it feels for the suffering of humans, creatures that are vulnerable to famine, who depend upon itself for their survival" (2014, 15–16).

6. Here, and throughout (taking my nod from Charles Taylor 2007), I take use the term "meaning" not in the sense of logical extrapolation or dictionary definition but, broadly, as the general significance, value, or importance of things.

7. Shepard's fascinating discussion of ontogenesis in hunter-gatherer society as compared with modern Western society deserves a far more detailed exegesis than this chapter can offer. The crucial point of Shepard's argument, which I outline here in brief, is not that the hunter-gatherer remains within an infantile world but that, for all humans, healthy maturity is the result of intimate understanding of, rather than separation from, the world into which one is born and the capacity for self-reflection and experiential recognition of one's capacities and limitations as an ambiguous being—"man as different and man as a kind of animal" (13). So mature personal identity involves understanding oneself as distinct from yet related to the Other (and, most especially, those Others—i.e., animals, plants, and also the inanimate—that differ most strikingly from oneself) in "spheres of meaning and participation" that widen from birth onwards to adulthood, old age, and death, and in which the life of the hunter-gatherer unfolds. In contrast, Western society severs the world of childhood from that of adulthood so that adolescence is a time not of maturation but of rupture from a trite, infantile world whose trivial meanings must be replaced by a world of meaninglessness over which the adult must learn to dominate or from which he/she must learn to retreat into abstraction. In contrast to that of the hunter-gatherer, the development of the modern Western individual is stunted and harbors compulsive infantile yearnings that cripple its own maturity, but that, Shepard argues, may be necessary to the various codependencies, hierarchies, and compulsive violence that undergird the basic methods of Western society (14–16).

8. In this, Zerzan gives a compelling comparative oversight in chapter 1 of *Future Primitive*.

9. Taylor (2007, 65–71) gives fascinating insight into the changing relationship with death through the processes of disenchantment and reform and the impact of these changes on individuation.

10. which appears to be due, in part, to the production of serotonin, almost all of which is produced in the gut; and partly to the protrusion of nerve fibers into the gut lumen, which then relay information into the brain via the vagus nerve [Carding, 37.00–41.00]

11. I can think of few more acutely worrying examples than that of the recent expansion of MAID (Medical Assistance in Dying, as it is called here in Canada) to include, beginning in the spring of 2024, those who are not terminally ill and whose death is not imminent but who are afflicted by mental distress or mental illness; and which is poised to become available to children over the age of twelve without parental consent. As I see it, this speaks to the catastrophic predicament

of Western society, the pathological hopelessness and helplessness of its responses and an astounding failure of imagination.

Bibliography

Adorno, Theodor W., and Max Horkheimer. *Towards a New Manifesto: Conversations Between Adorno and Horkheiner 1956*. Digital edition. https://files.libcom.org/files/Adorno_Horkheimer_NM-read.pdf.

Bachelard, Gaston. 1969. *The Poetics of Reverie*. Translated by Daniel Russell. New York: The Orion Press.

Bagga, Deepika, Christoph Stefan Aigner, Johanna Louise Reichert, Cinzia Cecchetto, Florian Ph. S. Fischmeister, Peter Holzer, Christine Moissl-Eichinger, and Veronika Schöpf. 2019. "Influence of 4-Week Multi-Strain Probiotic Administration on Resting-State Functional Connectivity in Healthy Volunteers." *European Journal of Nutrition* 58 (5): 1821–27.

Benjamin, Walter. 1979. *One-Way Street and Other Writings*. Translated by Edmund Jephcott and Kingsley Shorter. London: Verso.

Clastres, Pierre. 1989. "Society Against the State." In *Society Against the State*. Translated by Robert Hurley in collaboration with Abe Stein. New York: Zone Books.

———. 2010. *Archeology of Violence*. Translated by Jeanine Herman. Los Angeles: Semiotext(e).

Descola, Philippe. 2014. *Beyond Nature and Culture*. Edited by Marshall David Sahlins and translated by Janet Lloyd. Chicago: University of Chicago Press.

———. 2015. "Beyond Nature and Culture." In *The Handbook of Contemporary Animism*, edited by Graham Harvey, 77–91. Abingdon: Routledge.

Diderot, Denis. 2002. "Encyclopedia [1755]." In *The Encyclopedia of Diderot & d'Alembert: Collaborative Translation Project*, translated by Philip Stewart. Ann Arbor: University of Michigan Press.

Dreyfus, Hubert L. 1991. *Being-in-the-World: A Commentary on Heidegger's Being and Time, Division I*. Cambridge, MA: MIT Press.

Gut Bacteria and Mind Control: To Fix Your Brain Fix Your Gut! 2015. https://quadram.ac.uk/gut-bacteria-and-mind-control/.

———. 2008. *Being and Time*. Translated by John Macquarrie and Edward S. Robinson. New York: Harper Perennial.

Heidegger, Martin. 1994. *Basic Questions of Philosophy: Selected problems of "Logic."* Translated by Richard Rojcewicz and André Schuwer. Bloomington: Indiana University Press.

———. 1995. *The Fundamental Concepts of Metaphysics: World, Finitude, Solitude*. Translated by William McNeill and Nicolas Walker. Bloomington: Indiana University Press.

———. 2008. *Being and Time*. Translated by John MacQuarrie and Edward Robinson. New York: Harper Perennial.
Hirschman, Albert O. 2013. *The Passions and the Interests*. Princeton, NJ: Princeton University Press.
Kingsnorth, Paul, and Dougald Hine. 2014. *Uncivilization: The Dark Mountain Manifesto*. Bristol, UK: The Dark Mountain Project.
Limbana, Therese, Farah Khan, and Noha Eskander. 2020. "Gut Microbiome and Depression: How Microbes Affect the Way We Think." *Cureus* 12 (8) : e9966.
Lingis, Alphonso. 1986. *Phenomenological Explanations*. 96. Dordrecht: Martinus Nijhoff.
———. 1994. *The Community of Those Who Have Nothing in Common*. Bloomington: Indiana University Press.
———. 2018a. "Sensation and Sentiment." In *The Alphonso Lingis Reader*, edited by Tom Sparrow, 3–12. Minneapolis: University of Minnesota Press.
———. 2018b. "The Elements." In *The Alphonso Lingis Reader*, edited by Tom Sparrow, 43–54. Minneapolis: University of Minnesota Press.
———. 2018c. "The Levels." In *The Alphonso Lingis Reader*, edited by Tom Sparrow, 55–70. Minneapolis: University of Minnesota Press.
———. 2018d. "The Sensuality and the Sensitivity." In *The Alphonso Lingis Reader*, edited by Tom Sparrow, 13–24. Minneapolis: University of Minnesota Press.
———. 2018e. "The Unlived Life Is Not Worth Examining." In *The Alphonso Lingis Reader*, edited by Tom Sparrow, 183–90. Minneapolis: University of Minnesota Press.
Marcuse, Herbert. 1966. *Eros and Civilization: A Philosophical Inquiry into Freud*. Boston: Beacon Press.
———. 2007. "Remarks on a Redefinition of Culture." In *The Essential Marcuse: Selected Writings of Philosopher and Social Critic Herbert Marcuse*, edited by Andrew Feenberg and William Leiss, 13–31. Boston: Beacon Press.
Monbiot, George. 2014. "Cleansing the Stock." https://www.monbiot.com/2014/10/21/cleansing-the-stock/.
Nancy, Jean-Luc. 2015. *After Fukushima: The Equivalence of Catastrophes*. New York: Fordham University Press.
Naveh, Danny, and Nurit Bird-David. 2015. "Animism, Conservation and Immediacy." In *The Handbook of Contemporary Animism*, edited by Graham Harvey, 27–37. Abingdon: Routledge.
Rahmatia, and Tommy Christomy. 2020. "Eco-Phenomenology in the Local Concept of Buginese Agriculture Based on *Kutika* Manuscript." *E3S Web of Conferences* 211: 01008.
Ratcliffe, Matthew. 2015. *Experiences of Depression: A Study in Phenomenology*. Oxford: Oxford University Press.
Roszak, Theodore. 1973. *Where the Wasteland Ends: Politics and Transcendence in Postindustrial Society*. Garden City, NY: Anchor Books.

Sahlins, Marshall. 1972. "The Original Affluent Society." In *Stone Age Economics*, by Marshall Sahlins, 1–39. New York: Routledge.
Schürmann, Reiner. 1987. *Heidegger on Being and Acting: From Principles to Anarchy*. Translated by Christine-Marie Gros and R. Schürmann. Bloomington: Indiana University Press.
Serres, Michel. 1982. "Platonic Dialogue." In *Hermes: Literature, Science, Philosophy*, edited by Josué V. Harari and David F. Bell, 65–70. Baltimore: Johns Hopkins University Press.
Shepard, Paul. 1998. *Nature and Madness*. Athens: University of Georgia Press.
Sparrow, Tom. 2007. "Bodies in Transit: The Plastic Subject of Alphonso Lingis." *Janus Head* 10 (1): 99–122.
———. 2018a. "Editor's Introduction: A Philosopher of Transience." In *The Alphonso Lingis Reader*, vii–xvii. Minneapolis: University of Minnesota Press.
Steiner, George. 1971. *In Bluebeard's Castle: Some Notes towards the Redefinition of Culture*. The T. S. Eliot Memorial Lectures for 1970. New Haven: Yale University Press.
Suzman, James. 2017. *Affluence without Abundance: The Disappearing World of the Bushmen*. London: Bloomsbury.
Taylor, Charles. 2007. *A Secular Age*. Cambridge, MA: Harvard University Press.
Thoreau, Henry David. 1995. *Walking*. New York: Penguin Books.
Toadvine, Ted. 2014. "Apocalyptic Imagination and the Silence of the Elements." In *Ecopsychology, Phenomenology and the Environment: The Experience of Nature*, edited by Douglas A. Vakoch and Fernando Castrillón, 211–22. New York: Springer.
van Bruggen et al. 2021. "Indirect Effects of the Herbicide Glyphosate on Plant, Animal and Human Health Through Its Effects on Microbial Communities." *Frontiers in Environmental Science* 9.
Wallace, Caroline J. K., and Roumen Milev. 2017. "The Effects of Probiotics on Depressive Symptoms in Humans: A Systematic Review." *Annals of General Psychiatry* 16 (1): 14.
Wilde, Oscar. 2001. "The Soul of Man Under Socialism." In *The Soul of Man Under Socialism and Selected Critical Prose*, edited by Linda C. Dowling, 127–60. Penguin Classics. London: Penguin Books.
Zerzan, John. 2012. *Future Primitive Revisited*. Port Townsend: Feral House.
Zuboff, Shoshana. 2015. "Big Other: Surveillance Capitalism and the Prospects of an Information Civilization." *Journal of Information Technology* 30 (1): 75–89.

10

From Love of World to Love of Earth
Taking Responsibility for the Future of the Planet

KELLY OLIVER

> If we want to be at home on this earth, even at the price of being at home in this century, we must try to take part in the interminable dialogue with its essence.
>
> —Arendt 1953, 392

In her meditation on education, Hannah Arendt asks if we can love the world enough to take responsibility for it. What happens to Arendt's question if we ask instead: can we love the earth enough to take responsibility for it and for its future? In this chapter, I turn to some of Arendt's thoughts on love of the world as a springboard to imagine responsibility in relationship not only to the human world but also in relationship to the earth with all its creatures. I argue that we have a responsibility not only to other human beings but also to all living beings and to the earth itself. In the end, I propose an earth ethics based on a love of earth, which obligates us to our earthbound existence and fellow earthlings. In other words, I propose that earthlings rather than human beings are the subjects of ethics, including intergenerational ethics.

Arendt says, "In the last analysis, the human world is always the product of man's *amor mundi*, a human artifice whose potential immortality is always subject to the mortality of those who build it and the natality of those who come to live in it" (Arendt 2005, 203; cf. Beiner 1997). But what does Arendt mean by *amor mundi*? What kind of love is love of the world? Arendt is clear that romantic or sentimental love is a private affair and not part of the political world. Yet she also names love, along with friendship, as one of the oases in the desert of worldlessness that can restore the meaning of the world. Furthermore, she acknowledges the importance of intimate relations to sustain one's ability to enter into the public world and perform in the world of politics. What, then, is the relationship between love and politics if what binds us to the public world is love, *amor mundi*?[1]

Perhaps love of world is the primary political virtue. We might answer that love of the world is necessary for politics to become ethical. Certainly love of the world is the foundation for Arendt's famous claim for "the right to have rights," which is to say that ultimately *amor mundi* is the force behind universal or transnational norms.[2] For "the right to have rights" goes beyond any legal authority, national or transnational, and takes us into the realm of ethical norms grounded in our very belonging together on the earth and in the world.[3] This is the ethics based on our shared home, our cohabitation on the earth; and the unchosen nature of that cohabitation compels us to choose it, even to love it.[4] Love of world is the embrace of this plurality that makes world and worlds possible.

Insofar as Arendt emphasizes the importance of forgiveness, along with promises, to the political bond, her invocation of love, at least implicitly, resonates with the notion of *agape* as forgiveness. And yet her appeal to Augustine and his proclamation "I want you to be" suggests a form of love beyond forgiveness and towards acceptance. But even acceptance of the existence of the other, or stranger, is not enough to warrant the claim "I *want* you to be." Otherwise, Augustine could say, "I accept that you are." Embracing the existence of the other and our coexistence or cohabitation with others, including other creatures, takes us beyond either forgiveness or acceptance and towards love. To be political, and in our framework also ethical, this love is more than romantic or sentimental love. Rather, love of those with whom we cohabit the earth—along with love of other living beings and perhaps even nonliving things—is an ethical and political choice. The paradoxical situation in which we find ourselves that is essential to the human condition is that although we do not choose with whom to inhabit the earth, ethical and political bonds require making that choice. Choosing to love. This is to say, ethical relations to others require the Augustinean proclamation "I want you to be"; and political bonds require extending this proclamation to whole groups of people, perhaps including nonhuman animals. Imagine what it would mean to say to all animals, or all earthlings, "I want you to be." This would be an ethics of affirmation of all and each. In this regard, Arendt's extension of the Augustinean proclamation becomes the basis for an ethics of coexistence or cohabitation that grounds all political claims. Arendt's notion of *amor mundi* signals not only a love of one's own world, but also and moreover a love of the world of others. For Arendt, worldliness is always a matter of difference, diversity, and coexistence or cohabitation with others unlike me. *Amor mundi* is an embrace of the diversity of the world, and of worlds.[5] It is also an acknowledgment of our deep dependence on the plurality of the earth.

In this regard, we may think of love in terms of *eros* as the life force that compels us to bond with others.[6] *Eros* takes us out of ourselves and towards others; and through connections with others, human and nonhuman, we not only survive but also thrive as individuals and as species. For Plato, *eros* is a form of love as passion that gives rise to creativity and the highest forms of contemplation. The tensions inherent in *eros* move us towards something beyond ourselves. For Arendt, it is our relationships with other people that give rise to creativity, contemplation, and move us towards the political bonds through which we peacefully, more or less, cohabit. This creativity born from love provides an oasis of meaning in what she calls the desert of meaninglessness. That meaninglessness ensues from denying relationality, plurality, and the dynamic nature of the political world.

Ultimately, for Arendt, natality is the concept that signifies the plurality and diversity of the world as enabling both creativity and contemplation. The unpredictability of birth, which even in the most controlled and usual of circumstances results in the birth of a unique individual who is a stranger to his or her parents, becomes the symbol for the uncanny strangeness of the world.

We might compare this aspect of natality, namely the necessity to choose the unchosen, to Emmanuel Levinas's notion of "paternal election," which is the choice of this particular unchosen, even unbidden, child (Levinas 1969, 279). Can we expand this election of one particular child to every human being, and beyond? Can we elect each and every earthling because it is born, hatched, spawned, and therefore unique? Certainly, Arendt would never go so far since she reserves birth and uniqueness for human beings alone (Arendt 1958, 176). Yet what is more uncanny than another species?

Through friendship and love we not only come to terms with this uncanny strangeness, but also learn to embrace it, which is possible only when we give up the fantasy of being able to control or master it. Interpreting Augustine's love as affirmation of existence and cohabitation, Arendt says: "This mere existence, that is, all that which is mysteriously given us by birth and which includes the shape of our bodies and the talents of our minds, can be adequately dealt with only by the unpredictable hazards of friendship and sympathy, or by the great and incalculable grace of love, which says with Augustine '*Volo ut sis* (I want you to be),' without being able to give any particular reason for such supreme and unsurpassable affirmation" (Arendt 1966, 301). The ethical affirmation of each that grounds the political bond comes from the heart and not reason alone. Through natality, which Arendt calls a *miracle* that saves the world, this affirmation renews the bonds of the political world.[7] Although it is not always the case in practice, in principle, through the birth of each unique being, we come to accept, even love, the newcomer who is at first always a stranger. Natality renews the political world by injecting plurality with diversity since every individual is unique. And plurality, says Arendt, "is the law of the earth" (Arendt 1981, 19).

If, as Arendt claims, plurality is the law of the earth, and politics is based on this plurality and diversity, the affirmation of each one, what are the implications of our shrinking biodiversity on the planet for politics? What happens when climate change leads to the spread of a literal desert along with Arendt's metaphorical one? Could the earth itself become the "you" in Augustine's "I want you to be"? To answer these questions, we must extend Arendt's philosophy of plurality to include all earthly beings.

In *The Crisis of Education*, Arendt claims: "Education is the point at which we decide whether we love the world enough to assume responsibility for it and by the same token save it from that ruin which, except for renewal, except for the coming of the new and young, would be inevitable" (Arendt 1954, 196). Echoing but extending Arendt's sentiment, we might ask, what would it mean to love not only the world, but also the earth, enough to assume responsibility for it and for its future and the future of its inhabitants? Can we imagine a world in which the earth matters enough that we take responsibility for it? What is the relationship between love and responsibility?

Before we can extend Arendt's love of world to love of earth, we must consider the relationship between earth and world. Arendt opens *The Human Condition* with a description of the earth as "the very quintessence of the human condition" since it is most probably the only planet where we can "move and breathe without effort and artifice" (1958, 2). She defines the world, as opposed to the earth, as human artifice, or what she calls our "man-made home erected on earth" (1958, 134). In between earth and world, she introduces a third term, *nature*, which is associated with organic life "outside this artificial world," and through which "man remains related to all other living organisms" (1958, 2).

Although the earth provides the raw materials with which humans build their homes, and nature supports life, both are indifferent to the plight of humans. Only our created world shields us from this indifference and protects us from the many dangers inherent in life on earth. And for Arendt, protection, security, and safety are the building blocks of home, which come through a sense of belonging. The earth itself, then, is not our home until we make it home; before then (if we can imagine a time before the world, which would be a time when we were animals and not yet human), while we lived on the earth, it was not home. And although this is where we belong in the sense that our bodies cannot live anyplace else, in Arendt's account, as animals, we do not yet have the sense of belonging inherent in feeling at home. Belonging, it seems, is a property of the world and not of the earth. And world is distinctive of humankind.

In an important sense, for Arendt we do not share the earth, but only the world. Again, as animals on the earth, we share the planet with other species; but for Arendt, like Heidegger, animals are never properly *Mit-sein*; and therefore sharing, properly speaking, is reserved for the human world, which by its nature is necessarily shared (e.g., 1958, 176). Whereas in relation to the *earth*, homo sapiens is an animal species living among other animal species, in relation to the *world*, we are human beings relating in meaningful ways to other human subjects. The world is always plural and shared; there is no private world in isolation.

Arendt says: "No human life, not even the life of the hermit in nature's wilderness, is possible without a world which directly or indirectly testifies to the presence of other human beings. All human activities are conditioned by the fact that men live together . . ." (1958, 22). As an animal species, however—what she calls *animal laborans*—we are "worldless and herdlike" and therefore "incapable of building or *inhabiting* a public, worldly realm" (1958, 160; my emphasis). As an animal species we *live* on the earth, and only as human beings do we *inhabit* a world. The world is what makes the earth a home for human beings. In other words, our life on earth—if we can imagine life apart from world—may be necessary for sheer survival, but only when we create a world is it a meaningful life.

Although she repeatedly uses the phrase "a world" when discussing what human beings create, Arendt also refers to "the world" as what human beings inhabit together. The possibility of different worlds may be most apparent when she says that through the child, the lovers "insert a new world into the existing world" (1958, 242). As we have seen, however, she insists that any world is shared; no one has a world of her own. Yet it is unclear how many it takes to constitute a world. How many people make up a world? Is the child a world unto itself, or do the lovers and the child make up their own world? Allowing that there is no plurality of one, how many does it take to make a plurality?

For Arendt, there is a world only because there are perspectives. And there are perspectives only because there is plurality. Because human beings are diverse and relate to each other across differences, there is a world. "The world comes into being only if there are perspectives" (Arendt 1954, 175). And the more perspectives there are, the more world we have, not just in the sense of understanding the whole or the true world, or the real world, but also in the sense of enriching the meaning of the world. Arendt says, "the more peoples there are in the world who stand in some particular relationship with one another, the more world there is to form between them, and the larger and richer that world will be" (1954, 176). For Arendt, human beings are human by virtue of existing together in a world. And a world exists only through the plurality of human relationships. If this plurality or diversity disappears or is annihilated through war, then the world disappears. She couldn't be more forceful when she claims: "Human beings in the true sense of the term can exist only where there is a world, and there can be a world in the true sense of the term only where the plurality of the human race is more than a simple multiplication of a single species" (1954, 176). Without plurality, we are worldless.

We might push Arendt further at this point and argue that the human race is dependent on the plurality of species, and there is a human world only where there are interrelations between humans and other species. The plurality that is constitutive of the human condition extends beyond human diversity and into biodiversity. Even if, with Arendt, we separate world and earth by associating world with the human world of meaning and earth with our given physical limitations or animal bodies, still both the human world of meaning and our existence on the physical earth are dependent on not just human diversity but also biodiversity. Our imaginations are fueled by our cohabitation with different species, evidenced by our mythologies, literatures, and even our scientific research, inherently involved as they are with animals. Indeed, animal metaphors fill our language. And it is impossible to imagine what our world or worlds would be like without other animals species sharing our planet. Without our animal cohabitants, the life of the mind, as Arendt calls it, would be severely impoverished. In terms of our embodied existence, our very survival depends on other species and animals, especially an entire universe of microscopic organisms with whom we share a symbiotic relationship, not only on the planet, but also within our very bodies. Without plurality beyond mere human plurality, then, we can inhabit neither world(s) nor earth.

Going beyond Arendt's distinction between earth and world, the earth operates as both a limit concept and a concept of limit that has the potential not only to transform our thinking about political responsibility, but also to ground politics in an ethical obligation conceptually, if not chronologically, prior to the possibility of world or politics. As Arendt would be the first to admit, the world is radically dependent on earth. How does it transform Arendt's conception of *love of world* as an embrace of human diversity and human creativity if we consider that human beings are first and foremost earthlings? And what is love of earth if it includes not only human beings, but also all other beings who live on the earth, whether or not they have a language or concept with which to call it "home"? Can we conceive of love of earth as the basis for an ethics of earthbound creatures that share a planet even if they do not share a world? Can we imagine an ethics grounded on the fact that we share the earth but not the world? Finally, how is this earth ethics a form of *terraphilia* or love of earth?

Certainly an ethical notion of love cannot be reduced to stereotypes or fantasies of romantic or familial love. On the one hand, an ethics of love is an acknowledgment of the role of affects in ethics. Affects are the force that binds us to our obligations and compels us to act on them. Love of the earth, or *terraphilia*, is an emotional connection that binds us to others and to our environment. On the other hand, like our cohabitation on this planet, love is unchosen. And yet, to become ethical, it must be chosen and affirmed. In this sense, love is the affirmation of our bond to others and to the earth. To become ethical, and to ground political commitments, our dependence on others and on the earth must be avowed and then taken up, poetically or responsibly in the sense of opening onto, rather than closing off, possible interpretations, possible worlds.

Cohabitation is unbidden, and yet we can affirm it.[8] With Augustine, we can say, "I want you to be." Or, with Martin Luther King, we can say, "I decided to love." Or, without saying those words, perhaps without language, we can act in such a way as to affirm the other's existence. Love, like cohabitation, is an essential part of the human condition. But it is also an essential part of the animal condition if we consider that most animals rely on cooperation and empathy to survive and thrive. In this sense, love is an emotional bond and more; it is also a life force that bonds individuals to each other and to the earth. It is the connective tissue that binds each living being to others and to their environment. Obviously, this is a very different, and broader, notion of love than our everyday usage, or the romantic notion, of *love*, particularly insofar as the ethical responsibility to love, or the love that makes us responsible, paradoxically, requires that we choose the unchosen. We must cooperate and share to survive and thrive, yet we also must affirm cohabitation and the existence of each and all.

It is not just our own belonging to earth, then, that is at stake in earth ethics. Rather, all earthlings belong to earth. And the earth belongs to earthlings. In terms of earth ethics, this belonging requires an affirmation of the sort Augustine names when he says, "I want you to be." This affirmation of the other's existence can foster a sense of belonging. Rather than conferring belonging on another through a sovereign affirmation, this notion of the affirmation brings with it an ethical obligation to free other beings into their own belonging to their environments and to the earth. Indeed, acknowledging that all living beings belong to the earth is the beginning of such an affirmation. Furthermore, the realization that the earth belongs to us as our shared home through our cohabitation with others, rather than as our possession or a resource that we own, grounds an ethics of earth as an ethics of responsibility to care for that home. This earth ethics is necessary to ground a politics that is responsive to the needs of other earthlings, not just human beings, but all living beings, and "our" planet itself. This obligation to the earth is also an obligation to its future.

Love becomes the basis for political action when this ethical obligation is put into practice through civil law and public policy. This points to the affective and bodily dimension of cosmopolitanism driven by an ethics of earth. Of course, in practical terms, the unconditional principles of hospitality and affirmation of each and all must be tempered by the need to act and to navigate our world in proximity to others. Indeed, negotiating practical political concerns may require that we do not extend hospitality to all. For example, think of Arendt's remarks on Eichmann, or others who do not respect plurality or diversity, or those who brutally close off the possibility of the others' response; such people may not be welcomed.[9] And yet we are obligated to hold open that possibility. In this way, the force of the ethical—of loving enough to take responsibility—must jut through political practice.

Love provides the force of the ethical and political obligations to others (human and nonhuman) and to the earth (organic and inorganic) through the realization of our fundamental dependence on them. In this way, love of earth is not just altruism towards other living beings and the ecosystems that support them, but also a drive towards our own survival as creatures deeply embedded in those ecosystems with those others. As some biologists argue, we have evolved to share and care because those values are in our own best interests as well as the interest of the planet.[10] Today, as we contemplate man-made climate change and man-made pollution, however, we have to wonder whether our industrial evolution is putting the earth at risk. Ultimately, caring for the earth, acting as its steward, may involve moving beyond concerns for intergenerational, human survival and towards the survival of the planet along with its billions of nonhuman inhabitants.

Some biologists, most notably James Lovelock, maintain that the earth is a self-regulating living organism, made up of other living organisms in interlocking relations with rocks, oceans, and atmosphere. These interlocking relationships must be maintained in a delicate balance because if any one part comes to dominate, the whole is threatened. The most obvious example is the human dominance of the planet, which is threatening the whole with dangerous levels of pollution. This leads Lovelock to argue, "it is the health of the planet that matters, not that of some individual species of organisms" (Lovelock 1988, xix). And yet the health of the planet is intimately tied to, if not the consequence of, those interlocking individual species of organisms. Even so, considering the health of the earth rather than the survival of our own human species gives us a different perspective on what it means to "save the earth." The earth and its biosphere, however, are inseparable. For what is the earth without it? It would be just another lifeless planet. As inhabitants of earth's biosphere, we—that is, all living creatures—share the fact that we cannot live anywhere else. And while this fact in itself is not a prescription for ethical or political action, it should play an essential role in the development of our ethical and political norms.

Indeed, some biologists maintain that *biophilia* is not only essential to life, but also a prime motivator for human behavior. For example, Edward O. Wilson argues that *biophilia* "is the innately emotional affiliation of human beings to other living organisms" (Wilson 1993, 31). And extending Wilson's *biophilia hypothesis*, Stephen Kellert claims that human values and human fulfillment are inherently and profoundly tied to our relationship with nature and with other living beings on earth (Kellert and Wilson 1993, 42–43). These biologists see human values and human development as a result not only of our relationships with other life forms, but also of our love for, and affiliation with, them. *Biophilia*, they argue, has distinct evolutionary advantages for individual species, interspecies relationships, and ultimately for the biosphere itself. I propose, however, that it is impossible to conceive of the *biophilia hypothesis* without also the *terraphilia hypothesis*. For everything we know of life is supported by, and exists on, the earth. To love other living creatures and "lifelike processes" is to love the earth *and* its biosphere.[11] After all, the biosphere *belongs* to the earth.

How can we develop an earth ethics based on the *terraphilia hypothesis*? In other words, how can we develop the notion of responsibility to the earth based on love of it? To answer these questions, we need to clarify what we mean by *earth*, *responsibility*, and *love*. What becomes clear is that by earth we mean much more than a planet among other planets. Earth is the home to all living creatures (at least as far as we know). The earth is a network of relationships and connections that include its complicated biosphere, which is dependent on its lithosphere, hydrosphere, and atmosphere. What we mean by *earth* is a rich and complex relationality that sustains all earthlings, organic and not, in our shared *home*. *Our shared home* connotes belonging because *we belong to the earth* and not because the earth belongs to us, at least not as our possession.

What does it mean to love this earth, this rich network of relationality that sustains earthlings as our shared home? At this point, it is instructive to consider that the Ancient Greeks had several words for different kinds of *love*. *Philia* is usually associated with Aristotle's discussion of friendship, which has many different forms. At its best, *philia* involves affection and fondness for another or others, along with altruistic actions that benefit those others without concern for self. *Agape* is associated with spiritual or unconditional love and becomes a centerpiece of the Christian New Testament. This type of love is selfless and, at the extreme, even sacrificial. *Eros* means erotic or intimate love, passion, and longing. For Plato, however, this longing is associated with creativity, such that *eros* gives birth to the highest forms of thought.

All these forms of love contribute to love of the earth and of other earthlings. Our literal and figurative kinship with other species, and our dependence on them, may be conceived in terms of *philia*. Caring for the earth through what Heidegger calls its "telling refusal," which always points beyond our mortal existence, may be conceived in terms of *agape* (Heidegger 1995, 139). Indeed, caring beyond our own selfish needs may require *agape*. And *eros* as love and longing gives rise to our greatest creativity and contemplation through the strife of uncanny encounters with otherness. We could say that, as Arendt calls it, the "miracle" of cohabitation across vast differences—differences so great that we cannot even begin to understand each other—gives rise to creativity and contemplation. Creativity and contemplation, then, are not the result of sovereignty, autonomy, or mastery but rather of dependence, belonging, and deeply shared bonds with those whom we may not even know exist. For Arendt, the creativity born from love offers an oasis in the desert of meaninglessness that results from denying the plurality and natality of our existence. Creativity and contemplation are the result of unpredictability and not mastery, the uncanny unpredictability that is characteristic of our shared home, planet earth. Sigmund Freud links love with *eros* and *eros* with life. This connection between love and life may provide a starting place for thinking about love of earth. In his early work, Freud opposes *eros* to ego as the drive that connects us to others and thereby keeps us alive both as individuals and as a species. Ego, on the other hand, is what separates us off as individuals and puts us at odds with others. Eventually, Freud formulates *eros* as the counterbalance to *thanatos*. Again, *eros* is the drive for life that connects us to others and the world, while *thanatos* is the death drive that longs for equilibrium. In this regard, *eros* is dynamic and longs for relationships with all of their tensions and unpredictability, while *thanatos* wants stability and longs to overcome all tensions and return to a steady state. The death drive is the desire to avoid all tensions, even the pleasurable ones. *Eros*, on the other hand, is love as strife. *Eros*, then, is the dynamic life force that binds us to others. In this sense, it is from *eros* that we get compassion and tenderness, along with passion and erotic love (e.g., Freud 1920).

In Darwinian terms, *eros* is the social instinct that drives all sentient beings towards tenderness, compassion, and cooperation. In fact, Darwin imagines the evolution of tenderness and "sympathy," which become "virtues" that are passed on—initially by a few—until they spread and eventually become "incorporated" into life as we know it (Darwin 1981, 101). *Eros* not only gives rise to compassion, cooperation, and sympathy, but also to empathy and play. In other words, social bonds are formed through various manifestations of *eros* as the dynamic force of life.

Zoologists and primatologists have confirmed that play is important in establishing empathy and social bonding in many animal species, including humans.[12] For example, psychologist Alison Gopnik proposed that "humans' extended period of imaginative play, along with the traits it develops, has helped select for the big brain and rich neural networks that characterize Homo sapiens" (Dobbs 2013). And neuroscientist Paul MacLean argues that play is essential in the evolution of empathy in the human species. Moreover, he links play to the formation of a sense of social responsibility

(MacLean 1990, 380). There is increasing evidence that empathy and a sense of ethical responsibility for others within and across species is not only present in the so-called animal kingdom, but also is continuing to evolve in the human species. Primatologist Frans de Waal's pioneering work on the evolution of morality, from (and within) our animal ancestors to humans, makes evident that animals are empathic and have a sense of responsibility for others, which can be seen as a proto-ethical, if not also an ethical, response. Studies of rats and monkeys indicate that they would rather go without food themselves than witness pain inflicted on others (de Waal 2006, 28–29). Sharing and grooming behavior in animals also indicates a sense of gratitude and reciprocity that could be interpreted as proto-ethical behaviors (de Waal 2006). Following Darwin, de Waal argues that our moral sense or conscience evolved from animal sociability. Furthermore, he maintains that any animal that develops a certain level of intellectual ability will develop moral sensibility (de Waal 2009, 8). De Waal concludes that we can learn from nature and from animals about empathy and sharing, lessons that can only help us cooperate in our increasingly globalized world (de Waal 2009). His work suggests not only that empathy evolves within species, but also that empathy evolves between or across species. In this case, the biosphere is evolving to be more empathetic. Certainly, humans are becoming more empathic towards other animals.

As we have seen, biologist Edward O. Wilson proposes that human beings have evolved through *biophilia*, which is to say, through love of life and love of other living creatures. He argues that the biosphere is a dynamic system in which all parts are interrelated. Extinguish one microorganism, and you cannot predict the consequences as they ripple through the ecosystem. Human beings are the result of the great biodiversity of earth. "Biodiversity," says Wilson, "is the frontier of the future" (Wilson 1993, 39). He identifies biophilia with a "spiritual craving" inherent in our genes that cannot be satisfied through the colonization of space because other planets are not only inhospitable to life, but also too far away. There is more life, organization, and complexity in a handful of the earth's soil than on the surface of all the other known planets combined, which is why he concludes, "The true frontier for humanity is life on earth" (Wilson 1993, 39). We have evolved to love living beings and to be fascinated by other species. But given rapidly diminishing biodiversity, there is an urgent need for "an environmental ethic based on it" (Wilson 1993, 40). Affirming our dependence on the biodiversity of the biosphere may be a step in that direction, especially if we embrace biophilia as interspecies love. Given that the Greek *philia* is associated with mental love or friendship, however, we need to add the embodied sensual dimension of *eros* to imagine an embodied environmental ethic based on our radical relationality not only with other species but also with the earth that supports us all.

Interspecies love may be evolving for the sake of the biosphere. The biodiversity on which our biosphere depends may require interspecies cooperation and interspecies love. Given what human beings have done to destroy ourselves and to destroy the habitats of various species and slaughter others, human attitudes towards our earthly companions need to evolve if we are to learn to share the planet.[13] Our changing attitudes towards other animals signal a new era of interspecies relationships. Certainly the dramatic shift among many people in developed countries to consider companion animals as family, and to love and mourn them, is evidence of the evolution of *eros*. We could say that the life force is put into the service of interspecies cohabitation. And interspecies cohabitation becomes the ground for ethical responsibility to earth and its inhabitants. *Eros* is the groundless ground of interspecies ethics and the life force of earth ethics.

In *Interspecies Ethics*, Cynthia Willett develops a connection between ethics and *eros* manifest in her earlier work. Here, focusing on relationships between species and the evolution of ethics from play, she argues that ethics is thoroughly social and develops from play and laughter as ways of facilitating social relations, which are essential to all social animals, including human beings.[14] She argues that the "principleless principle" of ethics is not found in philosophical *logos*, but rather in playful encounters through *eros* as a biosocial drive that facilitates bonds between individuals and between species, and creates a sense of belonging and home. Willett describes *eros* as a drive towards home, but not the sentimental notion of home in popular culture or nationalist movements.[15] Contrary to this sentimental notion of home, *ethos* as habitat or home has everything to do with *eros* or love as the social bonding agent that brings creatures together and gives them a sense of belonging.[16] This drive towards home is not an individual enterprise, nor is it self-contained within one body. Rather, its means and ends are sociality itself and the bonds that make not just surviving but also thriving possible. Sociality and belonging are tied to earthly cohabitation and our shared, yet singular, bond to the earth.

In this earth ethics, an extended Arendtian plurality of worlds makes up the biosphere, which is held together through *biophilia*, or the love of different living beings. Through this biodiversity and cultural diversity, we share an inherent bond to the earth, and the need to belong to it, as well as to our own world(s) grounded on it. Animals too have their own cultures, which contribute to the cultural diversity and plurality of worlds on earth.[17] Moreover, the diversity of worlds and cultures on earth contribute to our uncanny home, both familiar and strange, but certainly where we belong. While earth may resist and refuse attempts to assimilate it into a notion of *home* as completely known and familiar, it grounds our sense of home as the uncanny mystery of cohabitation on this planet that we all necessarily make our home, whether we literally call it *home* or merely live by virtue of our connection to it. Even those of us who do call it *home* (or *Heimat, maison, casa,* or *hjem,* etc.) also live by virtue of belonging to the earth in ways unknown and unknowable to us.

To say that we are earthbound creatures is to say that we have a special bond to the earth. We belong to the earth, just as it belongs to us. Rather than ownership, this sense of belonging harkens back to a more archaic sense of the word that conjures *eros* as longing and companionship. Our life on earth is a longing for home, for a home that we can love, a home that we love enough to take responsibility for. Loving the earth as home enough to take responsibility for it entails an obligation to its future as a possible home for other earthlings. Climate change threatens the possibility of earth as home. Thus, we have an obligation to other earthlings to safeguard our shared earthly home.

Ethos as habitat or home brings with it a sense of belonging to an ecosystem or community.[18] This sense of belonging is not a familiarity that can be taken for granted, especially when we consider earth as home. For, as every creature "knows," the earth is populated with strange others and foreign landscapes that can be welcoming or threatening, and everything in between. For human beings, the earth as home is fore-given and must be interpreted and reinterpreted, even as it is also a prerequisite for meaning. Willett describes "biocultures of meaning" based on social bonds between companions, places, memories, histories, and interspecies relationships.

Meaning both requires social bonds and emerges through social bonds, which are tied to particular spaces or places and times or histories. The relationality of social bonds, including bonds to places and histories, makes meaning possible, even while meaning emerges through relationships. The dynamic of meaning as constituting, and constituted by, our relationships is akin to what I call the *witnessing* structure of response-ability, the structure of address and response.[19] Living creatures are responsive, and an earth ethics promotes our responsibility to open up, rather than close off, the response-ability of others, their ability to respond.

Witnessing or response ethics maintains that even in the face of our lack of understanding, the impossibility of mastery, and inherent unpredictability, we have a responsibility to act in ways that open up the possibility of response from our fellow earthlings and from the earth itself. Obviously this abstract "principleless principle" or "groundless ground" also opens onto the tension between ethics and politics. Ethics requires that we open up response and response-ability in the face of our ignorance—for if we knew with certainty, it would no longer be ethics but social or even natural science. By contrast, politics requires that we negotiate relationships within our living space to survive and thrive, which always necessarily means killing or excluding some others (e.g., deadly bacteria, fungus, and viruses). We might say that an ethical politics is one in which ethics juts through political policy and forces us to continually and vigilantly reassess and reinterpret our responsibility towards others, even if—perhaps especially if—those others are threatening.

Expanding on what I call response ethics, Willett argues for an ethics of "call and response" to recognize the vocal communication and expression of animality in both nonhuman animals and human animals.[20] Importantly, call and response also can refer to interspecies communication, which expands the notion of witnessing to nonhuman animals, and perhaps even beyond if we take a broad enough view of response. In *Animal Lessons*, I expand the notion of witnessing to include nonhuman animals. The basis for ethical relations has moved beyond reason or recognition and towards witnessing to response-ability itself, that is to say, witnessing to the ability to respond, which is the domain of not just humankind, but all animal-kind. In this way, witnessing ethics as response ethics can take us beyond human centrism and towards consideration of the ways in which all the creatures of the earth, and the earth itself, respond. Within response ethics, political and moral subjects are constituted not by their sovereignty and mastery but rather by address and response. Extending the analysis of witnessing, address, and response (broadly conceived) are the basis of earth ethics grounded on cohabitation and interdependence. And the responsibility to engender response, or facilitate the ability to respond, in others and the environment is the primary obligation of earth ethics. This earthly ethos is the result of pathos beyond rationality or recognition because it is based in our embodied relationality, which is bound to other living beings, not only through shared places and histories, but also through the larger biosphere and ecosystems that sustain us, and ultimately through our singular bond to the earth.

An ethics of earth is grounded on the affirmation of bio- and social diversity that make the earth a living planet. Earth ethics emerges from the tension between the absolutely unique place of each one and the collectively shared bond to the earth, both of which necessarily constitute the life of the planet. Earth's biosphere, which cannot be separated from the earth itself, is a dynamic of individuals and communities, species, and interspecies symbioses. And all life is dependent on nonorganic elements that also are terraforming. The earth is this complex of relationships. Insofar as our obligation is to the planet as a living organism, our obligation is also to the future of life on the planet and to sustaining the earth's capacity to sustain life.

Amor mundi based on *amor terra*—love of world based on love of earth—transforms the earth from the meaningless and solitary desert-island feared by Arendt into our uncanny home, as unsettling and mysterious as it is necessary for life. We started with the Arendtian notions that plurality is the law of the earth and that we have a responsibility to love the world. From there, we explored the idea that it is not just that we share physical space, or proximity, on the surface of the earth, but, more significantly, we share a special bond to the earth as our only home, whether home or habitat. This singular bond of all living beings to the earth and to other earthlings, directly and indirectly, obligates us to the sustaining possibility by virtue of which we not only exist and survive, but also live and thrive. All earthlings belong to earth and earth belongs to us. If we see *belonging* not in terms of property, but rather in terms of the longing and companionship of its archaic meanings, then our belonging to the earth is born from our singular bond to earth. Belonging as longing. *Eros* is the drive towards home that is grounded on love of the earth, a love that obligates us to the future of earth as the uncanny home of all earthlings.

Notes

1. Ella Myers develops an ethics based on Arendt's notion of *amor mundi* (2013). She extends Arendt's concept to include material aspects of the world. My concern is to think through love of earth rather than love of world. For Arendt, following Heidegger, earth and world are radically different. For a discussion of the difference, especially the difference between earth and world alienation, see Oliver 2015.

2. Cf. Honig 2006, 120.

3. Bonnie Honig reads Arendt's "right to have rights" in terms of Derrida's unconditional (2006, 107).

4. See Judith Butler's insightful and provocative analysis of Arendt on cohabitation and plurality in *Parting Ways*, 2012.

5. Cf. Chiba 1995, 509 and 534.

6. Chiba argues that Arendt's notion of love as the choice to live with others through friendship must be supplemented with *eros* as the drive toward stable relationships with other people and the world (Chiba 1995, 509 and 534). See also Myers 2013.

7. Cf. Arendt, *The Human Condition*, 247.

8. For a discussion of Arendt on cohabitation, see Butler 2012. See also Oliver, *Earth and World* for an extension of Arendt's notion of cohabitation in relationship to earth ethics (2015). There, I argue that the lack of limits leads to both what Arendt calls *earth alienation* and what I call *world alienation*. Taking a close look at these two concepts and the differences between them in Arendt's texts, I show why we need to think earth and world together as mutually dependent.

9. See Arendt *Eichmann in Jerusalem* 1992 and Butler 2012 on Eichmann.

10. See Rifkin 2009 for a survey of literature on so-called "selfish genes" and altruism as "hard-wired" into human infants and other species.

11. Cf. Kellert and Wilson 1993, 42.

12. For a discussion of the importance of play in the development of empathy in humans and other animals, see Rifkin 2009. See also Pellegrini et al. 2007. For a discussion of some of these studies in relation to philosophy, see Willett 2014. Rifkin cites studies on horses and play, particularly Rebecca Overton 2006.

13. For an assessment of diminishing biodiversity, see Wilson 1993.

14. Along with *Subjectless Sociality, Intersubjective Attunement*, and *Spirituality and Compassion*, Willett identifies *The Biosocial Network as Home* as one of what she calls the *Four Layers of Interspecies Ethics* (Willett 2014, 133).

15. Willett says, "*Eros* is not a bare striving for pleasure or wild intensity but a meaning-laden yearning. *Eros* is a drive toward home" (Willett 2014, 23).

16. Cf. Willett 2014.

17. Maurice Merleau-Ponty discusses animal cultures in his *Nature Lectures* (2003). For an analysis of Merleau-Ponty on animal culture, see Oliver 2009.

18. For a nice discussion of the relationship between rethinking Earth and community, see Brian Schroeder 2004.

19. See Oliver 2001.

20. Cf. Willett 2014.

Bibliography

Arendt, Hannah. 1953. "Understanding and Politics." *Partisan Review* 20 (4): 377–392.

———. 1954. *Between Past and Future*. New York: Penguin.

———. 1958. *The Human Condition*. Chicago: University of Chicago Press.

———. 1966. *The Origins of Totalitarianism*. New York: Harcourt, Brace, and World.

———. 1981. *The Life of the Mind*. New York: Harcourt.
———. 1992. *Eichmann in Jerusalem: A Report on the Banality of Evil*. New York: Penguin.
———. 2005. *The Promise of Politics*. Edited by Jerome Kohn. New York: Schocken.
Beiner, Ronald. 1997. "Love and Worldliness: Hannah Arendt's Reading of Saint Augustine." In *Hannah Arendt: Twenty Years Later*, edited by Larry May and Jerome Kohn. Cambridge, MA: MIT Press.
Benhabib, Seyla. 2006. *Another Cosmopolitanism*. New York: Oxford University Press.
Butler, Judith. 2012. *Parting Ways: Jewishness and the Critique of Zionism*. New York: Columbia University Press.
Chiba, Shin. 1995. "Hannah Arendt on Love and the Political: Love, Friendship, and Citizenship." *The Review of Politics* 57 (3): 505–35.
Darwin, Charles. 1981. *The Descent of Man and Selection in Relation to Sex*. Princeton, NJ: Princeton University Press.
Dobbs, Favid. 2013. "Zeal For Play May Have Propelled Human Evolution." *New York Times*, April 22. http://www.nytimes.com/2013/04/23/science/zeal-for-play-may-have-propelled-human-evolution.html?pagewanted=all.
Freud, Sigmund. 1920. *Beyond the Pleasure Principle*. Translated by James Strachey. New York: Norton Publishers.
Heidegger, Martin. 1995. *The Fundamental Concepts of Metaphysics: World, Finitude, Solitude*. Translated by William McNeill and Nicholas Walker. Bloomington: University of Indiana Press.
Honig, Bonnie. 2006. "Another Cosmopolitanism: Law and Politics in the New Europe." In *Another Cosmopolitanism*, by S. Benhabib and edited by Robert Post, 102–27. Oxford: Oxford University Press.
Kellert, Stephen R., and Edward O. Wilson, eds. 1993. *The Biophilia Hypothesis*. Washington, DC: Island Press.
Lévinas, Emmanuel. 1969. *Totality and Infinity*. Translated by Alphonso Lingis. Pittsburgh: Duquesne University Press.
Lovelock, James. 1988. *The Ages of Gaia: A Biography of our Living Earth*. Oxford: Oxford University Press.
MacLean, Paul. 1990. *The Triune Brain in Evolution: Role in Paleocerebral Functions*. New York: Plenum Press.
Merleau-Ponty, Maurice. 2003. *Nature: Course Notes from the Collège de France*. Translated by Robert Vallier. Evanston, IL: Northwestern University Press.
Myers, Ella. 2013. *Worldly Ethics: Democratic Politics and Care for the World*. Chapel Hill, NC: Duke University Press.
Oliver, Kelly. 2001. *Witnessing: Beyond Recognition*. Minneapolis: University of Minnesota Press.
———. 2009. *Animal Lessons: How They Teach Us to be Human*. New York: Columbia University Press.
———. 2015. *Earth and World*. New York: Columbia University Press.

Overton, Rebecca, and Darrell Doods. 2006. "Lonely Only." *Horse and Rider* 45 (3): 52–73.
Pellegrini, Anthony D., Danielle Dupuis, and Peter K. Smith. 2007. "Play in Evolution and Development." *Developmental Review* 27 (2): 261–76.
Rifkin, Jeremy. 2009. *The Empathic Civilization: The Race to Global Consciousness in a World in Crisis*. New York: Tarcher.
Schroeder, Brian. 2004. "The Inoperative Earth." *Studies in Practical Philosoph.* 4 (1): 126–45.
Vygotsky, Lev S. 1978. "The Role of Play in Development." In *Mind in Society: The Development of Higher Psychological Processes*, translated by M. Cole. Cambridge, MA: Harvard University Press.
Waal, Frans de. 2006. *Our Inner Ape: A Leading Primatologist Explains Why We Are Who We Are*. New York: Riverhead.
———. 2009. *The Age of Empathy: Nature's Lessons For a Kinder Society*. New York: Broadway Books.
Willett, Cynthia. 2014. *Interspecies Ethics*. New York: Columbia University Press.
Wilson, Edward O. 1993. "Biophilia and the Conservation Ethic." In *The Biophilia Hypothesis*, edited by Stephen R. Kellert and Edward O. Wilson. Washington, DC: Island Press.

Contributors

Hiroshi Abe is professor of philosophy and logic at the Graduate School of Human and Environmental Studies at Kyoto University, Japan. He received the Philipp Franz von Siebold Prize in 2017. He has published extensively on the topics of ontology, environmental philosophy, and Japanese philosophy. He coedited *Environmental Philosophy and East Asia: Nature, Time, Responsibility* (Routledge, 2022) with Matthias Fritsch and Mario Wenning.

Eva Buddeberg is professor of philosophy at the University of Wuppertal (Germany). Previously, she taught at the Universities of Frankfurt, Berlin (FU), Konstanz, and Mainz. Her research specializes in moral, social, and political philosophy. She is the author of *Verantwortung im Diskurs: Grundlinien einer rekonstruktiv-hermeneutischen Konzeption moralischer Verantwortung im Anschluss an Hans Jonas, Karl-Otto Apel und Emmanuel Lévinas*, Berlin 2011; her most recent publications include "Grenzen der Toleranz? Überlegungen im Anschluss an Rainer Forst, Pierre Bayle und Wendy Brown"; "Was Pierre Bayle Indeed a Feminist, or What Are the Implications of Bayle's Comments on Abortion for Feminist Theory?"; "Wozu noch Religion? Aneignung religiöser Gehalte als Ergänzung oder Korrektur liberaler Gesellschaften?"; "Moralismuskritik—wer kritisiert wen im Namen der Moral?"; "Kant on the Role of Religion for Moral Progress"; and "Justification Incorporated—a Discursive Approach to Corporate Responsibility" (together with A. Hecker).

Matthias Fritsch is a professor of philosophy at Concordia University, Montréal. In addition to more than fifty journal articles and book chapters, he has published the following books as sole author: *Taking Turns with the Earth: Phenomenology, Deconstruction, and Intergenerational Justice* (Stanford University Press, 2018); *The Promise of Memory: History and Politics in Marx,*

Benjamin, and Derrida (State University of New York Press, 2005). He has coedited the following anthologies: *Intercultural Philosophy and Environmental Justice Between Generations: Indigenous, African, Asian, and Western Perspectives* (Cambridge University Press, in press); *Environmental Philosophy and East Asia* (Routledge, 2022); *Eco-Deconstruction* (Fordham University Press, 2018); *Reason and Emancipation* (Humanity Press, 2007); Martin Heidegger, *Phenomenology of Religious Life* (Indiana University Press, 2004, cotranslator). He has been a Humboldt Fellow in Frankfurt and Berlin, visiting research professor in Kyoto, and senior research fellow at Western Sydney University.

Burkhard Liebsch is a professor of philosophy at the Ruhr University of Bochum (Germany). His phenomenological research focuses mainly on the areas of social and political philosophy. He is author and editor of more than thirty books. His most recent are *Geschichtskritik nach 1954: Aktualität und Stimmenvielfalt* (Hamburg, 2023), *Orientierung und Ander(s)heit* (with W. Stegmaier; Hamburg, 2022), *Einander ausgesetzt—Der Andere und das Soziale* (2 vols., Freiburg/Munich 2019).

Ferdinando G. Menga is a professor of legal philosophy and philosophy of politics at the University of Campania "Luigi Vanvitelli" (Italy). His phenomenological research focuses mainly on contemporary issues in the realms of law, politics, and ethics with a special interest for topics such as intergenerational responsibility, environmental ethics, as well as justice and care. He is author and editor of more than a hundred articles and twenty books, among which the most recent are *Cura* (Milan, 2023), *Rethinking Responsibility* (with E. Gräb-Schmidt and C. Schlenker; Tübingen, 2023), "When the Generational Overlap Is the Challenge Rather Than the Solution: On Some Problematic Versions of Transgenerational Justice" (*The Monist*, 2023), and *Etica intergenerazionale* (Brescia, 2021).

Anne O'Byrne teaches in the Philosophy Department at Stony Brook University. She works on radical democracy, identity, race, genocide, and natality, drawing on twentieth-century and contemporary European philosophy. Her most recent book is *The Genocide Paradox: Democracy and Generational Being* (Fordham, 2023), a study of kinship, taxonomy, and the failure of democracies to resist genocidal violence. She has also published *Natality and Finitude* (Indiana, 2010), and is coeditor of *Logics of Genocide: Structures of Violence and the Contemporary World* (Routledge, 2020), edited with Martin Shuster. She has translated several works by Jean-Luc Nancy including *Being*

Singular Plural (Stanford, 1996), *Corpus II: Writings on Sexuality* (Fordham, 2013), and *Derrida: Supplements* (Fordham, 2023). Articles and book chapters include "Generational Being," "Umbilicus: Toward a Hermeneutics of Generational Difference," "The Task of Knowledgeable Love: Arendt and Portmann in Search of Meaning," "The Ugly Psyche: Arendt and the Right to Opacity," and "Lessons from Anarchist Eugenics." See more at https://www.stonybrook.edu/commcms/philosophy/people/_faculty/byrne.php.

Kelly Oliver recently retired from Vanderbilt University, where she was distinguished professor of philosophy. She is the author of sixteen scholarly books, including *Response Ethics* (Rowman & Littlefield), *Carceral Humanitarianism* (Minnesota University Press), *Earth and World: Philosophy After the Apollo Missions* (Columbia University Press), and *Animal Lessons: How They Teach us to be Human* (Columbia University Press); the editor of another thirteen books, including her most recent coedited volume on *Gaslighting* (forthcoming), and the author of more than one hundred scholarly articles on a variety of topics including refugee detention, capital punishment, animal ethics, sexual violence, images of women and war, psychoanalysis, and film. Her work has been translated into eight languages. She has been interviewed on *ABC News*, appeared on C-SPAN *Book TV*, and published in the *New York Times* and *Los Angeles Times*, among other appearances and publications in popular media. Kelly is also the bestselling author of three award-winning mystery series.

Rebecca van der Post is pursuing her PhD in interdisciplinary humanities at Concordia University in Montreal. Drawing from her other life as a concert violinist, her research straddles phenomenology, Frankfurt School critical theory, anarchist political theory, and sensory anthropology to explore questions to do with sensory and aesthetic immersion, and to trace the environmental, social, and political significance of everyday absorption in the common-or-garden processes of making and doing.

Mario Vergani is professor of theoretical philosophy at the University of Milano "Bicocca" (Italy). His main interests lie in the realm of German and French phenomenology as well as post-structuralism, with a special focus on ethics and education. He is author of numerous articles and monographs, among which the most recent are *Dizionarietto di filosofia per educatori* (Brescia, 2024), "Husserl's Hesitant Attempts to Extend Personhood to Animals" (Husserl Studies, 2021), "Vulnerability: Phenomenological Premises of Juridical Categories in Levinas's Thought" (*Ethics & Politics*, 2020), and *Nascita* (Rome, 2020).

Bernhard Waldenfels is emeritus professor of philosophy at the Ruhr University of Bochum (Germany). He is one of the most prominent living figures in the realm of phenomenological studies. His pathbreaking works have focused on topics such as alterity, interculturality, responsivity, corporeality, as well as a dialogue between German and French contemporary philosophy. Among his many books one may recall *Antwortregister* (Frankfurt a.M., 1994), *Order in the Twilight* (Athens OH, 1996), *Bruchlinien der Erfahrung* (Frankfurt a.M., 2002), *Phenomenology of the Alien* (Evanston, 2006), *Hyperphänomene* (Berlin, 2012), *Sozialität und Alterität* (Berlin, 2015), and *Globalität, Lokalität, Digitalität: Herausforderungen der Phänomenologie* (Berlin, 2022).

Index

alienation, 183, 195; natal, 16, 181, 183–86, 191, 192–93, 195
alterity, 10–11, 48, 55, 76, 83, 88, 111, 119, 121–125 passim, 141, 197, 213–14; Other, 10, 27–28, 37–42 passim, 48, 51, 54–55, 65, 80–88 passim, 92–98 passim, 118–20, 133–41 passim, 190; otherness, 35, 39, 41, 42, 54, 57, 58, 59, 82, 97, 119, 121, 124, 125, 175, 248; others: future, 3, 10–11, 13, 55, 84, 87, 93, 97, 121, 123, 134; sexual, 88
Arendt, Hannah, 18, 124–25, 171, 174, 185–86, 189, 191, 192, 239–49 passim, 251, 254
Augustine, 240–42, 245–46

Bachelard, Gaston, 226–29
biophilia, 247–48, 250, 251
biopolitics. *See under* politics
birth, 11, 12, 27–28, 31, 36–42 passim, 47, 58–59, 74, 79, 98, 170, 189, 191–92, 241–42. *See also* natality
Butler, Judith, 109–10

climate change, 1, 65, 111, 151, 196, 242, 247, 252

Darwall, Stephen, 135–37
death, 16, 27, 30, 31, 39–40, 47, 49, 59, 74, 77, 79, 80, 85–86, 98, 169, 188–91, 193–94, 196, 214, 219; death drive, 167–68, 249; death: of imagination, 229, death: social, 184–85. *See also* mortality
Derrida, Jacques, 40, 83, 97, 118, 126, 187, 197
Descola, Philippe, 213–14
Dilthey, Wilhelm, 33

Edelman, Lee, 167–69
Enlightenment, 184, 195, 216–17
ethics, 32, 117, 133–34, 138, 174, 240, 241, 253; anarchist, 174; discourse, 6, 13, 144–45, 147; earth, 18, 239–40, 245–46, 248, 251–53; future-oriented, 3, 112, 113; intergenerational, 1, 2, 18, 111, 187, 188, 239; interspecies, 251; of love, 245; of the Other, 48, 133; present-centered, 120; response, 253; of responsibility, 246
Eurocentrism, 182, 183

fecundity, 2, 10–11, 16, 59, 88, 97, 187, 190, 194, 197, 214. *See also* generativity

fraternity, 58, 143
freedom, 14–15, 16, 54, 59, 61, 66, 88, 90, 119, 155, 156–57, 163–75 passim; responsive, 54; sexual, 168

Gardiner, Stephen, 111–12
Gauthier, David, 115
generation (verb), 28, 57–58, 171; concept of, 34–35, 73, 76, 81–82
generativity, 6, 9–11, 14–15, 16, 27–42 passim, 57, 66, 73–91 passim, 96, 97, 98, 99, 192, 194; human, 36, 74, 79, 82, 87, 89, 91, 94, 97–98

Habermas, Jürgen, 13, 134, 144–46
Hegel, Georg W. F., 75
Heidegger, Martin, 33–34, 39, 79, 85, 188–91, 194, 221–22, 243, 248
Husserl, Edmund, 35–37, 50, 57, 188

image: of the Human, 14, 156–160
injustice, 41, 62, 122; intergenerational, 193. *See also* justice

Jonas, Hans, 14, 30–31, 91–92, 95, 144, 151–61
justice: generational, 78; intergenerational (IGJ), 3, 6, 7, 8, 9, 111, 113–17, 120, 122, 193, 209. *See also* injustice

Kant, Immanuel, 11, 62, 73–74, 75, 76–77, 85, 98–99, 123–24, 134, 138, 144, 146, 188, 195

Levinas, Emmanuel, 10, 11, 12, 13, 16, 39–41, 48, 49, 54, 55–56, 58, 59, 62, 63–65, 66, 84–85, 87–88, 89, 97, 118–123 passim, 133, 134, 137–147 passim, 190–92, 193, 196–97, 241
lifeworld, 2, 6, 7, 56, 63, 187, 195
Lingis, Alphonso, 17, 210–13, 217–18, 224, 226–233 passim
love (noun), 18, 36, 48, 64, 92, 163, 167, 191, 239–54 passim; *agape*, 240, 248; *eros*, 58, 59, 241, 248–49, 251–52, 254; ethical notion of, 245; free, 15, 166, 172; interspecies, 250–51; of the neighbor, 48, 64, 141; *philia*, 248, 250

Marcuse, Herbert, 17, 220, 226, 227, 229
Marx, Karl, 63–65, 181–84
modernity, 11, 16, 17, 77, 187, 193, 195, 197, 210, 217, 221, 226, 229, 232; critical theory of, 181, 184, 195; Western, 17, 207, 209, 221, 224, 226, 233
mortality, 16, 74–75, 98, 188–91, 194, 239

natality, 6, 8, 16, 98, 125–26, 189, 191–92, 194, 239, 241–42, 249
nature, 77, 79, 95, 151, 152, 166, 171, 181, 194, 216, 217, 226, 229, 230, 243, 247, 250
Nietzsche, Friedrich, 50, 52, 54, 58, 62, 66, 12

obligation: to future generations, 4, 113, 115; intergenerational, 3, 115, 116, 121; moral, 3, 116, 117–18, 138, 146
otherness. *See under* alterity

Parfit, Derek, 29–30, 116
pathos, 10, 49, 50, 52, 54, 253

Patterson, Orlando, 16, 184–86, 189, 193
politics, 142–43, 165, 167, 174, 240, 242, 245, 246, 253; anarchist, 174; biopolitics, 165, 174; of others, 48; responsive, 64, 66
presentism 16, 111–12, 113, 117, 187, 188, 193, 195–96, 209
primitive accumulation (PA), 186, 195–97

Rawls, John, 29, 114–15, 196
reciprocity, 5, 115, 192–93, 250; asymmetrical, 192, 195; nonreciprocity, 4, 30
relations: intergenerational, 6, 7, 11, 30, 89, 186–87, 191–95
representation, 12–13, 55, 109, 110, 152, 164, 173, 227; process of, 55
reproduction, 15, 28, 58, 60, 82, 84, 88, 93, 165–72 passim. *See also* generativity
responsibility: to earth, 251; to future generations, 3, 14, 29, 31, 114, 134, 151, 155, 160–61; generative, 96, 97; towards the Idea of the Human, 14, 151–52, 155, 159–60; parental, 91, 152–154; for the other, 119, 139, 141
Ricoeur, Paul, 34

sacrifice, 77, 122, 124, 173, 197
Schütz, Alfred, 33, 56–57
sex, 15, 165–72 passim; education, 15, 163, 173–174
Shepard, Paul, 215–16, 218, 220, 224–25, 226, 235n7
slavery, 16, 182–85, 193, 225
solidarity, 11, 12, 73–81 passim, 98–99, 143; intergenerational, 11, 74, 81, 99; diachronic, 11, 80; generative, 81, 97

Taylor, Charles, 17, 214–16
Toadvine, Ted, 228–29, 230

de Waal, Frans, 250
Wilson, Edward O., 247, 250

www.ingramcontent.com/pod-product-compliance
Lightning Source LLC
Chambersburg PA
CBHW020643230426
43665CB00008B/302